The Road to Sustainability

The Sustainable World

Aims and Objectives

Sustainability is a key concept of 21st century planning in that it broadly determines the ability of the current generation to use resources and live a lifestyle without compromising the ability of future generations to do the same. Sustainability affects our environment, economics, security, resources, health, economics, transport and information decisions strategy. It also encompasses decision making, from the highest administrative office, to the basic community level. It is planned that this Book Series will cover many of these aspects across a range of topical fields for the greater appreciation and understanding of all those involved in researching or implementing sustainability projects in their field of work.

Topics

Data Analysis
Data Mining Methodologies
Risk Management
Brownfield Development
Landscaping and Visual Impact Studies
Public Health Issues
Environmental and Urban Monitoring
Waste Management
Energy Use and Conservation
Institutional, Legal and Economic Issues
Education
Visual Impact
Simulation Systems
Forecasting
Infrastructure and Maintenance
Mobility and Accessibility
Strategy and Development Studies
Environment Pollution and Control
Land Use
Transport, Traffic and Integration
City, Urban and Industrial Planning
The Community and Urban Living
Public Safety and Security
Global Trends

The Road to Sustainability

GDP and future generations

Federico M. Pulselli,
Simone Bastianoni,
Nadia Marchettini
&
Enzo Tiezzi

University of Siena, Italy

WIT*PRESS* **Southampton, Boston**

F. M. Pulselli, S. Bastianoni, N. Marchettini & E. Tiezzi
University of Siena, Italy

Published by

WIT Press
Ashurst Lodge, Ashurst, Southampton, SO40 7AA, UK
Tel: 44 (0) 238 029 3223; Fax: 44 (0) 238 029 2853
E-Mail: witpress@witpress.com
http://www.witpress.com

For USA, Canada and Mexico

WIT Press
25 Bridge Street, Billerica, MA 01821, USA
Tel: 978 667 5841; Fax: 978 667 7582
E-Mail: infousa@witpress.com
http://www.witpress.com

British Library Cataloguing-in-Publication Data

A Catalogue record for this book is available
from the British Library

ISBN: 978-1-84564-140-5
ISSN: 1476-9581

Library of Congress Catalog Card Number: 2007939221

The texts of the papers in this volume were set individually by the authors or under their supervision.

Printed in Great Britain by Athenaeum Press Ltd.

Contents

Presentations

The Road to Sustainability: GDP and Future Generations

Environment, welfare and lifestyle

The Province of Modena has decided to pursue a quality of development in line with the principles of sustainability. The challenge of environmental quality will be decisive for the economic and social future of the province. Environmental quality means focussing on regional excellence and localisation of firms. Environmental sustainability is linked to the development of the human and social capital of our area and is based on social cohesion and the capacity to reinforce community identities. The aim of sustainable development and quality stimulates and guides innovation in our area. We are therefore investing in the environment, developing knowledge, research, innovation and creativity, mobilising resources and talents.

Significant examples of this are quality agriculture with the 2008 World Organic Agriculture Conference in Modena, the quality of parks and reserves (more than 10% of the area of the province) and export of quality manufactured goods. The production scene of the province is becoming dynamic and has gone beyond the old dichotomy of environment versus industry. Firms no longer ignore questions such as efficient use of resources, optimisation of primary materials, reduction of wastes, waste recycling and limitation of emissions. The whole ceramics sector has EMAS certification and more than 200 firms are presenting requests for integrated environmental authorisations in a climate of strong collaboration with the provincial administration.

In order to move in this direction, instruments are needed to indicate possible innovations in local policy. National systems of accounting and their indicators, such as GDP, have proven inadequate for measuring the sustainability of an economy: because they do not consider depreciation of natural and social capital, they do not reflect the perception of welfare and the opinion that families have of local development. It is therefore essential to consider environmental and social components as well. Today the concept of welfare is no longer linked exclusively to the earning power of a population, but overlaps with the concept of quality of life. This is why we chose to use the index of sustainable economic welfare, ISEW, which corrects GDP, including social costs and short and long term environmental damage.

The analysis was conducted by the Department of Chemical and Biosystem Sciences and Technology, Siena University, under the supervision of Professor Enzo Tiezzi. It not only enabled us to assess the current situation regarding the quality of development in the province, but also to examine long time trends from 1971 to 2003. The situation in our province has the problems typical of a heavily anthropised area with a strong industrial sector, however there are signs that the path already undertaken can have positive results. The study shows that the environment must be the basic discriminant of planning policy in order to achieve a quality of development that improves quality of life.

The Environment and Sustainable Development Department of the province has therefore undertaken a series of concrete steps towards territorial sustainability, with the priority aim of greater environmental protection and thus protection of the health and welfare of citizens. We are acting on all the major environmental fronts, involving all local stakeholders through the forum of Agenda 21. In May 2005, the Provincial Council approved the Provincial Waste Management Plan, the main aim of which is to reduce waste production and to increase differentiation (55%), recycling and reuse. In March 2007 we approved the Air Quality Plan with a strong commitment as regards transport and collaboration between firms and local bodies. The Water Quality Plan is being adopted with strong measures regarding the quantity and quality of water resources. The Regional Quarry Plan is also being adopted and aims at reducing land and resource consumption to improve environmental quality and landscape. We are also reinforcing the system of parks and reserves. The province has two regional parks, three nature reserves, three areas of ecological restoration, fauna sanctuaries and sites of the Nature 2000 network covering 10% of the province. It is an important resource for a heavily anthropised province, improving quality of life. We think that good land management, both environmental and cultural, that considers those who live and work in the province, is a strong point of the Modena system in the panorama of wealthy European areas.

Let us examine how the path towards sustainability divides into many parallel paths. Each area of direct planning has had the environment and society as a prime aim, but this is not enough. It is also necessary to spread environmental awareness in order to optimise relationships between persons, social groups, society and the environment. By becoming aware of their role and responsibility, individuals can improve their own lives and contribute to sustainable development. The Province has therefore taken different initiatives to support and increase environmental communication and education, because investment in knowledge and awareness is a necessary condition for creating a society capable of developing, not just of growing, in other words a society on the path towards sustainability.

Alberto Caldana
Modena Provincial Administration Environment Policy Officer

Index of Sustainable Economic Welfare (ISEW) – for a sustainable Province of Rimini

For a number of years, the economy of our province has been flagging. Our model of development, which produced a good level of general wealth over the years at the expense of 'Riminisation', is showing its limits. The model is largely based on unlimited consumption which has increased bank accounts while generating striking social and environmental contradictions. I therefore took on the task of changing the model and aiming for a more sustainable type of development. This is a difficult task, and if people are to accept it, much attention and participation is needed. It was necessary to talk to local actors, the true protagonists of growth, and reach an agreement about what sustainable development is. It was decided to request an analysis of sustainability by the group of Professor Enzo Tiezzi at Siena University, which led to the calculation of ISEW.

The project 'Sustainable Province of Rimini' set out to obtain insights into the province from different points of view. We began with two information sources:

- Report on the Economy of the Province of Rimini 2006–2007 by the Chamber of Commerce and the Fondazione Cassa di Risparmio di Rimini which indicated a healthy economy in all sectors, with upturns in tourism and industry. Employment increased to 65.8%, approaching the Lisbon objectives, GDP increased by 5.6% in all sectors, the number of firms increased by 8.4%.

- Report on the State of the Environment 2001 and 2006 and Sustainability Analysis 2005, which indicated major signs of stress in different environmental compartments: land use along the coast is the main cause of these problems. In summer, air pollution and sewage often exceed safety levels. The main economic sectors place the province in a very critical position with regard to imports and local resources. In 2005, 70 external resources were imported for every local resource. Indices of sustainability such as

> eMergy and per capita emission of greenhouse gases are high and the Ecological Footprint is double that of the average Italian. Water resources have a high regeneration capacity, they are overexploited and river estuaries are polluted and drying up, with negative repercussions on coastal water quality. Ecosystems have become artificial in more than 80% of the province and only 10% of the area has a good level of naturalness. Taken together, these results indicate a situation of environmental risk for ecosystems and for human health. Though some may consider these problems negligible at local level, at global level the same problems exist on a very worrying scale, as shown by the fourth report of the Intergovernmental Panel on Climate Change (IPCC, February 2007), and ought to make us think.

Both sources provide clear indications, but they are two different ways of looking at the situation, two studies that do not seem to have any relation between them. Economy and environment are represented as separate and independent.

With regard to the first report, economists have always proposed GDP as a measure of the production of final goods and services per year and GDP is still considered a strategic value for defining the growth of a community. Governments and politicians are preoccupied with GDP, especially with how to increase GDP. However this index has many limits. Indeed, Senator Robert Kennedy questioned the importance attributed to GDP, claiming that it represents "*everything except that which makes life worthwhile.*" GDP does not distinguish between activities that produce welfare and those that damage welfare, nor does it consider the depreciation and devaluation of natural capital caused by human activities.

With regard to environmental sustainability, our province began to adopt measures in this sense many years ago, but challenges still await us if we really want to make development more sustainable. The process began with the First International Conference on Sustainable Tourism, held in June 2001, and the signing of the Rimini Charter. The forum of Agenda 21 was signed in 2002 and its action plan led to the creation of 20 ecosustainable bathing establishments with energy self-sufficiency and reutilisation of water. There have been initiatives promoting sustainable urban and sea transport, such as methane and hydromethane scooters, door-to-door differentiated rubbish collection, a passive-house school, an off-shore wind farm and calculation of ISEW.

After their collaboration with scientists at Siena University, the Provinces of Rimini and Modena published an analysis based on indicators alternative to GDP. ISEW was developed by Herman Daly and John Cobb in 1989 and includes aspects of economic life ignored by GDP. It combines positive factors (like services of domestic labour, services of durables, area of nature reserves) with negative factors (defensive expenditures, loss of natural capital, use of non renewable resources...), integrating different economic, social and environmental components. ISEW therefore enables regions to be represented in a more realistic way.

The time trend of ISEW of the Province of Rimini shows a progressive increase in costs of environmental impact in various sectors and due to increasing use of non renewable energy. To this is added a set of environmental costs, common to all post-industrial economies, due to air and water pollution, noise and road accidents. As noted, natural areas and habitats of protected species are a grave weakness: the absolute value is low and growth has been less than the regional average.

Positive factors are widespread economic welfare.

When all the values are summed, ISEW is seen to have grown less than GDP. In the mid eighties GDP overtook ISEW and has exceeded it ever since. Thus ISEW confirms the vitality of the provincial economy but a fraction of GDP (almost €800,000,000) creates many problems that severely affect welfare. Environmental and social sustainability are therefore sectors in need of improvement, for example by reducing pollution, increasing natural areas, remediating coastal environments, restoring wetlands and reducing private defensive spending for health and education.

My sincere thanks to the group from Siena University who enabled this pilot project to come to fruition, especially Federico M. Pulselli and Enzo Tiezzi.

Cesarino Romani
Environment Policy Officer, Rimini Provincial Administration

Preface

James Maitland, Earl of Lauderdale, a classical economist, noted in 1819 an important distinction between 'public wealth' and 'private riches.'[1] Public wealth 'consists of all that man desires that is useful or delightful to him'. Private riches consist of 'all that man desires that is useful or delightful to him, which exists in a degree of scarcity'. Scarcity is a necessary condition for something to have exchange value and be counted as private riches. In the Garden of Eden (no scarcity) private riches were zero, but public wealth was at its maximum. Creating scarcity indeed may increase private riches, but at the expense of diminishing public wealth. Lauderdale felt that, 'the common sense of mankind would revolt at a proposal for augmenting wealth by creating a scarcity of any good generally useful and necessary to mankind.

Goods can be rival or non-rival. My shirt is a rival good because if I am wearing it you cannot wear it at the same time. The warmth of the sun is non-rival because my enjoyment of it does not preclude the same enjoyment by others. Rivalness is a physical property of a good that precludes its simultaneous use by many people. Goods are also excludable or non-excludable. Excludability is a legal right to prevent another from using your property. For example you could wear my shirt if I let you, but that is up to me because it is my property. My shirt is thus both rival and excludable, as are most market goods. The warmth of the sun is both non-rival and non-excludable. We cannot buy and sell solar warmth. The categories that cause problems and will be of interest to us are the remaining combinations: rival and non-excludable, and non-rival and excludable.

The economy as a commonwealth

A national economy itself constitutes a commonwealth and used to be referred to as such[2]. The resources, customs, laws, division of labor, distribution of

[1] Lauderdale, J.M., (1819) *An inquiry into the nature and origin of public wealth and into the means and causes of its increase*, Archibald Constable, Edinburgh.

[2] As defined by the *OED*, commonwealth = 'the whole body of people constituting a nation or state, the body politic; a state, an independent community, esp. viewed as a body in which the whole people have a voice or an interest.'.

purchasing power, labor markets, etc. of a nation constitute a community, cohesive internally, but with strict limits to access from the outside. Imports of goods and services are controlled, imports of capital are controlled, and immigration of people is controlled, all in the internal interests of citizens of the commonwealth. Traditionally, national markets have not been thought of as an open-access commons. Globalization aims to change that – to erase national boundaries for economic purposes (free trade, free capital mobility, and free, or at least uncontrolled, immigration). The consequence of open access is the tragedy of the commons, the disintegration of the national commonwealth, which is welcomed by many in the questionable pursuit of an integrated global economy. In the absence of world government, however, such a global economy is not a commonwealth writ large, but a kind of global feudalism in which corporate individualism has free reign.

More narrowly, social institutions such as legal systems, language, moral codes, and monetary systems also constitute a kind of social wealth or commonwealth, that is different from knowledge and nature, and that, like knowledge, seem to be inherently non-rival. I would like to consider only one of these in closing, namely money.

Money, at first glance may seem to be rival, since if I have a dollar you cannot simultaneously have it. Yet the only reason for having a dollar is to be able to give it in exchange for something else, and so its value depends on the willingness of everyone to accept it in exchange and hold it at least temporarily. The more people use a dollar, the more useful it is, and in that sense it is non-rival. We use money without using it up. But is money a commonwealth? Indeed, is it wealth at all? It depends – if it is commodity money, then it circulates at its commodity value, and is a rival commodity that can be privately produced and owned, e.g. gold – then it is not really commonwealth. It is private wealth that serves a social function. However, token or fiat money is different. Its commodity value is nil (it has only a trivial cost of production), but it circulates at an exchange value independent of its commodity value. The amount of token money that people are willing to hold rather than exchange it for real commodities is the 'virtual wealth' of the community. People are willing to hold token money balances to avoid the inconvenience of barter. They can convert their money balances into real wealth at any time, and thus reasonably count these balances as part of their personal wealth. Yet if everyone tried to convert their money balances into real wealth at once it could not be done, because someone would have to end up holding the money. Thus the aggregate of individuals in a community considers itself richer than it really is by the amount of virtual wealth, which is equal to the exchange value of stocks of token money.

Although we all benefit from the convenience of money, the issuer of token money, the one who creates and first spends it, gets a transfer of real wealth from the rest of the community. He pays the negligible cost of production of token money, but receives the full exchange value when he spends it. Everyone else must give the full exchange value's worth of something in exchange for money. The profit to the issuer of fiat money is called 'seigniorage' and really should be public income since it derives from the socially created commonwealth of token money.

Seigniorage used to accrue to the king. The privilege largely passed, not to the State, the legitimate heir of the king, but to the private banking sector via the institution of fractional reserve banking. Seigniorage on currency still goes to the Government, but that on demand deposits, over 95% of our money supply, goes to the commercial banks in the first instance, and is probably in large part competed away to the rest of the private sector (commercial banks' customers).

One hundred percent reserves would eliminate the ability of the commercial banks to create money, and put our money supply back under the control of the government rather than the private banking sector. Money would be a true public utility, rather than the by-product of commercial lending and borrowing in pursuit of growth. Under the fractional reserve system the money supply expands during a boom, and contracts during a slump, reinforcing the cyclical tendency of the economy. Demand deposits are loaned into existence at interest, and a new loan will only be taken if the project it finances is expected to grow at a rate greater than the interest rate. Therefore it would seem that under fractional reserve banking, economic growth is required just to keep the money supply from shrinking as old loans are repaid.

The seigniorage from creating and being the first to spend token money would, with 100% reserve requirements, accrue to the government rather than the private sector. It could be used for interest-free financing of public goods. The reserve requirement, something the Fed manipulates anyway, could be raised gradually to 100%. Commercial banks would make their income by financial intermediation (lending savers' money for them), and by service charges on checking accounts, etc., rather than by lending money they simply create. Lending only pre-existing money that someone has actually saved brings about a greater discipline in lending, and enforces the classical balance between marginal time preference and marginal productivity of capital.

The two leading American economists of the 1920s, Irving Fisher[3] of Yale and Frank Knight[4] of Chicago, both strongly advocated 100% reserves. Why this issue disappeared from the policy agenda is an interesting question for historians of economic thought – if there are any left. And why there are so few left is another interesting question.

In sum – I argue that the commonwealth of nature should be enclosed as property, to the extent possible as public property, and administered so as to capture scarcity rents for public revenue. The commonwealth of knowledge should be freed from enclosure as property and be treated as the non-rival good that it is.

[3] Fisher, I., (1935) *100% Money*. An Adelphi Publication, New York.

[4] Knight, F., (1927) *Review of wealth, virtual wealth, and debt.* Saturday Review of Literature.

A third category of commonwealth, the institutional, is here mentioned with the example of the institution of fiat money and the suggestion of capturing seigniorage for public wealth through one hundred percent reserve requirements. These three policies establish basic directions in which to move. How fast we should move in each direction is an important question that I have not attempted to answer. However, the policies advocated in each case (fewer and shorter patent monopolies; cap-and-trade plus ecological tax reform; and 100% reserve requirements) can all be imposed with varying speeds and to varying degrees. We can try them out a little at a time.

If what I have argued is even more or less correct, then I am faced with a difficult question. Why do so many neoclassical economists continue to teach, by and large, the opposite – namely, that nature is not really scarce; that knowledge must be made scarce in order to increase it; and that our private banking institutions must create money out of nothing and lend it at interest as a necessary part of the economic order?

They may be right – I may be crazy. But crazy people should be easy to refute, shouldn't they? So let's see what happens!

The economy as a subsystem

The economy is a subsystem of the finite biosphere that supports it. When the economy's expansion encroaches too much on its surrounding ecosystem, we will begin to sacrifice natural capital (such as fish, minerals and fossil fuels) that is worth more than the man-made capital (such as roads, factories and appliances) added by the growth. We will then have what I call uneconomic growth, producing 'bads' faster than goods – making us poorer, not richer. Once we pass the optimal scale, growth becomes stupid in the short run and impossible to maintain in the long run. Evidence suggests that the US may already have entered the uneconomic growth phase. Recognizing and avoiding uneconomic growth are not easy. One problem is that some people benefit from uneconomic growth and thus have no incentive for change. In addition, our national accounts do not register the costs of growth for all to see. Humankind must make the transition to a sustainable economy, one that takes heed of the inherent biophysical limits of the global ecosystem so that it can continue to operate long into the future. If we do not make that transition, we may be cursed not just with uneconomic growth but with an ecological catastrophe that would sharply lower living standards.

The economic parachute

To judge from how gross domestic product (GDP) is discussed in the media, one would think that everything good flows from it. Yet GDP is not a measure of well-being or even of income. Rather it is a measure of overall economic activity. It is defined as the annual market value of final goods and services purchased in a nation, plus all exports net of imports. 'Final' means that intermediate goods and services, those that are inputs to further production, are excluded. GDP does not subtract either depreciation of man-made capital (such as roads and factories) or depletion of natural capital (such as fish and fossil fuels). GDP also counts so-called defensive expenditures in the plus column. These expenditures are made to protect ourselves from the unwanted consequences of the production and consumption of goods by others – for example, the expense of cleaning up pollution. Defensive expenditures are like intermediate costs of production, and therefore they should not be included as a part of GDP. Some economists argue for their inclusion because they improve both the economy and the environment. We can all get rich cleaning up one another's pollution! To go from GDP to a measure of sustainable well-being requires many more positive and negative adjustments. These adjustments include uncounted household services (such as those performed for free by spouses); increased international debt; loss of well-being resulting from increasing concentration of income (the well-being induced by an extra dollar for the poor is greater than that for the rich); long-term environmental damage such as ozone layer depletion or loss of wetlands and estuaries; and water, air and noise pollution. When all these adjustments are made, the result is the index of sustainable economic welfare (ISEW), as developed by Clifford W. Cobb and John B. Cobb, Jr, and related measures. These indices have been used by ecological economists but are largely ignored by others in the field. For the US, it appears that, beginning in the 1980s, the negative factors in the ISEW have been increasing faster than the positive ones. Similar results have been found for the UK, Austria, Germany and Sweden. In other words, for some countries in recent years, the costs of growth are rising faster than the benefits. As important as empirical measurement is, it is worth remembering that when one jumps out of an airplane, a parachute is more beneficial than an altimeter. First principles make it abundantly clear that we need an economic parachute. Casual empiricism makes it clear that we need it sooner rather than later. More precise information, though not to be disdained, is not necessary, and waiting for it may prove very costly.

This book deals with all these things. It is important to highlight that Enzo Tiezzi and the members of his staff are physical chemists. Some years ago, I dedicated Enzo a booklet of mine on Frederick Soddy, Nobel Prize in Chemistry in 1921, and I wrote: to Enzo Tiezzi, the Frederick Soddy of the 21st century.

Soddy played a fundamental role for a two reasons:

a) in 1920, he acknowledged the importance of the laws of thermodynamics in economics

b) he guessed that money drives us to confuse the symbol with real wealth: the former can grow indefinitely within mathematical theories of economic growth; the latter follows physical laws that determine constraints and dimensions.

H. Daly, 2008

Part I

Foundations

Chapter 1

The megaptera's song, or what the GDP does not tell us

Conservation without evolution is death,
Evolution without conservation is madness.
Gregory Bateson

Suppose we have four planets for the land available to us: the first for humans, their houses, roads, schools, hospitals, churches and factories; the second for agriculture to produce food and textile fibres; the third for biomass for fuel to avoid global warming and absorb the exact same quantity of CO_2 from the atmosphere as the fuel emits when it burns (zero greenhouse effect). The fourth part would be left wild for the conservation of natural biodiversity, as taught by St Francis of Assisi, patron saint of the International Society for Ecological Economics (ISEE).

Our metaphor continues in the sea, in an attempt to provide further epistemological foundations for this book.

A musical story

There is a piano on a floating platform in the ocean. A pianist plays and his note dies in the silence of the sea. Then the pianist presses the sustaining pedal and the note expands. The song of a whale, a megaptera, is heard in reply. The sustaining pedal maintains or sustains the sound in time.

The megaptera's song, different from that of other whales and other megaptera, is a metaphor for biodiversity. It is the voice of nature. Today, Prigogine's strange attractors can be used to demonstrate that every whale has its own song; biodiversity is life, life's symbol.

The sustaining pedal is a metaphor for sustainability. Biodiversity and sustainability are the two conditions for maintaining life on this wonderful planet. The sustaining pedal is linked to the role of time in science, an evolutionary science represented by the megaptera that swims the oceans and is not shackled to safe linear quantitative moorings: a science based on the irreversibility of time (Prigogine) and on aesthetics (Bateson), which sails the sea of chaos and free choice, unconditioned by obsolete mechanistic and reductionist views.

The two entropies

In our opinion, it is necessary to recover cultural forms forged by particular habitats in order to discover the structures connecting our minds with nature, as Gregory Bateson taught.[1] On the other hand, we also need to be global, to enter into new sustainable relations with all ecosystems, to know how to exploit the creative side of cultural diversity.[2] The global being is born through creativity and is the opposite of globalisation, which is the death of creativity by *entropic euthanasia*.

The second principle of thermodynamics, one of the fundamental laws of nature, indicates the roads to avoid if life is to continue to exist on the Earth. It points to the universal trend towards disorder (in thermodynamics, the trend towards maximum entropy), which amounts to loss of information and useful energy. This trend, called *thermal death* by Clausius, is the death of biological systems and ecosystems through destruction of diversity.

Two roads lead to this condition:

1. when temperature differences decrease during heat exchange, leading to levelling of energy, making it impossible to do anything because useful energy exchange is impossible;
2. when a system remains isolated and undergoes a great increase in internal entropy through consumption of resources, amounting to self-destruction.

This is why living systems try to avoid thermodynamic equilibrium, staying as far away from it as possible, self-organising by virtue of flows of energy and matter received from the outside and from systems under different conditions of temperature and energy.

The economy and society cannot ignore the second principle of thermodynamics. Globalisation, destruction of biological and cultural diversity, levelling and *one-dimensional* thought inevitably lead to thermal death (entropic euthanasia), or final destruction. A country, nation or system that adopts the political dogma of isolation, rejection of cultural cross-fertilisation and conservative fundamentalism will meet the same fate. Excessive defence of difference and loss of diversity are two aspects of the same thermodynamic nonsense.

---

1. Bateson, G., *Mind and Nature: A Necessary Unity*, Dutton: New York, 1979; Bateson, G., *Steps to an Ecology of Mind*, Chandler Publishing Company: New York, 1972.
2. Bocchi, G., & Ceruti, M., Complessità e incompiutezza del divenire umano. *OIKOS*, **6**, pp. 29–48, 1999.

Camus underlined the Mediterranean character of St Francis of Assisi, so aptly praised by father Ernesto Balducci[3] who left us a parable about sustainability:

> We are on the fast descending curve of a parabola. If the metaphysical god is dead, so is the god of history. The future is in the hands of humans and humans of consumer societies shorten the future because they consume, denying existence to future generations. This is bankrupt humanism and indicates the need for a change which we could call a change from a *having* to a *being* society, from a society whose evolutionary law is competition to a society whose law, imposed not just by conscience but also by science, is love for all living creatures, including those of the future.

Choose the greater good and the lesser evil

It is the day before the Battle of Zama. Hannibal is exhausted after the campaign in Italy, crossing the Alps with elephants and his victories won by strategy. He decides to talk to Scipio. Humbly, he admits defeat but wants to avoid a bloodbath. This is Polibio's[4] version of Hannibal's meeting with Scipio:

> I'm afraid, Scipio, that you will not be persuaded by what I have to say, because you are young. So far everything has gone according to plan for you in Spain and Africa and you have not yet experienced a change of fortune. I invite you to consider the course of human affairs on the basis of what I am about to say. I will not use examples from the past but today's facts. I am Hannibal, who was lord of almost all of Italy after the battle of Cannes, and who reached the gates of Rome and was arbiter of your life and homeland. Now I find myself in Africa, forced to negotiate my own safety and that of the Carthaginians, with you, a Roman. I therefore urge you to consider all this and not to give way to pride, but to act as a man in the present circumstances: always choose the greater good and the lesser evil. What prudent man would tackle a danger such as the one that now looms over you? If you win this battle, it will not greatly enhance your fame, nor that of your country; if you are defeated you will destroy the fruit of all your previous noble and splendid enterprises.

Scipio did not listen but wanted Hannibal dead in battle or in chains for a triumphant return to Rome. In the Battle of Zama thousands of Carthaginians and Romans died. Hannibal was not found among the bodies or among the prisoners; he lived quietly for many years afterwards on the shores of the Black Sea.

---

3. Balducci, E., *Francesco d'Assisi*, Edizioni Cultura della Pace: Firenze, 1989.
4. Polibio, *Le Storie, III*, Mondadori: Milano, 1955.

In certain ways, sustainability is the path of the lesser evil. It is not the illusion of never-ending economic growth, impossible in a biosphere of finite space and resources; it is not the illusion of magnificent progress; it is not the illusion of developing countries following the Western economic and industrial model: the biophysical constraints of the planet exclude this possibility.

Laura Conti[5] understood these contradictions and described them with great clarity:

> Marx rejected both hypotheses of Malthus, that of decreasing productivity of the Earth and that of unlimited reproductive pressure. Not only did he reject the latter hypothesis, but could not understand why Darwin, who had convinced him of biological evolution and whom he deeply admired, claimed to be a disciple of Malthus. This idea seemed madness to Marx: indeed, he believed that Darwin had not realised the incongruence of attributing unlimited reproductive pressure to one species as Malthus seemed to do. If other species also have this propensity, then does Marx consider that human reproduction matches that of wheat so that humans will never be without grain? Strangely, he does not seem to realise that humans have the same basic reproductive pressure as other species, but their capacity to achieve it, multiplying it by reproduction of survivors, is greater.
>
> Marx's comment on Malthus's hypothesis of decreasing soil productivity was that fertility of the soil depended on human work: it would therefore increase. However, a non-controversial observation of daily experience is a decreasing world trend in soil productivity.
>
> Marx argues that when soil is cultivated it does not lose its original fertility but durably incorporates the costs of improvement. Today we know that this is untrue: much of the Fertile Crescent became desert due to *improvements* and the Amazon forest will become desert after very few crops.

Hans Immler,[6] who defined Malthus an ecological economist *ante litteram*, recently showed that the material wealth of industrial society is totally derived from mass exploitation of natural potential through labour, science and technology. This is done in the name of abstract laws of economics and technology, based on mind–nature separation and on Descartes's anti-aesthetic assumption that only quantities count in science. According to Immler, the industrial lifestyle has become a *negative natural practice* in its attempts to deny nature.

---

5. Conti, L., *Entropia e Potere*, eds A. Baracca & E. Tiezzi, CLUP-CLUED: Milano, 1981.
6. Immler, H., *Welche Wirtschaft braucht die Natur? Mit Ökonomie die Ökokrise lösen*, S. Fischer Verlag GmbH: Frankfurt am Main, 1993.

The end of certainty

Prigogine's ants are transgressive, leaving habitual routes to look for new resources and new paths. The Nobel laureate laid the foundations of a new science, evolutionary physics, to apply to evolving systems: the complex systems of biology and ecology.[7]

If we want tools to study the relationship between ecology and economics, if we want to govern complexity with complexity, we will have to obtain ideas and predictive models from this new science. It is a science *without foundations*,[8] like biological evolution. The certainty and determinism of classical mechanics and molecular biology are questioned, the complexity of the natural world and the fundamental role of time that governs it are finally considered, and the science of space and quantity is flanked by the new science of time and quality. In this new view of the world, there is at last room for the evolutionary creativity of nature and for the creativity of humans, which is also evolutionary. Thermodynamics becomes the basis for interpreting environmental and economic problems, which can no longer be studied in reversible mechanistic terms, but with irreversible evolutionary models. The answers are no longer simple or the fruit of deterministic logic of cause and effect. They call for new questions and they teach us to travel new paths where bifurcations, correlations, networks and change are the new non-rules to follow, the paths of Prigogine's ants.

Mauro Ceruti tells the story of a new civilisation in which plurality weighs more than homogeneity, in which creation prevails over elimination of the obsolete, in which experimentation and diversification predominate over standardisation. These new epistemological paths, which will necessarily be the foundations for constructing the theories of sustainable development, are characterised by innovative words and concepts, from the *connecting structures* of Bateson to the *autopoiesis* of Maturana and Varela. Indeed, Francisco Varela[9] guessed the relations between the disciplines, the structures and cognitive pathways *to mitigate the various forms of dogmatism that infest our world.*

In the preface to his book, *The Web of Life*, Fritjof Capra[10] quotes Ted Perry, inspired by the Indian Chief Seattle:

> Everything that happens on the Earth happens to the sons and daughters of the Earth.
> Humans do not weave the web of life, they are only a thread.
> Whatever humans do to the web, they do to themselves.

---

7. Prigogine, I., *The End of Certainty – Time's Flow and the Laws of Nature*, The Free Press: New York, 1997.
8. Ceruti, M., *Evoluzione senza fondamenti*, Laterza: Bari, 1995.
9. Varela, F., *Connaitre les sciences cognitives*, Seuil: Paris, 1989.
10. Capra, F., *The Web of Life*, Doubleday–Anchor Books: New York, 1996.

Capra points out that molecular biologists have discovered the bricks of life, but this does not help them to understand the fundamental processes of integration of organisms. A type of development that considers nature will therefore not draw its epistemological lymph from molecular reductionism but from the theories of complexity.

The essence of time

The last 50 years have seen humans make incredible advances in scientific knowledge and technology, solving many problems and increasing health care and economic welfare. What, then, is the recent source of increasing discomfort of people like ourselves, who do not see science as a means for dominating the world and nature but as a path of knowledge for living in harmony with nature? Scientists have been known to make discoveries that, if applied by a sorcerer's apprentices for profit and power, could gravely damage humans and the environment. While science celebrates new peaks, it is clear to everyone that the quality of life has deteriorated, also in the psychological realm, with destruction of nature and high unemployment of youth, despite economic and industrial growth.

A striking example of the work of the sorcerer's apprentices is the attempt to clone humans, when *clonation* or *replication* of living species (plant or animal) is completely contrary to biological evolution and the origins of life, both of which are based on biodiversity and the diversification of forms, individuals and species.

The planet Earth has grave environmental problems today, global problems, since the Earth is a single complex system composed of interdependent parts. Environmental problems apparently afflicting a nation, or part of a nation, are actually part of a global problem affecting the whole planet. With their style of life and production, humans are affecting the biogeochemical cycles of the biosphere, and major and minor environmental catastrophes are signs of a general planetary disorder.

Today, the true world problem is a problem of interdependence, of relations between producer and consumer countries, between holders of primary resources and holders of know-how, between polluter countries and countries with a rich, uncontaminated, environmental heritage. Hence it is necessary to understand the complex relations between energy and resources, between natural capital and man-made capital, between local and global.

Geological, meteorological, ecological, oceanographic and biological studies have shown that the life of every organism is part of a large-scale process that involves the metabolism of the whole planet. Biological activity is a planetary property, a continuous interaction of atmospheres, oceans, plants, animals, microorganisms, molecules, electrons, energies and matter, all part of a global whole. The role of each component is essential for the maintenance of life.

The fundamental scientific novelty is indeed the discovery that the system in which we live, the planet Earth, is a finite system and as such has limits and constraints: limited land, limited capacity to absorb wastes and pollution, constraints related to the great life cycles of air, water, oxygen and so forth, constraints that limit an indiscriminate increase in population and production. The physical world is subject to constraints which can pose limits. Just one example: if the population increases, more food is necessary; to have more food, more must be produced per hectare, but this leads to soil depletion, erosion, pollution of underground water and eutrophication of the seas. Alternatively, we can clear forests to make more land to cultivate, but this leads to loss of biodiversity and upsets the equilibrium of the carbon and oxygen cycles (greenhouse effect) causing climate change which affects agriculture, and so forth.

The Earth has a long history, 4500 million years of evolution. The story of biological evolution is wonderfully complex, a story of energy and matter, of molecules and cells, a story that has given rise to living forms of great diversity, plants and animals including humans. Continuous flows of solar energy to the Earth's surface and photosynthesis drove the evolution and multiplication of the many biological species: this is the natural capital entrusted to us, a capital of biodiversity, consisting of air, soil, rivers, seas, forests and animals. Biodiversity is fundamental for the maintenance of life, because everything is linked to everything on this planet. It is a story that our great grandmother, the blue-green alga, began hundreds of millions of years ago, inventing the process of photosynthesis, the process that builds the bricks of life (the biological structure of all living beings) using energy from the Sun, water and CO_2 from the air: the first of the two conditions essential for life.

On the surface of the Earth,photosynthesis counteracts entropic degradation[11] (inevitable in biological time on a universal scale) by 'ordering' disordered matter. Powered by solar energy, plants use disordered matter (low energy molecules of water and CO_2 in disorderly agitation) and organise it into complex structures. Photosynthesis is therefore the process that paved the way for biological evolution, by capturing solar energy and decreasing the entropy of the planet. Photosynthesis is the green talisman of life, a sort of Maxwell's devil that decreases the entropy of the biosphere. All living systems on the Earth need a continuous flow of energy from outside them ('negative' entropy) and this flow consists of the solar energy captured by plants via photosynthesis. To maintain the carbon cycle, this input of solar energy is indispensable.

Thus we can read the whole story of life on the Earth, the story of photosynthesis and evolution, as the story of a singular planet that learned how to

11. Tiezzi, E., *Fermare il tempo*, Raffaello Cortina: Milano, 1996; Tiezzi, E., *The Essence of Time*, Series: The Sustainable World, 2, WIT Press: Southampton, UK, 2003.

capture solar energy and feed on 'negative' entropy from the Universe to create complex structures (living organisms).

Unfortunately, by wasting energy and using technologies not integrated with nature, humans run the risk of destroying this vital interrelated mechanism. The limits of photosynthesis are not imposed by the energy source, the Sun, which is practically infinite, but by the reckless human production of today. The Sun is an enormous machine that produces energy and offers the Earth the possibility of receiving a great amount of 'negative' entropy (organisation, life), permitting an overall global balance that does not violate the second principle of thermodynamics. Each year, the Sun sends 5.6×10^{24} joules of radiant energy to the Earth: this quantity is more than ten thousand times greater than all the energy that humans consume in a year.

However, if the Earth were surrounded by an adiabatic membrane, preventing heat exchange, the planet would heat so much that all life would die. The increase in CO_2 in the atmosphere is promoting this (greenhouse) effect. The atmosphere of Venus, which is rich in CO_2, has created temperatures of more than 400°C. Life is impossible at such temperatures: we beings of the biosphere are made largely of water that boils at 100°C.

Nature created the second condition essential for life when it relegated reduced carbon to the depths of the Earth (fossil deposits, the garbage dump of evolutionary history) because it knew that CO_2 molecules could not escape the Earth's gravitational field. Today the stupidity of human technologies is inverting this mechanism. This is why oil and carbon are not and can never be sustainable energy sources.

The false prosperity of the consumer society is based on the exploitation of three classes of people:

1. the younger generations who will be left with depleted resources and a polluted environment;
2. underprivileged groups who incur health hazards, pollution, etc., without enjoying the economic advantages of consumerism;
3. the third world which pays for our consumer needs with monocultures, destruction of the natural and social environment and hunger.

These three points demonstrate that purely historical and economic analyses cannot further our understanding. We are concerned with a biological time scale, but today's parameters are changing more rapidly than ever in the past: natural changes that previously occurred over thousands of years may now, with the impact of new technologies, practically occur overnight. The biological tempos between generations today are much faster; the speed with which the younger generations seize and assimilate new technologies is enormous; the rate at which production methods and relationships evolve is also growing rapidly.

The problems of nature and resources concern everyone, including the third world. In mathematical terms, we must extrapolate both in space and time and take the rapidly emerging younger generations into account as social agents.

At this historical crossroads between survival and destruction of the planet, the environment and future generations can no longer be excluded from the market. *The economy cannot continue to be based on reversible sciences (mechanics) but needs sciences which penetrate into the future (biology, thermodynamics).* Living systems do not possess the determinism of technology. Living systems cannot be reduced to a quantity. *Neoclassical economics is a form of reductionism.*

Aesthetic feeling

The word *aesthetics* is derived from the Greek word which means *to feel*, distinguishing sensory from rational knowledge.

As pointed out by the spokesman of the Mapuche people, Jorge Nahuel: 'Biodiversity, which is the source of all original cultures, is threatened by an ecological disaster. It is essential to discuss the consequences and impacts of the current irrational, even despicable, *development model* from the point of view of the impact and consequences that it wreaks in the life, culture, cosmos and spirituality of the native nations.'

We must not let the wonders of the planet be destroyed by self-destructive technological processes, but protect them by conserving their self-organisation.

We call environmental wisdom the explicit knowledge that emerges from long periods of co-evolution of people and nature in local systems. Environmental wisdom arises both from trial-and-error processes and from more subtle kinds of knowledge, involving aesthetics and intuition. It settles out as tradition or religion and contributes to the creation of landscapes, sustaining ecosystems and humans together.

Scientific enterprise has diverged radically from this path and does not blend naturally with environmental wisdom. Scientific ideology has played a large role in abandoning environmental wisdom. However, environmental wisdom is blind outside its local domain and is therefore no longer enough to achieve sustainability.

This book discusses ecodynamic models as a first bridge between scientific thought and environmental wisdom, which can re-establish the interrupted dialogue between local communities and nature.

Argentine tango on the Atlantic

After 30 years of organic farming and sustainability studies in the Argentine pampas and in Chaco, Enrique Cresta returned to Florence, where he had attended university, with much to say. He could see that Argentinian agriculture was damaged by subsidies to European agriculture, but he also knew that Italian agriculture (with salaries ten times the average Latin American salary) had no other chance. He knew that without agriculture, Italy would suffer an environmental disaster: the uncultivated Apennines would slump into the Tyrrhenian and Adriatic seas. He discussed four solutions with our research group.

1. Subsidies to Italian and European agriculture are necessary because agriculture, not industry, can save the environment.
2. Subsidies should be conditional on agriculture producing at least 30% of biofuel crops to decrease the impact of greenhouse gases and save on fines imposed by the Kyoto Protocol.
3. Import the food, fibres and feedstocks replaced by energy crops from developing countries (e.g. meat from Argentina).
4. Use the money saved on Kyoto fines and fewer oil imports for these food imports.

We adopt point 3 of Enrique Cresta and call it *indirect emissions trading* because that is exactly what it is, and it enables us to avoid a portion of the Kyoto fines.

The disappearing island

From an article that appeared in *Corriere della Sera* on 17 January 2007:

> Tennis Schmitt, who discovered it, called it 'the heating island', *ununartoq qeqertop* in Inuit. Until September 2005 it was considered a peninsula of Greenland known as the three-fingered promontory by virtue of its three mountains. On that date, Schmitt, a Californian explorer with more than 100 polar expeditions behind him, sailed along the coast and discovered that it was actually an island, joined to the mainland by a melting glacier. This month, Schmitt returned to explore it and found that it had separated from Greenland and was surrounded by icebergs, the remains of the glacier. 'It is a frightening discovery', he declared to a journalist of the *New York Times* in January 2007. 'This island is a product of global warming. It is not an isolated phenomenon. I know many others that have formed or are in the process of forming.'

From an article that appeared in *La Repubblica* on 28 December 2006:

> Lohachara, a small island in the Bay of Bengal, has been reclaimed by rising seas and its 10,000 inhabitants have been evacuated. It is the first inhabited island to pay the price exacted by 'carbon dumped in the sky'. The news, first reported in Britain's *The Independent*, follows the calvary of islands already taken by the sea for days or weeks, challenging the physical and psychological survival of their inhabitants. Climate change has begun to change geography, starting from one of the most populated areas of the planet. The obliteration of Lohachara Island, in India's part of the Sundarbans

> where the Ganges and the Brahmaputra rivers empty into the Bay of Bengal, marks the moment when one of the most apocalyptic predictions of environmentalists and climate scientists has started coming true. As the seas continue to swell, this is the first inhabited land swallowed, the first land paid as 'collateral damages' for carbon dumped in the sky.

The megaptera will not drown. Hear how it sings!

Chapter 2

Economics and environmental sensibility

Though still met by scepticism and accusations of alarmism by a part of public opinion, the debate on environmental questions is currently lively, and lately a profusion of scientific and experimental evidence on the negative effects of certain human activities, particularly economic and industrial enterprise, is considerably weakening the position of optimists. In the period of a few weeks between the end of 2006 and the beginning of 2007, many reports on the condition of our planet and of part of the world population, on climate change and the availability of resources were presented to the scientific community and world public opinion.

Ninth October 2006 was designated *Overshoot Day*. What was overshot? Cyclically, from year to year, the Earth produces a great quantity of environmental resources and services that humans can use. For example, the water cycle supplies domestic, agricultural and industrial uses. Food production, by both plants and animals, depends on nature's services. Forest production is an important part of the carbon cycle. Humans may draw on natural capital, namely the set of elements and mechanisms that, through natural laws, transform primary materials and solar energy into flows of products and services. At current rates of consumption of resources and production of wastes and emissions, it has been calculated that this flow of products is insufficient to satisfy annual human needs. Overshoot Day is the day in the solar year when humans have used up the year's supply and begin to consume their capital. Greenhouse gases build up in the atmosphere, wastes and contaminants accumulate, resources become depleted and minerals are increasingly expensive to extract. The mechanisms of the machine called nature grind painfully and its cogs are losing some teeth. The capacity of the environment to provide the same quantity of goods and services as it did the previous year is threatened. Future generations will pay the price in natural capital loss and lost natural production. Calculations show that Overshoot Day was 19 December in 1987, whereas in 1995, yearly resources were depleted by 21 November. Now Overshoot Day is 9 October. If we compare the levels of consumption with national resources, we find that Overshoot Day was 27 June in USA, 14 April in Great Britain and 27 March in Italy. These calculations are done systematically by an international research organisation, the Global Footprint Network (Oakland, California), directed by Mathis Wackernagel.

On 24 October 2006, WWF presented its *Living Planet Report.* This report is published every two years and summarises, among other things, the results obtained by applying the ecological footprint[1] to a vast number of national economies. The ecological footprint is a well-known system of environmental accounting that considers the area of the planet (in hectares) as a limiting factor for material growth of human society. It is said that infinite growth is impossible on a finite planet and the ecological footprint demonstrates this. Let us assume that everything we consume requires a certain area of land for its production. If we sum all the hectares needed to produce all the goods consumed by the population of a nation, we obtain a certain area. If the area (calculated using a set of standardised conversion coefficients) is then compared with the area of biologically productive land available in that nation (calculated by conversion coefficients), it is possible to determine whether the system provides for its own needs or whether it depends on supply from outside. The mean per capita ecological footprint calculated for the whole Earth is 2.23 ha, whereas biocapacity is only 1.78 ha. To meet our current needs, the Earth should therefore be 25% larger than it really is. This is clearly impossible. This situation, known as 'ecological deficit', applies to all industrialised countries, which consume much more than what local ecosystems can offer. This means that they grow into the productive space of nations that consume less than them (e.g. economically 'backward' countries).

On 29 October 2006, the United Nations Food and Agricultural Organisation (FAO) published an alarming world report on food supply. *The State of Food Insecurity in the World* asserts that 854 million people live in hunger. In 1996, 180 heads of state committed to halving the number of undernourished, bringing it down to 412 million by 2015 (Declaration of Rome). In 2006, half way to that deadline, nothing has changed; rather, the situation has drastically deteriorated in certain underdeveloped countries, where the line between life and death is now blurred. Something is wrong with our lifestyles and societies, as suggested by the slogan of the report: 'The existence of hunger in a world of plenty is unacceptable'.

On 30 October 2006, Nicholas Stern, economist and consultant to the British government, announced the results of *The Stern Review on the Economics of Climate Change*. After a panorama of future scenarios related to man-made CO_2 emissions and their consequences for mean global temperature and its effects, Stern provides some interesting figures and paints an alarming picture. A major finding is the risk of losing 20% of the gross world product due to consumption

1. For more details on the ecological footprint method, see Chapter 8.

loss caused by global warming. International cooperation, concerted reduction of emissions well beyond the Kyoto objectives and investment in environmental technology and management are measures that could save us, costing only 1% of the gross world product, an acceptable figure when compared to the other scenarios. 'The conclusion of the Review is essentially optimistic. There is still time to avoid the worst impacts of climate change, if we act now and act internationally. Governments, businesses and individuals all need to work together to meet the challenge. Strong, deliberate policy choices by governments are essential to motivate change. The task is urgent. Delaying action, even by a decade or two, will take us into dangerous territory. We must not let this window of opportunity close'. British Prime Minister Tony Blair described the Stern Review as the most important document issued by his government; in the view of certain commentators, an invitation to the US administration.

On 10 January 2007, a communiqué entitled 'Limiting Global Climate Change to 2 degree Celsius: policy option for the EU and the world for 2020 and beyond', was issued by the Environmental Directorate of the European Commission on Climate Change. The Council and the Parliament of Europe confirmed the objective of limiting the increase in mean global temperature to less than 2°C above pre-industrial levels. The importance of this limit was recognised in the Second Assessment Report of the Intergovernmental Panel on Climate Change (IPCC) and was emphasised in the Third Assessment Report, which illustrated that the risk of severe climate change could increase sharply if mean global temperature were to rise by more than 2°C. Major consequences for ecosystems and water resources are, however, considered likely with increases of 1–2°C, but the intensity of the phenomena would be less. The European report states that a 50% cut in greenhouse gas emissions by 2050 (with respect to 1990 values) is necessary to obtain this objective. The novelty of the report is that the EU commits to promoting and leading the fight against climate change. The countries of the EU are committed to a 30%, autonomous, unilateral reduction of emissions by 2020. This ambitious project is a clear signal to the international community of the leading role that Europe intends to play. Indeed, the EU cannot win the challenge of climate change alone, but must be a point of reference and set a convincing example. This should help to convince industrialised countries, which have not ratified the Kyoto Protocol (such as USA and Australia), as well as developing countries, to reduce their emissions.

On 2 February 2007, the summary of the Fourth Assessment Report of the IPCC was approved in Paris by the 10th Session of Working Group I. The report describes scientific progress in the understanding of the natural and man-made causes contributing to climate change. IPCC experts sustain that the increase in mean global temperature in the second half of the 20th century was due to greenhouse gas emissions by human activities. This statement is sustained with a greater probability (>90%) than in the previous report (>66%). Atmospheric concentrations of CO_2, the most abundant greenhouse gas, increased from 280 ppm in the pre-industrial period (1750) to 379 ppm in 2005.

Recent research on ice cores confirms that CO_2 levels have never been so high in the last 650,000 years. Moreover, the rate at which the concentration of CO_2 is rising has accelerated in the last 10 years from 1.4 ppm/year in 1960–2005 to 1.9 ppm/year in 1995–2005. The increase in temperature in 1906–2005 was 0.74°C compared to 0.6°C in 1901–2001, as shown in the last report. By the end of the century, the surface temperature of the Earth may rise by 2–4.5°C. It is unlikely that the increase will be less than 1.5°C, and temperature increments of up to 6°C cannot be excluded. The increase is greater at higher latitudes, and satellites have estimated that since 1978 the mean annual area of Arctic ice has decreased at the rate of 2.7% for every 10 years. Warming also tends to reduce the absorption of CO_2 by land and oceans, increasing the fraction of man-made emissions remaining in the atmosphere, and thus establishing positive feedback. Between 1961 and 2003, world sea levels have risen by about 1.8 mm/year. This rate rose to 3.1 mm/year in the period 1993–2003, though it is unclear whether the acceleration falls in the range of 10-year variability or whether it is part of a long-period trend. However, there is a high probability (>80%) that the rate of sea rise increased in the 20th century. The total rise amounts to 17 cm due to the increase in the mean global temperature of oceans to a depth of about 3000 m, and it is estimated that it could be between 19 and 58 cm by 2100. Certain models and new data suggest that the rise could be as much as a metre. Meteorological observations have shown long-term trends in precipitation in the period 1900–2005 in large areas of the planet: increasingly abundant rain in eastern America, Western Europe and central and northern Asia; increasing drought in the Sahel, Mediterranean, southern Africa and certain parts of southern Asia. In general, the frequency of intense precipitation has risen. The Mediterranean emerges as an area highly subject to future climate change.

When these reports are presented, many authorities are heard. International conferences on environmental protection and saving the human race are important events. Many authorities and institutions clamour to participate in these activities. The vortex of speeches and parallel sessions is counterproductive for efficacy. Thus, these initiatives often conclude without any major results. Jacopo Giliberto[2] commented, for example, on the Johannesburg Summit in 2002, 10 years after the Earth Summit of Rio de Janeiro:

> Though at first sight it did not seem to be, the Johannesburg Summit in 2002 was an environmental summit. If the topic no longer seemed to be ecology but rather economics, the reason is that ecology itself has changed. Likewise, environment was the central theme of the Social Forum in Porto Alegre in January 2003. Ecology still means defending threatened seals and admiring the elegance of *Poinsettia pulcherrima*, but though it is legitimate to defend the few eggs of *Caretta caretta* (the turtle of Lampedusa), ecologists are spending

2. Giliberto, J., *La guerra dell'ambiente*, Editori Laterza: Roma-Bari, 2003.

> their energy in quite different directions. With reckless joy, humans have multiplied their capacity to consume, reproduce, burn, kill and have fun. The damage that a billion rich men could cause in the 1970s is different from the damage caused by rich countries and the tumultuous growth of emerging countries today, and different from the damage that two billion Chinese and Indians will cause when they soon approach western levels of consumption [...]. The survival of threatened species will not be fought on the front of industrial consumption and the availability of resources, including the resource *World*, but the future of the whole Earth and human existence.

International meetings are generally dedicated to scientific description of phenomena, such as questions of climate change, and to political discussion on how to tackle the problems. The result of this duality is often a difficult composition of special interests that makes mediation useless and disregards scientific knowledge. An example of this is the fact that the United Nations Framework Convention on Climate Change (UNFCCC), a non-binding document produced by the Summit of Rio in 1992, is renewed every year by the Conference of Parties (COP), an operative instrument for implementing measures against the emergencies of climate change. The famous Kyoto Protocol, that only became binding in 2005, was the product of COP3 (Kyoto 1997); the other COPs concluded with many proclamations but few solutions. For example, at the COP12 (Nairobi, November 2006) the umpteenth exhortation of scientists alarmed by the greenhouse effect led only to non-binding measures, many noble words and *see you at the next meeting* on the political side.

Date	Event or report	Institution
9 October 2006	Overshoot Day	Global Footprint Network
24 October 2006	Living Planet Report	WWF
29 October 2006	The State of Food Insecurity in the World	FAO
30 October 2006	The Stern Review on the Economics of Climate Change	Nicholas Stern – British government
6–17 November 2006	United Nations Climate Change Conference and COP12 – Nairobi (Kenya)	United Nations
10 January 2007	Limiting Global Climate Change to 2 degree Celsius: Policy option for the EU and the world for 2020 and beyond	Environmental Directorate of the European Commission
2 February 2007	4th Assessment Report	IPCC

Why is it so difficult to reach a compromise, or why do compromises lead to such weak provisions and solutions? Is it because the foundations of international politics are not solid enough to build anything other than non-binding general agreements? Or is the political-institutional element only a façade of the economic edifice that guides the behaviours of states and populations? This is likely, because otherwise it is impossible to explain why 20% of the world population owns 80% of the world's resources, and why 85% of the CO_2 released into the atmosphere by burning of fossil fuels is the direct or indirect responsibility of developed countries, which constitute less than 16% of the world population, or why USA contributed to 30% of world emissions between 1860 and 1990.

Environmental signs in economics

The economic system is orientated towards objectives that are limited in time and space and operates with instruments that are not coherent with the complexity of the ecosystem on which it rests, apparently oblivious to long-term prospects and its own capacity to survive indefinitely. However, certain aspects of the concept of sustainability stem from economic thought.

Sir John Hicks,[3] Nobel Laureate (economics), defined income as the maximum amount that can be spent without reducing the possibilities of real future consumption. Herman Daly,[4] citing Hicks, claims that the aim of calculating income is to give people an indication of how much they can consume without becoming poor. When a person saves, he/she is therefore planning to be richer in future; when a person lives beyond his means, he is going to be less well off in future. The idea of income, Daly continues, also holds at national level. Income is not an exact theoretical concept, but rather a practical indication of the maximum amount that can be spent by a nation without becoming impoverished. The central feature of income is its sustainability, but note that this is a concept of sustainability or permanence in time belonging exclusively to the economic sphere. In other words, one must not damage the capacity of the economic system to produce the same level of (economic) wealth in the period following that in which the income is spent. This capacity is maintained by not liquidating capital.

Another important advance was the advent of environmental economics, a branch of traditional economics established in the early 1960s, with the aim of accounting the effects of human activity on the environment, and vice versa.

3. Hicks, J.R., *Value and Capital*, 2nd edition, Oxford University Press: Oxford, 1946.
4. Daly, H., *Beyond Growth. The Economics of Sustainable Development*, Beacon Press: Boston, 1996.

It emerged at a time when problems associated with agricultural and industrial contamination began to be evident as damage to the environment and to resources caused by economic growth. Sometimes this damage was irreparable, other times it was very expensive to repair. In the course of its evolution, environmental economics has certainly had many achievements, including awareness of the limits to growth and the importance of goods and services existing outside the market. However, the collocation of this discipline has always been the market, which has meant that its position in economic theory has remained marginal. In the wake of milestones in economics, such as the work of Arthur C. Pigou[5] and Ronald Coase,[6] the motivation of the first environmental economists was to try to correct externalities (external effects) produced by economic activity, by viewing the problem as market failure. The so-called 'internalisation' of externalities involves expressing environmental events induced by economic activities in monetary terms or counterparts, and can be achieved in many ways, such as through taxation, emission quotas, standards and subsidies, about which discussion continues. The main criticism of environmental economics has been that it often neglects global questions that emerge on a large scale and over long periods, while concentrating on the limits of the market. By its very nature, environmental economics has always maintained great faith in market instruments. A typical example is an incentive or environmental tax on goods, which is assumed to automatically favour reallocation of resources towards environmentally more friendly sectors and productions, inducing everyone to reduce pollution or the rate of exploitation of resources within the desired limits. The mechanical approach to the behaviour of economic agents, whether individuals, firms or the aggregate economy, ensures the survival of reductive views that often ignore the complexity of relations. Today, when speaking about the environment in a traditional economic context, externalities and market failures are still the only concession of dominant theory to something external and alien.

The reasoning of environmental economics does not consider certain essential elements:

1. The uncertainty permeating relationships between human activities and available resources. Consider, for example, the fact that today's use of environmental goods and services can have future consequences. It is not possible to extract resources forever or to produce and dispose of unlimited quantities of wastes. What we do today has consequences in the long period that we do not know. This is not the uncertainty entered in mathematical

5. Pigou, A.C., *The Economics of Welfare*, Macmillan and Co.: London, 1932.
6. Coase, R., The problem of social cost. *Journal of Law and Economics*, **3**, pp. 1–44, October 1960.

and statistical models in the literature. It is actually the Heisenberg's uncertainty of knowledge, calling for application of the precautionary principle.[7]

2. Things may have intrinsic values and rights by virtue of the interaction between subject and object, in this case humans and the environment, without there being any market transaction. Such values could be the basis of economic implications or of social and ethical values, which transcend the purely economic and market aspects. To ignore them for lack of a way to measure them leads to large errors. Today, Ricardo's concept of 'free gifts of nature' is a dangerous equivocation.
3. Many decisions involving the environment are characterised by irreversibility, so that any decision limiting future choices about alternative forms of utilisation becomes an irreversible decision. Neoclassical economic theory rests on a view of the economy as an isolated system. The fundamental image of the process of production and consumption is that of a flow of goods, services and money from factories to families and vice versa, without any exits or entrances. Dominant economic theory lacks a complementary physical perspective, according to which the economic process is described as a one-directional, irreversible entropic process in which energy and matter are transformed into economic goods and services and in the end into degraded energy and matter, namely contaminants, effluent, garbage and heat.

The watershed of the 1970s

In the 1970s, a number of events touched the sensibilities of economists and non-economists, to different degrees, with regard to the relationship between human activity and the natural environment. Much essential literature was published.

In 1974, there was a violent oil shock when Arab countries decreed an oil embargo on countries supporting the military and financial policy of Israel after the war of Yom Kippur (October 1973). Between October and January, the price of crude oil quadrupled with respect to pre-war prices, triggering a recessive phase that took a long time to overcome. This event shook those who, sensitive to economic questions, posed the problem of the survival of the economic system under certain conditions. With their objective of maintaining positive per capita consumption for an indefinite time (as implied by Hicks's definition of income), economists were faced with the problem of the depletion of resources. Robert Solow claimed that the fact that certain resources

7. Tiezzi, E., *Steps Towards an Evolutionary Physics*. WIT Press: Southampton, 2006; especially the third step – thermodynamic uncertainty.

are only available in limited quantities does not necessarily modify the possibility of indefinitely increasing output. He sustained that previous generations took limited resources for as long as they could increase the stock of reproducible capital, which means that the introduction of exhaustible resources in intertemporal optimisation does not imply any great inversion of basic principles, provided certain conditions are met, the first of which is the possibility to substitute natural resources with reproducible resources.[8] In other words, the subject of the model is the economic system with its capacity to produce goods and services and to generate income. Hence it does not matter what type of resources (input) are used to obtain flows of products (output), nor the value or role they have in other contexts (e.g. the environmental context). It only matters that capital, or the totality of means of production, maintains its productive capacity. This concept was formalised by John Hartwick in the rule that bears his name, according to which the way to have an eternal and constant flow of per capita consumption is for society to invest all current incomes obtained from use of the stock of exhaustible resources.[9] In other words, to maintain a constant flow of consumption indefinitely, it is necessary to make sure that the totality of available capital remains intact.

The implications of the concept of 'maintaining capital intact or constant', where 'constant' is an abbreviation of 'non-decreasing' regard the presence of inputs of natural capital (resources) and man-made capital in the production function. In order to meet the condition for sustainability proposed by Hartwick and Solow, it must be possible to substitute the second type of capital for the first, since it is assumed that resources, especially non-renewable ones, are subject to depletion.

Considering the two forms of capital as perfect substitutes, it is possible to explain why an economy can grow indefinitely while resources are subject to depletion, and on Solow's side, why this limit does not undermine the basic principles of growth theory.

This argument is collocated in the neoclassical framework of growth theory with exhaustible resources, and although it is unsatisfactory, being calibrated only on the economic system with its parameters of consumption, production, optimal allocation, technological progress and the like, it is an important step in the definition of certain categories relevant to sustainability.

However, its flanks are bared to many criticisms, based especially on the dignity of the role of natural capital as support for human activities and as a vital element in its own right and essential for life on the Earth. The definitions

8. Solow, R.M., Intergenerational equity and the exhaustible resources. *Review of Economic Studies, Symposium on the Economics of Exhaustible Resources*, **41**, pp. 29–46, January 1974.
9. Hartwick, J.M., Intergenerational equity and the investing of rents from exhaustible resources. *American Economic Review*, **66(5)**, pp. 972–974, 1977.

of weak and strong sustainability are crucial because they are derived from the role that natural capital is considered to play.

On one hand, weak sustainability does not consider the special nature of the environment but puts it in the same category as other forms of capital, without this meaning excessively rapid exploitation of non-renewable resources or implying that environmental degradation goes unnoticed. Indeed, the latter scenarios would cause loss of future well-being, unless accompanied by adequate compensation with investments in alternative forms of wealth.

On the other hand, strong sustainability rejects any degree of substitutability of natural goods with man-made goods, because it considers the special irreplaceable nature of the environment.

Weak sustainability is a different way of expressing Hartwick's rule, which is achieved by maintaining the stock of capital constant, provided there is a high degree of substitutability between man-made and natural capital and technological change balances the physical limits opposing unlimited growth, making it possible to increase the productivity of capital stocks, to ensure a constant flow of per capita consumption (even if certain resources become depleted) and to compensate population growth and its effects on the level of consumption.

Criticisms of weak sustainability arise from the fact that the concept does not include the important links between environment and economy, such as the need for natural capital to produce manufactured capital, and especially the role of the former as provider of services that sustain life.

Another major event in the 1970s was the publication of research by Dennis and Donella Meadows with Jorgen Randers and William Behrens, commissioned by the Club of Rome and conducted at MIT in Boston: *Limits to Growth*.[10] One conclusion of the study was that if current growth continued unchanged in the five basic sectors (population, industrialisation, pollution, food production and consumption of natural resources), humankind would reach the natural limits of growth in less than 100 years. The most likely result would be a sudden, uncontrollable decline in population and of the industrial system. However, it was possible to modify this line of development and achieve a condition of ecological and economic stability that would last into the future. The condition of global equilibrium could be defined to satisfy the material needs of the inhabitants of the Earth and to give everyone the same opportunity to develop human potential. If humankind opted for the latter alternative instead of the former, the probability of success would be greater, the sooner work in this direction began.

The aim of the research was to analyse the future of human activities in the long period, given the physical constraints preventing infinite growth. A model known as *World III* was developed to construct development scenarios. The book

10. Meadows, D.H., Meadows, D.L., Randers, J. & Behrens III, W.W., *Limits to Growth*. Universe Books: New York, 1972.

deals with growth, economics, relations of economics with the environment and resources, population and standard of living, in some cases advising changes in direction. The path of growth was constructed in three stages: growth, gradual approach of physical limits and overshoot, followed by collapse, when an uncontrolled decline in population and well-being would occur. Unchecked material growth leads to collapse when the Earth's limits (carrying capacity of the planet, pressure on resources and mechanisms of absorption of waste) are surpassed. In 1972, the authors were optimistic that the carrying capacity of the planet was still far away; 20 years later, they proposed an update of the research in which the limits had been exceeded.[11]

We can now read the third publication of these authors.[12] They are now less optimistic because new data confirm that the limits have been exceeded. Their pessimism is shown by their conviction that human society lacks the ability to take intelligent, altruistic and long-sighted measures to meet the challenge. This can be appreciated by a glance at emission trends and oil production, evidence of hunger and degradation of the planet's living species, aquifers and forests. The causes of overshoot are basically the usual three: (1) development, acceleration and rapid change; (2) limits beyond which the system cannot go without damage; (3) delayed or defective perception of the limits and of responses aimed at keeping the system within these limits.

Far from being a pageant of pessimism and resignation towards imminent ruin, the book continues to be constructive and to appeal to consciences about the urgent need for action, because 'collapse is not a desirable future'.

Economic quantification of environmental phenomena has been a subject of research for many economists. In the 1970s, after contact with Simon Kuznets, Christian Leipert, economist at the Berlin Institute of Economic-Ecological Research, began his work at the frontier between the two disciplines.[13] He observed that the environmental problems emerging at that time could be defined as co-products of economic growth, with negative side effects on quality of life and well-being. The term 'quality of life' was heard with force in the 1970s and certain politicians as well as whole movements began to speak of qualitative growth. Leipert followed Kuznets in his conviction that economic activity should aim at satisfying human needs, and inspired a series of criticisms of the national accounting system. The idea was based on the fact that certain

11. Meadows, D.H., Meadows, D.L. & Randers, J., *Beyond the Limits*, Chelsea Green Publishing Company: Post Mills, 1992.
12. Meadows, D.H., Meadows, D.L. & Randers, J., *Limits to Growth. The 30-year Update*, Chelsea Green Publishing Company: Post Mills, 2004.
13. Leipert, C., *Unzulänglichkeiten des Sozialprodukts in seiner Eigenschaft als Wohlstandsmaß* (Inadequacies of the National Product as a Measure of Welfare), PhD Thesis (Paul Siebeck), Tübingen, 1975.

expenditures of families, firms and the public sector were (and are) in actual fact costs induced by the negative effects of economic growth on living and working conditions of the population and on the environment.

Leipert introduced the concept of defensive expenditures. Defensive costs are those connected with certain economic activities by means of which we defend ourselves from the side effects of economic growth. They include expenditures to remedy, neutralise, eliminate, avoid or anticipate damage to the environment and to living conditions in general caused by the economic process of industrialised nations. They are fundamentally an economic expression of social and environmental problems related to the development of the economy.

Leipert identified three key elements that generate social and environmental costs in modern industrial societies: (1) the emergence of structures of production, consumption and construction with heavy environmental impact; (2) the aim of minimising microeconomic costs which simultaneously externalises factors of cost onto third parties or onto society in general, and especially onto the use of environmental functions and natural resources which are practically cost-free; (3) a persistent uncontrolled process of growth of production and consumption that leads to increasing exploitation of environmental resources beyond the carrying capacity of the Earth. Although the conceptual origin is essentially microeconomic, defensive expenditures manifest as an increase in macroeconomic costs that society as a whole has to foot by redirecting an increasing portion of economic resources to restoring environmental functions.[14]

At the International Institute of Environment at the Science Centre in Berlin, in the framework of a project to calculate defensive expenditures in West Germany and their trend between 1970 and 1988, Leipert observed an increase in defensive expenditures of the preventive type (to avoid environmental degradation) and of the remedial type (to compensate or repair environmental damage, e.g. pollution abatement). The weight of society and the economy on the environment, measured by total defensive expenditures, grew from 1.5% of the GDP in 1970 to 3.4% in 1988. GDP grew by 50% in this period, while total environmental defensive expenditures grew by 300%.[15]

In the 1970s, various authors expressed the need for a system of indicators that could represent the complex world of economic and social dynamics in their relation to the environment, to replace or at least complete the one-dimensional nature of economic information. Despite much criticism, most economists continue to use GDP and its rate of growth as an objective function.

---

14. Leipert, C., National income and economic growth: the conceptual side of defensive expenditures. *Journal of Economic Issues*, **3**, pp. 843–856, 1989.
15. Leipert, C., Defensive expenditures. *Taking Nature into Account. Toward a Sustainable National Income*, ed. W. van Dieren, A Report to the Club of Rome, Copernicus-Springer Publishers: New York, 1995.

Today, Leipert writes:

> An obsolete concept of economic growth reigns: it counts the consumption of natural resources and degradation of the environment positively as income. The prevailing concept of growth produces a big illusion of growth and welfare. Politically speaking, the policy of pursuing the highest possible economic growth is discredited by the exposure of defensive expenditures. Under the present conditions of economic development, in which productive as well as destructive forces are at work, it can no longer be taken for granted that economic growth is equated with an increase in welfare. What is needed is a policy of differentiated development focussing on addressing the structural causes of environmentally damaging and costly patterns of production and consumption. Economics has long neglected the difference between wants and needs. Needs are finite, unlike wants which emerge continually in new forms and are therefore insatiable. Economics should address the political-ethical question of balancing the legitimacy of the demands of the living and of future generations for consumption/depletion of natural resources.[16]

Ecological economics

Leipert continues:

> Environmental problems were first perceived as micro-problems in economics, but almost overnight, the precarious co-evolution of economic and ecological systems in the last decades has transformed these micro-problems into macro-problems, which the analytical instruments of environmental economics are not prepared for. The new experience is that the system as a whole, the global ecosystem, is threatened, and not only in its different parts. Actually, ecological knowledge becomes decisive to determine the maximum physical expansion of the economic system: it is no longer a question of determining which and how many resources can be fed into production or what portion of natural capital, being an essential tool of production of goods and services, can be sacrificed on the altar of income, provided it is artificially reconstituted. Today, we can speak of the necessary ecologizing of economics that complements the economizing of ecology in the micro-context, the central theme of neoclassical environmental economics.[17]

Ecological economics is a meta-discipline established at the end of the 1980s as a point of encounter between different disciplines, methodologies and

16. Leipert, C. & Pulselli, F.M., The origins of research on defensive expenditures: a dialogue with Christian Leipert. *International Journal of Design & Nature and Ecodynamics*, **3(1)**, 2008 (in press).
17. Ibid.

philosophies orientated to create a new relationship between human activities (represented by the noun *economics*) and its environment in the broad sense (represented by the adjective *ecological*). Far from being a new branch of traditional economics, ecological economics is an attempt to exceed the frontiers of traditional disciplines by studying the links between ecological and economic systems, according to Robert Costanza, one of its founders. A key aim of this research was to develop sustainable models of economic development, distinct from economic growth, which is not sustainable in a finite planet. A key aspect of developing sustainable models is the role of constraints: thermodynamic constraints, biophysical limits, limits to natural resources, limits to absorption of pollution, demographic limits, constraints imposed by planetary carrying capacity and, above all, our limited knowledge of what these limits are and how they influence the system.

Ecological economics is not a discipline, nor does it aspire to become one. For lack of a better term, we call it a 'transdiscipline'.[18] It is still 'under construction', and therefore no fully accepted methodologies or tools exist. Instead, its practitioners draw on methodologies and tools from various disciplines to address specific problems. Ecological economics seeks to ground economic thinking in the dual realities and constraints of our biophysical and moral environments. Current 'canonical assumptions' of insatiable wants and infinite resources, leading to growth forever, are simply unrealistic and their dire consequences are evident.[19]

In 1990, the International Society for Ecological Economics (ISEE) promoted its first conference in Washington, during which specialists of many disciplines attempted to change the direction of economics towards community, environment and a sustainable future.

Regarding the second conference, Paul Ekins, Carl Folke and Rudolf De Groot write:

> In November 1990, at a café in the central square of Siena, Italy, the theme of the upcoming ISEE conference in Stockholm in 1992 was discussed. The working title of the conference *Maintaining Natural Capital* did not really capture the essence of the issues to be raised. In an intense discussion Herman Daly suddenly proclaimed 'Let's use *Investing in Natural Capital* instead!' The shift from maintaining (in essence preserving the stock of capital) to investing marked recognition of renewable natural capital as a dynamic entity that needs to be understood and actively managed. The shift gave credit to the fact that it is not sufficient to assume that if we only live

18. See Chapter 7.
19. Daly, H. & Farley, J., *Ecological Economics – Principles and Applications*, Island Press: Washington, DC, 2004.

> on the rent of the natural capital stock it will be conserved. Instead we will have to find ways to value and manage the capacity of natural capital to generate and sustain the rent, actively adapt to the dynamic nature of complex systems and learn to live with uncertainty and surprise.[20]

The second ISEE conference took place in Stockholm in August 1992. About a thousand scientists from all over the world tackled the theme *Investing in natural capital – a prerequisite for sustainability*.

The third ISEE conference was held at San Jose, Costarica, in 1994 and is known as the *Down to Earth* conference. A balanced group of scholars attended: one-third were economists, one-third biologists and ecologists and the other third were experts in various disciplines (sociologists, political scientists, demographers, etc.).

ISEE meetings have continued on a two-yearly basis, with increasing emphasis on interdisciplinarity, on the role of natural capital primarily as a support system for life and secondly as an instrument for human activity, and finally on global environmental problems such as climate change and loss of biodiversity.

The conference in New Delhi in December 2006 had *sustainability and human well-being* as its theme, as if to emphasise the true objective of economics: regulation (nomos) of the environment and resources (oikos) for human welfare (and not for plunder and accumulation).

The line taken by ecological economic theorists asserts the importance of the role of environmental goods as input for production, contrasted with growth theory with exhaustible resources; it criticises growth theory's principle of substitutability of man-made and natural capital.

The main proponent of ecological economic thought is certainly Herman Daly. He sustains that if natural resources, N, are included in a production function together with the factors capital, K, and labour, L:

$$Y = f(K, L, N),$$

the marginal product of K and L, for constant resources, will be zero since there can be no extra unit of output if labour and capital are increased because there is no further physical substance from which further product can be derived.

This may seem a subversion of neoclassical economic theory, but it follows as a direct consequence of analysis of human activity when not only economic but also biological and physical aspects are taken into consideration. Natural resources are the only material factor of production, the crucial importance of which implies optimal management if they are to be enjoyed

20. Ekins, P., Folke, C. & De Groot, R., Identifying critical natural capital (Editorial). *Ecological Economics*, **44(2–3)**, pp. 159–163, 2003.

by future generations, and calls for adjustment of production, including production of wastes, to the laws of physics, especially thermodynamics, which govern life.

According to Daly, what is usually known as production is actually transformation. Labour and capital are agents of transformation (*efficient causes*), whereas resources are what is transformed (*material causes*). We may substitute an efficient cause with another, or a material cause with another, but the relation between efficient and material causes is complementarity, not substitutability. Once we recognise the truth about inputs from nature, we have to inform ourselves about their scarcity and the ecological processes that regenerate them. Once we recognise the fact that output wastes are returned to nature, we have to adjust to the capacity of ecosystems to absorb them. This said, as ecological economists, we can no longer fail to see that the economy is a subsystem of a finite, non-growing, materially closed, complex ecosystem.[21]

On this basis, it is also possible to appreciate Daly's ideas about the possibility of substituting man-made (or artificial) capital for natural capital. Daly sustains that transformed material and the means of transformation are complementary and not substitutes. Can an increase in sawmills replace decreasing forests? To the contrary, the productivity of sawmills, refineries and fishing nets (human capital) decreases with decreasing forests, oil and fish (natural capital). Natural capital, as a supplier of primary material and energy, is therefore complementary to man-made capital. But natural capital as absorber of wastes is also complementary to the man-made capital that generates these wastes. Once we understand the complementarity of natural and man-made capital, it becomes clear that development is limited by whichever of the two is less available. If the two factors were interchangeable, then neither would be a limiting factor because the productivity of one would not depend on the availability of the other. The world is in transition from an era in which the limiting factor was man-made capital to an era in which the limiting factor is *what remains* of natural capital: the fish catch is limited by the scarcity of fish populations, not by the number of fishing trawlers; wood production is limited by the scarcity of forests, not by the number of sawmills; the quantity of crude oil pumped out of the Earth is limited by the availability of oil from the wells (or by the capacity of the atmosphere to absorb CO_2), not by extraction capacity; agricultural production is limited by the availability of water, not by tractors or harvesters.

We have gone from a world relatively rich in natural capital and poor in man-made capital (and humans) to a world poor in natural capital and rich in man-made capital. The aim is still to find compatibility between human activities and the environment and to act in a way that this compatibility is durably maintained.

21. See, e.g. Daly, H., Georgescu-Roegen versus Solow/Stiglitz. *Forum. Ecological Economics*, **22** (special issue), 1997.

Daly inaugurates the line of research that makes this project operative and dictates the principles of sustainability:

> For the management of renewable resources there are two obvious principles of sustainable development:
>
> 1. harvest rates should equal regeneration rates (sustained yield)
> 2. waste emission rates should equal the natural assimilative capacities of the ecosystems into which the wastes are emitted.
>
> Regenerative and assimilative capacities must be treated as natural capital, and failure to maintain these capacities must be treated as capital consumption, and therefore not sustainable.
>
> There remains the category of non-renewable resources which strictly speaking cannot be maintained intact short of non-use (and if they are never to be used then there is no need to maintain them for the future!). Yet it is possible to exploit non-renewables in a quasi-sustainable manner by limiting their rate of depletion to the rate of creation of renewable substitute.
>
> The quasi-sustainable use of non-renewables requires that any investment in the exploitation of a non-renewable resource must be paired with a compensating investment in a renewable substitute (e.g. oil extraction paired with tree planting for wood alcohol).[22]

From here to a definition of sustainability,[23] the distance is short: sustainability is the set of relations between human activities with their fast dynamics and the biosphere with its generally slower dynamics. These relations must be such as to permit human life to continue in time, for individuals to satisfy their needs and for the different human cultures to develop, *but* in such a way that changes to nature caused by human activities remain within limits and do not destroy the global biophysical context.

The process of environmental degradation can only be slowed down by re-establishing an agreement with biological equilibrium and with the complexity of natural systems. From a biological point of view, many agree that increased complexity and diversity of genetic information increases ecosystem stability. Biological complexity is therefore synonymous with stability.

To understand these things, disciplines must be combined. A general integration of scientific disciplines, humanities, social sciences, economics and law is needed. Matthias Ruth attempted to do this. Using basic thermodynamic concepts, he represented the economic system as an open system that exchanges

22. Daly, H., Toward some operational principles of sustainable development. *Ecological Economics*, **2**, pp. 1–6, 1990.
23. For more about sustainability, see Tiezzi, E. & Marchettini, N., *Che cos'è lo sviluppo sostenibile?* Donzelli: Rome, 1999.

flows of matter and energy with a larger system (environment) which contains it. He defined sustainability as a state of the ecosystem, which consists of interconnected components, such as biotic components and economic systems, in which the structure and function of each component can be maintained in the long period. Thus, assessment of sustainability can be made on the basis of flows of matter and energy, while any deviations can be corrected by socio-economic intervention.[24]

We believe that the environmental and the socio-economic aspects have a different hierarchical value: economic advantage can be induced or driven by laws, social behaviours, political decisions, etc., if (necessary condition) ecological-physical sustainability is already achieved. If we consider a system that is not economically profitable but ecologically sustainable, a change in the socio-economic framework can (and should) enhance economic performance, maintaining the same physical conditions. The contrary, however, is not true: if the goal is economic profit, some environmental aspects could be irreversibly damaged. At most, we may have a 'compatible', but not a sustainable, development.

---

24. Ruth, M., *Integrating Economics, Ecology and Thermodynamics*, Kluwer: Dordrecht, 1993.

Chapter 3

The foundations of sustainability

The idea of *sustainable development* is not new. It was formalised by the Brundtland Commission about 20 years ago. Since then, many eminent scholars in different disciplines have worked to understand and explain what is meant and what is *not* meant by the expression. There have been many scientific contributions, symposia and international conferences inspired by the need to find the most appropriate behaviour to ensure prosperous survival of the human species for an indefinite time. These events have adopted the theme 'development that satisfies present needs without compromising the possibility of future generations satisfying theirs'.[1]

Nevertheless, the concept of sustainability remains elusive and vague. This is because it has become an advertising slogan, marketing tool and electoral manifesto through common usage, rather than an objective with deep epistemological, cultural and scientific foundations. Today, associating the adjective *sustainable* with something means attributing a positive connotation, by virtue of the erroneous common perception that sustainability and feasibility or compatibility are the same thing. It is understood that something sustainable probably has something to do with the environment, similar to a cycling track in a city.

The pillars of sustainability

The foundations of sustainability are biophysical foundations that obey the laws of nature that govern all human behaviour. In speaking of sustainability,

1. WCED, *Our Common Future*, Oxford University Press: Oxford, 1987.

it is always necessary to bear in mind the three great pillars that support it: (1) time, (2) biophysical limits and (3) relationships.

Time

The concepts of carrying capacity and sustainable development are linked. Carrying capacity is the number of individuals of a population that the population's environment can support. The concept was originally defined for relatively simple population–resource systems, e.g. the number of cattle or sheep an area of pasture could maintain without deteriorating. For the human population, it is much more complex due to the great variety of resources that humans take from the environment, the great quantity of wastes they put back, and the range of their possible technologies, institutions and life-styles. Carrying capacity is a dynamic concept; it is not constant but varies with meteorological conditions and other external factors, as well as the pressure exerted by the species it carries.[2]

Dynamicity, or the fact that carrying capacity varies in time, means that it is a concept close to, but not the same as sustainable development. The verb *to carry* means to hold, contain or support something, whereas *sustain* means to maintain in time. To consider time in the ambit of sustainability therefore means considering the dynamics of human activity and of ecosystems, but not as a simple sequence of changes of state and modifications, but as evolution. This helps us to understand which of these modifications are positive and which should be avoided, and whether or not the future is merely a destiny to accept fatalistically and adapt to.

In December 2006, the world conference 'Ravage of the Planet'[3] was opened by the plenary lecture of Adolfo Pérez Esquivel, winner of the Nobel Peace Prize in 1980 for his work for human rights in relation to processes of development, especially in Latin America, and for his commitment to environmental conservation:

> The equilibrium between man and nature has been broken. Science and technology have caused an acceleration of the natural cycle. Every being has its own cycle and this acceleration has changed life's objectives and conditions, resulting in marginalisation. The main novelty of technology is the acceleration and velocity of time. It is no coincidence that Galileo, at the moment of the birth of modern science, was studying acceleration, and that the most expensive piece of nuclear physics equipment, nowadays, is for the acceleration of particles. Time in technology is different from cosmic time and human time, and because of that, technology has the awesome power of modifying not only human nature, but Nature itself.

---

2. Meadows, D.H., Meadows, D.L. & Randers, J., *Beyond the Limits*, Chelsea Green Publishing Company: Post Mills, 1992.
3. The First International Conference on Management Resources, Sustainable Development and Ecological Hazards – 'Ravage of the Planet'. Bariloche, Argentina, 12–14 December 2006.

On one hand, the avalanche of technology cannot be stopped; a type of fatality exists in all fields leading towards the most complete technology. It is no longer the machine that must adapt itself to man, but he who must adapt to the rhythm of the machine. This situation leads to the human being becoming more and more divorced from nature, because of the use and abuse of natural resources, by developed countries in particular, and their responsibility for the transfer of pollutants to developing countries.

The application of these policies gives priority to financial capital over human capital in a process of accumulation but not redistribution of goods and resources, destroying harmony between human beings and nature.

Time becomes a critical factor in the production process. It is now evident that in all cost-benefit relations, the time factor intervenes decisively, and a new system of individual and social values operates under the surface. The great danger in the current millennium is that the fast world and the slow world are out of phase. Everything seems to indicate that there is an imminent and progressive isolation of the dispossessed towards a fatal solitude, due to the accelerated isolation of the world, of wealth with its control of vital mechanisms. In our present world, which is characterised by the process of acceleration, life in our planet is at risk.

Biophysical limits

Sustainability is an anthropocentric concept. It would be useless to talk about sustainability for nature. The Earth has existed for 4.5 billion years, during which wonderful, slow, biological evolution occurred through practical application of winning strategies. Nature diversified: biodiversity is a strong general attribute for survival. Nature used the most abundant and certain energy source, solar energy, learning how to feed primordial vital mechanisms, including photosynthesis, from this source. Nature succeeded in optimising resource management and in disposing of wastes and excess degraded energy, e.g. by closing cycles or retransmitting heat into space. Nature has been successful in surviving in time.

The human species, on the other hand, tends to ignore the winning strategies that nature has demonstrated, behaving, paradoxically, in quite the opposite manner.

Modern man's counterpart for biodiversity is homologation: the fact that humans dress so similarly in different parts of the globe, is homologation; the fact that most young people the world over like British pop or gangsta rap of the American slums, though all populations have different musical traditions, is homologation; the fact that humans want to dissolve geographical borders and national diversity in favour of globalisation of markets, is homologation. These trends spring from the common root of all world economies: economic growth.

Modern man's counterpart for solar energy is the energy of fossil fuels, since the latter can apparently be exploited without time constraints. The speed of use is limited solely by technical capacity to extract and refine. Nobody asks how long we can use fossil energy resources, as long as they can be extracted and exploited to our heart's desire.

Modern man's counterpart for nature's capacity to use and re-use all resources and dispose of degraded (high entropy) matter and energy that can no longer be used, is irrational use of natural capital and waste of energy and materials. Indeed, the increase in greenhouse effect is a direct consequence of the great quantity of greenhouse gases emitted by combustion of fossil fuels in complete disregard of the natural capacity of ecosystems to absorb them.

To ignore nature's ways means ignoring the limits beyond which the natural phenomenon of life can *no longer maintain* itself (sustain). In nature, the struggle for life is sometimes fierce and cruel. It is a battle for survival in the prey–predator chain. However, as life and death alternate to the rhythm of nature and drive evolution, every being has its chance. Even the tiny, apparently insignificant butterfly *Caligo memnon* can win its struggle by deceiving predators into seeing an owl instead of a butterfly with eyes painted on its wings.

It is necessary to follow the strategy of nature. She diversifies instead of depleting; she re-uses, leaves possibilities open, waits her turn and observes limits. Today, nobody is prepared to wait or to observe limits.

On this topic, Enzo Tiezzi writes:

> Freedom is a sort of flag for me, and my own freedom is very dear to me, but this does not stop me from recognizing that in nature there are certain universal limits. For example we cannot go below –273°C, we cannot exceed the speed of light, everything that exists is in three dimensions and no more. All these limits have always existed and will continue to exist; they are limits which man cannot do anything about. To obey and respect the laws of nature does not mean renouncing one's freedom.
>
> I am an incurable optimist but my optimism does not come from the type of scientific ignorance which induces people to say that nature is great and strong and can withstand man's onslaught. Nor is it based on a shallow hope of some technological miracle. It is based on the conviction that man has the capacity to make the right decisions to get himself out of this dilemma.[4]

Relationships

Thermodynamics is the science of limits. It sets limits to the total availability and capacity to exploit energy. According to the first principle of thermodynamics,

4. Tiezzi, E., *The End of Time*, WIT Press: Southampton, 2003.

the energy in the universe is constant: energy cannot be created or destroyed. This principle of the conservation of energy can be expressed by saying that the total energy existing in the universe, in all its possible forms, is constant. Energy can pass from one form to another, but the total of the various forms is always constant. The first principle is a law defining the very existence of energy and matter and establishes its conservative character. The second principle of thermodynamics states that energy cannot be freely transformed from one form to another and that thermal energy (heat) can go freely from a hot source to a cold body, but not in the opposite direction. The second principle of thermodynamics therefore says that a machine cannot transfer heat from a cold body to a hot one without expending energy. In the universe, a degraded form of energy, heat, is favoured. For any transformation of energy, such as transformation of energy into mechanical work, part of the energy used is degraded. This loss of capacity of do work is called entropy and the universe, or any isolated system, tends towards maximum entropy or disorder. In other words, energy tends towards complete degradation, culminating in so-called thermodynamic equilibrium or 'thermal death'. Entropy is therefore a concept that indicates the direction of events.

Biological systems (open systems) seem to violate the second principle: they have extremely ordered structures that evolve in the direction of greater order or lower entropy. Thermodynamics adds an approach based on relationships and the concept of evolution to the mechanistic approach to studying systems. Relationships and time are obviously fundamental for studying living systems. Thermodynamics tells us about relationships that all natural phenomena must conform to, in space and time.

For a correct interpretation of processes in open (or non-isolated) systems, such as living systems, it is necessary to calculate the decrease in entropy (or increase in order) produced inside the system and the increase in entropy (disorder) created outside. It emerges that the creation of order is only apparent and occurs at the cost of order in the surrounding world.

This change in entropy was formalised by Prigogine[5] for open systems far from thermodynamic equilibrium. The variation in entropy, dS, consists of two terms: d_eS, entropy crossing system borders and d_iS, entropy produced by irreversible processes inside the system:

$$dS = d_iS + d_eS.$$

Certain processes occur inside the system, without any input from outside, as if the system were isolated, hence d_iS is always positive. In isolated systems, entropy increases to a maximum and the system goes towards thermal death. On the other hand, open systems receive flows of negentropy and release high entropy.

5. Prigogine, I., *Introduction to Thermodynamics of Irreversible Processes*, C.C. Thomas: Springfield, 1954.

The result of this exchange, d_eS, may be positive or negative. If d_eS is negative and if

$$|-d_eS| > d_iS,$$

the total change in entropy of the system, dS, is negative: the system evolves and moves away from thermodynamic equilibrium. This is only possible if a negentropy source meets the system's need to constantly dissipate energy and matter in its surroundings, and if a cold sink receives the degraded energy. The sink is just as necessary for life as the source of negentropy.[6]

The entropy balance must be global and must include biological organisms and the environment with which they continually exchange energy and matter. Living organisms therefore develop and live by virtue of the increase in entropy that their metabolism induces in their surroundings. The overall change in entropy (system + environment) is positive, the entropy of the universe increases, the second principle is not violated.[7] On this topic, Erwin Schrödinger wrote:

> A living organism feeds on negative entropy, attracting a stream of negative entropy upon itself to compensate the entropy increase it produces by living and thus to maintain itself on a stationary and fairly low entropy level. [...] The fact that we give off heat (thermal entropy) is not accidental, but essential.[8]

All this shows the importance of relationships for living systems and the dependence of all such systems on their contexts.

Prigogine defined systems that decrease in entropy as they exploit flows of energy as *dissipative structures*. The complexity of these structures manifests in the relations that these open systems entertain with their surroundings and in the way they self-organise.

Human behaviour and its manifestations resemble dissipative structures: economic systems, social systems, regional systems, urban systems all develop by exploiting flows of energy and matter, releasing entropy into their surroundings.

The concept of sustainability therefore rests on three pillars: time, biophysical limits and relationships. A project cannot be called sustainable without these foundations: the use of the word sustainable would be inappropriate, misleading, illusory and false. Human behaviour generally violates the laws of nature for ends that are often in contradiction with the ultimate aim of survival of the species.

---

6. Morowitz, H., *Energy Flow in Biology*, Ox Bow Press: Woodbridge, Connecticut, 1979.
7. For a correct description and interpretation of the work of Prigogine, see also: Tiezzi, E., *The Essence of Time*, WIT Press: Southampton, UK, 2003.
8. Schrödinger, E., *What is Life? The Physical Aspect of the Living Cell*, Cambridge University Press: Cambridge, UK, 1944.

1. *Time:* Western society does not evolve coherently with the environment's capacity to produce the inputs the former requires. Our system is driven by prevalently non-renewable resources, which are exhaustible in a definite determinate time. We help ourselves, ignoring the needs of future generations, contaminating their water, soil, air, as well as our own. If this trend does not change, we will do so increasingly in future.
2. *Biophysical limits:* In the same way, the model of development of industrial countries makes self-sufficiency unlikely. We cannot meet our needs for materials, energy, land, waste sinks and information with our own resources. We therefore help ourselves to the resources of other populations, and if this trend does not change, we will do so increasingly in future.
3. *Relationships:* Care of the Earth and of natural resources will certainly not be promoted by the scramble for increasing levels of financial wealth. Economic instruments lack the criterion of efficient allocation of resources, since they do not consider things not directly linked to the market. We help ourselves to resources, ignoring their real value and scarcity. If this trend does not change, we will do so increasingly in future.

What will that future be?

Historical time, biological time

In 1984, a book denounced the disappearance of two of the four seasons. The book was *Tempi storici, tempi biologici* by Enzo Tiezzi.[9] The book was a long-term project, which began in the 1960s after collaboration of the author with Barry Commoner at Washington University. It is about environmental problems, population, economics, agriculture, energy and society and uses the language of physics, biology, chemistry and ecology. In proposing an interpretation of the reasons for human presence on the Earth in evolutionary and holistic terms, it laid the basis for what was subsequently distilled in the concept of sustainability.

Chapter 2 is about entropy, time and economics:

> Entropy means waste of resource and pollution, energy crises and destruction of the environment. The fundamental Malthusian dilemma of today is related to entropy increase. Georgescu-Roegen and J. Rifkin have brought these concepts into the field of economics. E. Schumacher, Commoner and the European green movements have converted these theories into political

9. Tiezzi, E., *Tempi Storici, Tempi Biologici*, Garzanti: Milano, 1984. The book had a second edition in 1992. In 2001, it was published by Donzelli, Rome, in the updated version, *Tempi storici, tempi biologici Venti anni dopo*, and in 2005, *Tempi storici, tempi biologici Venticinque anni dopo*. It was translated into Portuguese (*Tempos históricos, tempos biologicos*, Livraria Nobel: São Paulo, 1988), Spanish (*Tiempos históricos, tiempos biologicos*, Fondo de Cultura Economica: Città del Messico, 1990) and English (*The End of Time*, WIT Press: Southampton, 2003).

issues. Dominant economic theory, based as it is on mechanistic principles, remains ignorant of the law of entropy and the role of the time variable. The classical dynamic concept of time and its reversibility has nothing to do with reality and nature. Time has direction: it is not isotropic as is space. Thermodynamics introduces 'knowledge of the unidirectional flow of time', tracing the limit between past reality and future uncertainty, and indicating the orientation of time in natural processes.

Chapter 3 is about entropy, evolution and human behaviour:

> Entropy and evolution are one-way processes. Time cannot be made to run backwards but we can influence the speed of these processes, their time derivative. Our way of living, consuming, behaving decides the speed of the entropic process, the speed of dissipation of useful energy, the period of survival of the human species. Being convinced about the second law of thermodynamics does not mean accelerating it, just as being convinced evolutionists does not mean accelerating evolution. [...] If we can understand which parameters in the entropic and evolutionary processes should be slowed, this will be a step towards an overall framework in which human behaviour can be evaluated and a step towards construction of a new society of the future.

According to Tiezzi, their intelligence and culture can elevate humans to the role of arbiter of their own survival (Chapter 4):

> [...] man, because he is a cultural being, runs serious risks when his reproductive pressure exceeds that of wheat. He is the only living creature able to destroy his own species and natural equilibrium by choice. There is no doubt at all that man has the potential to choose a path which leads to a dead end for himself and the entire natural environment. We only need to think of the existing nuclear deterrent or the capacity to modify climate. On the other hand, because he is a cultural being, he can avoid the dead end and make a responsible choice for the future of his species and the delicate equilibrium of the planet Earth. This is the goal of 'species consciousness', the optimism of Sartre's last appeal: 'Sub-men, do not despair!'
>
> Environmental deterioration and dissipation of resources continue to penalize social development. The gap between rich and poor countries and the scarcity of resources point in the direction of unacceptable inequities and increased probability of war. Man has sufficient history and culture not to blindly obey the laws of nature like an animal. He can slow down evolution rather than accelerate it in order to promote social equality. He can slow entropy production with appropriate choices; he can oppose reproductive pressure with conscious choices of birth control; he can work for an international society of peace instead of a balance of terror.

Tiezzi also writes about technology and science in relation to environmental limits and quality of life (Chapter 9). The lines for a new economic approach emerge from this broad treatise. These lines are reflected by the principles of ecological economics:

> Science, within the limits of its uncertainties and non-neutrality, tries to increase our understanding; technology tries to make use of it. Science has improved our knowledge of matter; technology takes practical advantage of it. As such, technology is completely conditioned by the social, economic and institutional environments. The supremacy of science over technology in terms of priority of choice and intellectual analysis, is undisputed. A purely technocratic state would be an imbecilic state.

He continues:

> The quality of our existence depends on the quality of our land (nature, towns, country) and the quality of the human activities which it hosts. Any attack upon this quality to the advantage of a few and the detriment of the rest is unacceptable, even if motivated by allegedly inexorable economic necessity (the 'iron laws' of the market, competition and the like). It is to the advantage of few to build a villa in a natural reserve or to maintain a factory of poisons (dioxin, synthetic bioproteins for feedstock, nuclear power) even with employment considerations. In the long run, the destruction of natural resources and the environment does not pay in economic or social terms.
>
> Science and technology cannot perform miracles, nor can the laws of the market: the only truly 'iron' laws with which our culture must come to terms are the laws of nature.

Tiezzi goes on to criticise the mechanistic economy and its fixation with growth of the gross domestic product:

> The natural and social limits of growth show that the GDP has become a myth. The definition of welfare requires other sciences and other parameters. Universal limits are posed by thermodynamics and the law of entropy on one hand, and biology and the delicate equilibrium of the biosphere on the other. All man's activities must reckon with this law and these limits. [...] to recognize the supremacy of biology and the limits imposed on growth by the laws of nature is revolutionary. It introduces an astounding novelty into economics; it opens new perspectives and rekindles hopes. It enables us to attack consumer society at a higher level based on understanding of a universal culture which is man's heritage. Contemporary economic theory is still linked to the positivist mechanism and Newtonian cosmology: the modern scientific concepts of entropy, indeterminism and uncertainty have not yet undermined the erroneous assumptions of determinism and certainty in

> economic theory. Unlimited scientific progress is postulated as a remedy for diminishing returns, and research and development are confused with miracles. [...]
>
> A relationship between economics and ecology has not yet been established, but certain points are clear: a) ecology teaches economics that there are economic costs distant in space (the whole planet) and time (future generations); b) ecology reveals that many environmental and human costs cannot be reduced to economic units; c) if production only obeys economic laws, what is produced will not necessarily be to man's benefit. [...] Political, social and economic choices first need to pass an ecological-economic filter: if an investment does not fulfil certain essential requirements indicated by Daly or Odum-type analysis, it should be considered bio-economically risky or wrong, and refused.

Chapter 11 was added in the 2001 and 2005 editions of the book and springs from more than 20 years of work in the environmental field: scientific work, quasi-popular science writing and political and social commitment. The following passage reflects the complexity of topics and relations between the human species and the dynamics of life.

> Millions of years have elapsed since our great grandmother, the blue–green alga (as Laura Conti called it), brought about the photosynthetic revolution, giving rise to life on the planet Earth. If we look at this great story of evolution, from which we sprang, we discover three protagonists ignored by the dominant physical sciences: beauty, time and biodiversity.
>
> The limits of a purely quantitative view of nature, which denies the fundamental ecological category of quality and the importance of the aesthetic element, are emerging before the complex temporal dynamics of the biosphere and global ecosystem. These temporal dynamics are based on multiple relations in a process of coevolution based on forms, colours, sounds, odours and flavours. The history of nature is a systemic and evolutionary history, one in which quantity and quality are ever present, a story in which the aesthetic element plays a determinant role. [...]
>
> Observation of nature tells us two important things: that quality and time are not external values but intrinsic properties of living organisms. This is the great lesson of Darwin's theory of evolution, a theory which, among other things, has the merit of not indicating aims or certainties for evolution. Darwin repeatedly underlined the fundamental role of chance and the absence of an end towards which life as a whole moves.
>
> Time modulates forms and structures, sounds and colours: these properties are an uninterrupted thread throughout evolution. Colours, forms and structures pass information between different living species, between plants and animals, between us and the environment. 'Objective science' has reduced colours to a mere parameter, blue to radiation with a wavelength

of 440 nm, just as 'subjective art' regards colour as subjective, as mere sensation.

If we want to see an orange also as a blue orange, without giving up the orange, if we want to contaminate science with art and art with science, we need to consider relations, connections and interactions between observer and observed. The colour green of a plant exists irrespective of whether we see it, because it existed for millions of years before the human mind. Before man appeared on the Earth it was recognised by millions of plants and animals. However, it is also true that when we look at a plant, our mind begins a series of interpretations, of rational and intuitive synthesis, and weaves a series of relations with the plant itself and with the emotions engendered by it. All this is influenced by our culture and our genes.

What we have to do is to fuse microscopic and macroscopic, supersede the dichotomies of reductionism and antireductionism, study biological phenomena in terms of relations and self-organisation, so that the behaviour of the parts becomes coherent. We need a philosophy of nature that I would define as Lucretian, in which rediscovery of aesthetics is determinant in science, economics and politics. It means weaving the first new alphabets that enable us to converse with nature.

[...]

Western science has put nature in a cage of geometric rules and mechanistic laws. We know that they do not hold for living systems, ecosystems, events of biology or events of ecology.

Chapter 4

Sustainable management of resources: commons, knowledge and nature

Resource management is a fundamental question for sustainability and cannot be answered simply by attributing an economic value to resources. Attributed values often do not reflect the real value of a resource, because the market ignores non-economic functions that resources play in ecosystems. In other cases, there is no economic value or no economic value can be determined. For example, it may be difficult to establish criteria for property rights, which almost always leads to unsustainable behaviour.

Herman Daly made important contributions to the concept of sustainability, tackling the problem of commons, especially knowledge and nature.[1] These two categories of goods are closely linked to individual and collectively perceived welfare. He analysed the problems associated with forms of social wealth based on nature and knowledge, as two extreme examples of non-economic capital.

Management based on traditional economic instruments leads to unsustainable behaviour. It is therefore necessary to think of the problem in a different way. In the Preface to this book, Daly defines two characteristics of goods: rivalness and excludability. He asserts that goods can be rival or non-rival: rivalness is a physical property of a good that precludes its simultaneous use by many people; goods are also excludable or non-excludable: excludability is a legal right to prevent another from using your property. Different goods have different combinations of these qualities. The categories that cause problems and are interest to us here are the combinations rival and non-excludable, and non-rival and excludable.

1. Daly, H., Sustaining our commonwealth of nature and knowledge. *International Journal of Ecodynamics*, **1(3)**, pp. 236–244, 2006.

Certain things in our lives are difficult to express in market terms. We are familiar with the market because we deal with money every day, but we also deal with things of great intrinsic value that we are not always able to translate satisfactorily into economic language. The value of these things is evident and real but it has no economic counterpart. When forced into economic terms, it may create problems that lead to incorrect or unsustainable management.

Knowledge and nature are commons essential for the survival of society, and are difficult to evaluate in economic terms. Daly considered their management in relation to the categories of rivalness and excludability.

Knowledge

> Knowledge is easy to use sustainably because it is a non-rival good. If I use the Pythagorean theorem I don't use it up, and I don't prevent you or any number of other people from using it at the same time. We can all use it as much as we want without using it up. The problem of sustainable use of knowledge is trivial – sustainability is guaranteed by the fact that knowledge is non-rival. Knowledge is multiplied among users, not divided. However, expenditure of rival resources in the pursuit of new knowledge, or the teaching of old knowledge, may indeed be unsustainable – but not existing knowledge itself. Once it exists, knowledge is non-rival, has zero opportunity cost, and its efficient allocation requires that its price be zero.

According to Daly, the production cost of knowledge may be high or negligible. Knowledge may arise from an intuition or by chance. Passion for research may drive the production of knowledge, irrespective of material incentives.

> Nevertheless, the idea has somehow grown up that new knowledge would never be discovered unless some people were paid a great deal of money to provide them with the incentive to undergo the drudgery, pain and expense of discovery. Patent monopolies, intellectual property rights, are urged as the way to provide an extrinsic reward for knowledge production. The dominant view is that knowledge, a non-rival good, must be made artificially rival, i.e. legally excludable, so that it will command a market price, which in turn will stimulate its production.
>
> [...] it seems we create a scarcity of knowledge precisely to give it a positive price so it can be counted as private riches, which we mistakenly consider to represent an increase rather than a decrease in public wealth.

Those who justify this apparently illogical mechanism (create scarcity in order to establish a price) hold that unless knowledge becomes scarce enough to have a significant price, nobody in the market will be incentivated to produce it. They cannot conceive that anything could be produced outside the market system.

> But even within that restricted vision, keeping knowledge scarce makes little sense because the main input to the production of new knowledge is existing knowledge, and making that key input more expensive will surely make the production of new knowledge more expensive. [*Furthermore,*] not all new knowledge is equally beneficial, and private profit does not provide the best social filter for selecting what kind of knowledge should be developed.

Nature

The many relationships between humans and their environment make management of the resources and services of nature a complex problem that cannot be forced into a pre-existing framework:

> Nature, in the form of natural resources, is rival. The timber cut to make a table for me cannot be used to make a chair for you. In the form of natural services nature is sometimes rival and sometimes non-rival. Even when it is rival it is sometimes so plentiful relative to the existing scale of demand that it is effectively treated as non-rival, (i.e. legally non-excludable) even though physically it is rival. For example, drinking water is rival, but may be so plentiful as to be non-excludable and command no price. Yet, unlike the Pythagorean theorem, if enough people use it, its inherently rival nature will become apparent. Solar energy provides natural services of light and warmth that are non-rival. But if your photovoltaic panel shades mine, then it is rival, at least during part of the day or year. Furthermore, some resources are rival within a generation but may be either rival or non-rival between generations. For example, renewable resources like timber and fish, while rival at a given time, are non-rival over time if exploited at sustainable yields, but rival over time if exploited beyond sustainable yield. Metals are rival within generations but largely non-rival between generations through recycling. Fossil fuels, however, are rival both within and between generations.

Nature provides a great quantity and variety of goods and services that can be used by humans. Humans can modulate their use of environmental goods and services as they like, in relation to their needs and aims. These two facts mean that goods with different physical characteristics and different degrees of rivalness require different management, case by case.

> The price system, the market, works only for rival goods that are sufficiently scarce to command an opportunity cost, and also to have been declared excludable by a legal system. My shirt is inherently rival, but unless I have exclusive use rights to it then you may take it from me – it would not really be my shirt, it would be a loose shirt up for grabs. So for market exchange to replace conquest, rival goods must also be legally excludable.

Daly explains the need to declare progressive scarcity of environmental resources due to their appropriation by humans. Humans' use of nature does not actually depend on the physical characteristics of environmental resources. Instruments are therefore needed to sustainably modulate resource use.

> [...] for rival goods that are only now becoming scarce and are consequently still treated as non-excludable – the open access commons – it does make sense to institute a regime of excludability, thereby enclosing the resource in the market domain. This combination of rival and non-excludable gives rise to tragedy of the open access commons (overuse and unsustainability). The opposite combination, non-rival and excludable, gives rise to what might be called 'the tragedy of artificial or self-inflicted scarcity' – for example, the inefficient under-use of knowledge due to intellectual property and patent monopoly. This is also a tragedy because treating what is non-scarce as if it were scarce is at least as big an error as treating what is scarce as if it were non-scarce.

Market instruments for the management of commons

Instruments must represent behaviour and may suggest how to obtain a desired result. However, if the aim of behaviour is to please the instrument, distortions and problems may arise. Daly asks whether it is appropriate or fair to make knowledge, a physically non-rival good, legally excludable. The answer is obviously no.

> It is curious that Watson and Crick received no royalties for the discovery of the structure of DNA, yet second-rate gene jockeys are getting royalties by tweaking the monumental discovery of their scientific betters. Nor did Gregor Mendel get any royalties for discovering the principles of heredity – but then he was a monk, motivated by pious curiosity about how God's creation works – however politically incorrect that may be today! [...] So why not cut back on intellectual property – why not rely more on public finance and joy of discovery as the means, motivation, and filter for producing new knowledge? [...]
>
> The relation of profit to new knowledge is nevertheless an important issue in economics. Joseph Schumpeter's theory of profit[2] holds that new knowledge, by virtue of its novelty, confers a temporary monopoly on the firm discovering it, and consequently temporary monopoly profits. These monopoly profits are competed away as the new knowledge gradually spreads to other firms. It is the continuing stream of new invention, followed by temporary

2. Schumpeter, J., *The Theory of Economic Development*, Harvard University Press: Cambridge, MA, 1934.

> monopoly profits, that Schumpeter argued was the source of profit in a competitive market whose tendency is to compete profits down to zero in equilibrium (a necessary condition for efficient allocation, you will remember!).
>
> The benefit of new knowledge does not disappear as it spreads, but rather that benefit is maximized. The benefit from the increased use of the non-rival good (knowledge) is realized in higher productivity of the rival goods (labour, capital and resources).
>
> It is silly to enclose non-rival goods in the market and impose artificial scarcity (excludability) on what is inherently non-rival. [...] Also, if we thought clearly about it, it would be apparent that international development aid should consist more of freely shared knowledge, accompanied by small grants – and less of interest-bearing loans for large projects that require rival goods that create unrepayable debts and dependency.
>
> In sum, my conclusion regarding the sustainable use of the commonwealth of knowledge is that it is in no danger whatsoever of unsustainable overuse, but is in fact grossly underused. Knowledge is both inefficiently allocated and unjustly distributed as a result of excessive reliance on intellectual property. The fundamental error is to treat a non-rival good as if it were rival in order to fit the Procrustean bed of free-market ideology. This has led both to converting a non-rival good into an artificially rival good, and to converting a commonwealth into private property, essentially by 'enclosure' or 'silent theft', as David Bollier[3] calls it in his insightful book of that title. Abolishing all intellectual property tomorrow would be draconian, but a minimum policy implication is that fewer discoveries should be eligible for patent monopolies, and these should be granted for shorter periods of time. Unfortunately, both trends are in the opposite direction.[4]

With regard to the common *nature* (i.e. natural goods and services that are rival and up to now have been non-excludable), Daly advises inclusion in the market in order to avoid 'tragic incentives' for unsustainable use. He states that excludability can be in the form of individual private property or collective social property. What needs to be avoided is open access. Access can be restricted to a community and managed by the community, or it can by restricted at the individual level by private property. How that new property is distributed among individuals then becomes an important issue.

3. Bollier, D., *Silent Theft*, Routledge: New York, 2003.
4. The big danger to the sustainability of knowledge is not overuse, but the incomplete and biased transfer between generations. Witness the fact that few universities any longer offer a course in the history of economic thought.

Daly considers a market-based institution to deal with this broad class of rival but non-excludable goods – the cap-and-trade system. It is worthy of consideration not only because of its practical value, but also because of the light it sheds on a fundamental problem in economics.

> Traditionally, some environmental assets, say fishing rights or rights to emit SO_2, have been treated as non-excludable free goods. Then, as economic growth increases the scale of the economy relative to the biosphere, it is recognized that these goods are in fact rival and impose an opportunity cost at the new larger scale of use.

The cap-and-trade system consists of two phases. The first involves defining a limit, known as the cap, that may be placed at the source or sink end of resource throughput, whichever is more scarce, or easier to control. Setting the cap at a sustainable level is a social–ecological decision, not a market decision. Once a limit has been fixed, the right to extract or emit up to that limit is now a scarce good which has a price. In the second phase, the owner of the scarce good is decided politically, outside the market, since it is a problem of distribution. For example, Daly states that ownership could be social with yearly quotas to deplete or emit auctioned to highest bidders and proceeds entering the public treasury. The emissions trading scheme of the Kyoto Protocol is a cap-and-trade system. Once the good, the limits of its use (scale) and the owners of rights or quotas (distribution) have been defined, exchange in a free market (allocation) can begin.

> The practical problem of cap-and-trade policies confronts us squarely with the logically separate issues of scale, distribution, and allocation. The cap-and-trade system is not 'free market environmentalism' as frequently labelled – it is 'social market environmentalism'. Social constraints on scale (sustainability), and on distribution (fairness) must be politically imposed before markets are allowed to trade permits and determine prices.
>
> Allocation, distribution, and scale are separate problems. Neo-classical economics has dealt mainly with allocation (the apportionment of scarce resources among competing commodity uses – how many resources go to produce beans, to cars, to haircuts, etc.). A good allocation is efficient – in the sense that no reallocation can increase anyone's welfare without decreasing the welfare of someone else. Properly functioning markets allocate resources efficiently in this sense (called Pareto optimality). But this concept of efficient allocation presupposes a given distribution (the apportionment of goods and resources among different people – how many resources embodied in beans, cars, etc. go to you, how many to me). A good distribution is one that is just. A third issue is scale (the physical size of the economy relative to the ecosystem that sustains it – how many of us are there and how many beans, cars, etc. do we each get on average, and how large are the

> associated matter-energy flows relative to natural cycles). A good scale is sustainable. A sustainable scale, like a just distribution, cannot be determined by the market – both are conditions which the market must take as given, which must be politically imposed on the market, and subject to which the market finds the efficient allocation and corresponding prices. Economists' legitimate concern with efficient allocation should not be allowed to obscure the critical presuppositions regarding just distribution and sustainable scale.

The 'free' market does not provide the necessary signals to obtain a sustainable scale, fair distribution and optimal allocation. According to Daly, the causation goes from given scale and given distribution to market prices that are allocatively efficient on the basis of those two givens. But the values of sustainability and justice are set politically, not by market prices. Prices cannot produce optimal allocation, optimal distribution and optimal scale at the same time. We need a separate equation for each variable; likewise, we need an independent policy instrument for each independent policy goal.[5]

> Is our goal optimal allocation? Fine, then supply equals demand pricing in competitive markets can be our policy equation. We also want just distribution? Fine, but we need a second policy instrument (not prices again). We also want a sustainable scale? Fine, now we need a third policy instrument (not prices yet again). Let us by all means keep prices and markets for solving the allocation problem. Now what are our independent instruments for solving the distribution and scale problems? Following the logic of cap-and-trade, which conforms nicely to Tinbergen's rule, scale is set by ecological criteria of sustainability effected by setting aggregate quotas (caps); distribution is set by ethical criteria of fairness effected by distribution of ownership of the quotas; and that leaves only allocation to be settled by efficiency criteria effected through market prices.

The question of the scale of human activity is an essential point on the agenda of ecological economics.[6] It is a priority topic, since the size of the economy must be compatible with the functions and limits imposed by nature. It is impossible to ignore the absolute barriers of finite resources and space. The problem of optimal or sustainable scale is often disregarded by economists.

Sometimes scale is treated as infinitesimal – the economy is thought to be very small relative to the ecosystem, which is consequently considered infinite

---

5. Tinbergen, J., *On the Theory of Economic Policy*, North Holland Publishing Co.: Amsterdam, 1952.
6. See, e.g. Daly, H.E., Allocation, distribution, and scale: towards an economics that is efficient, just, and sustainable. *Ecological Economics*, **6(3)**, pp. 185–193, 1992.

and non-scarce. Alternatively, economists sometimes seem to consider scale as total, the economy is the whole. If everything is economy then nothing is left over as environment, and scale disappears as an issue with allocation taking its place. Then it is no longer necessary to use a specific instrument to determine optimal scale, and prices remain the best instrument. The question thus reduces to giving everything a price, calculating the so-called 'shadow price' for things not traded on the market. This holds for most things in the world, creating a big information problem.

The impossibility of understanding everything through prices is another reason for using composite instruments to manage resources and for institutions to design systemic programmes or tax reform to manage commons.

> A further advantage of the cap-and-trade system is that, if the ownership of the quotas is public, they can be auctioned off for public revenue. The resource-scarcity rents, unearned income, from the newly scarce part of the natural commonwealth, can go to the public, not privileged private parties.
>
> An important proposal of ecological tax reform arises from the above.
>
> Ecological tax reform advocates shifting the tax base away from value added (income earned by labour and capital) and on to 'that to which value is added', namely the throughput flow of resources, preferably at the depletion end (at the mine-mouth or well-head, the point of 'severance' from the ground). Many states have severance taxes. Taxing the origin and narrowest point in the throughput flow, induces more efficient resource use in downstream production and consumption, and facilitates monitoring and collection. Taxing what we want less of (depletion and pollution), and ceasing to tax what we want more of (income) would seem reasonable. [...]The shift could be revenue neutral and gradual. Begin for example by forgoing $x revenue from the worst income tax we have (payroll tax, perhaps). Simultaneously collect $x from the best resource severance tax we could devise (perhaps a carbon tax). Next period get rid of the second worst income tax, and substitute the second best resource tax, etc. Such a policy would raise resource prices and induce efficiency in resource use, while encouraging value added and employment. The regressivity of such a consumption tax could be offset by spending the proceeds progressively, and by instituting a sumptuary tax, or retaining an income tax on high incomes. Also offsetting the regressivity of a consumption tax is its advantage of bringing the underground economy into the tax base.

Daly admits that any change in the tax system is politically very difficult. However, people resent having their earned income, value added, taxed away, and they also resent seeing unearned income in the form of scarcity rents accrue to people who added no value. Ecological tax reform would remove much of the cause of these two justified resentments, while raising public revenue. That is a substantial political advantage to set against the political opposition of the extractive industries.

To summarize, managing the commonwealths of nature and knowledge present us with two rather opposite problems and solutions. For nature, the truly scarce is often treated as non-scarce. Therefore we must recognize the scarcity of natural resources and enclose the resource commons as public property from which we capture the scarcity rent as public revenue. Examples of natural commons are: mining, logging, and grazing rights on public land, the electromagnetic spectrum, absorptive capacity of the atmosphere, orbital locations of satellites, etc. For knowledge, we often treat the truly non-scarce as if it were scarce, enclosing a non-rival good in the prison of excludability. Instead we must free knowledge from this perverse enclosure, allowing it to be allocated efficiently as a non-rival good at its proper price of zero. Especially knowledge financed by government and university research should quickly be freed from enclosure, and even privately financed knowledge should be granted shorter monopoly protection, and eventually be recognized as a non-rival good.

Epilogue

A colleague told me a story that illustrates how far we have strayed. He was on a review panel for awarding large government research grants. In interviewing one of the final candidates he asked for some specific information referred to vaguely in the proposal. The applicant replied that he was not allowed by his university to disclose that information since it was their intellectual property.

Chapter 5

Thermodynamics and the economic system: autarchy and globalisation

The second principle of thermodynamics states that the universe, or any isolated part of it, tends towards a state of disorder, of maximum entropy, or in the words of Clausius, of thermal death. Progressive loss of information and useful energy is a spontaneous, irreversible process towards the condition of thermodynamic equilibrium, which is equivalent to loss of diversity and the consequent disappearance of biological systems and ecosystems.

Life seems to contradict the second principle because living systems create ordered structures by self-organisation. There are actually different ways of describing the evolution of systems with respect to the conditions imposed by the second principle, though the conditions are always valid and never contradicted.

First it is necessary to distinguish between isolated systems (that do not exchange energy or matter with the outside), closed systems (that exchange energy but not matter with the outside) and open systems (that exchange energy and matter with the outside). The Universe is regarded as an isolated system. The biosphere can be considered a closed system. Living organisms and ecosystems are examples of open systems.

In biological systems, as on the Earth (both are non-isolated systems), ordered structures form as a result of energy inputs and outputs. In physical terms, the creation of order means a decrease in entropy within the system, which is always compensated by an increase in entropy in the environment. Clearly, therefore, creation of order in an open system is always associated with an increase in disorder in its surroundings.

Processes regulating the survival of an open system far from thermodynamic equilibrium were modelled by Harold Morowitz,[1] who showed that it is not

1. Morowitz, H., *Energy Flow in Biology*, Ox Bow Press: Woodbridge, CT, 1979.

energy that makes life possible but the flow of energy through an open system. Systems, if non-isolated, are in contact with different hot sources and cold sinks. Constant flows of energy through systems go from hot sources to cold sinks, as in the following flow diagram:

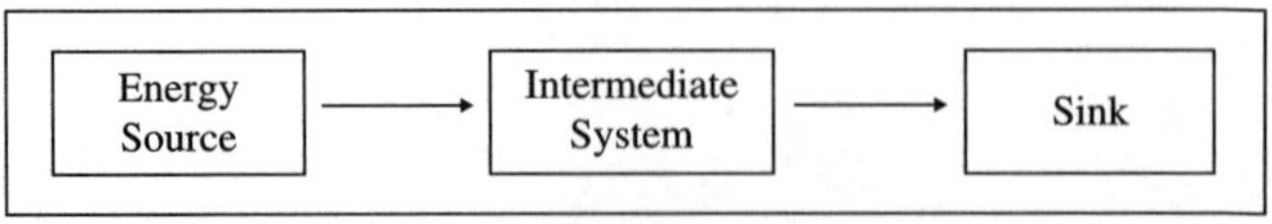

The system represented in this diagram can be divided into two parts:

1. source + sink (ss);
2. intermediate system (int).

According to the second principle of thermodynamics:

$$dS_{ss} + dS_{int} \geq 0,$$

where S_{ss} is the entropy of the system 'source + sink' and S_{int} is the entropy of the intermediate system. The flow of energy from the source to the sink always involves an increase in entropy:

$$dS_{ss} > 0,$$

while the only restriction placed on dS_{int} by the second principle is that:

$$-dS_{int} \leq dS_{ss}.$$

Thus, the entropy of the intermediate system may decrease if there is a flow of energy. This variation in entropy can be explained by Prigogine's formalisation[2] for open systems far from thermodynamic equilibrium, expressed by the concept of *dissipative structures* (see Chapter 3). Open systems absorb negentropy and discharge 'positive' entropy outside themselves. In this way, they evolve and move away from thermodynamic equilibrium. The variation in entropy of the open system (the intermediate system in the model of Morowitz) is negative, and this is only possible if an external energy source meets its requirements for negentropy and if it can somehow get rid of degraded energy. Dissipation is possible if there is a cold sink. This sink is just as necessary for life as the source of negentropy.

As we have already seen, there is a *necessary condition* for the decrease in entropy of an open system: the overall change in entropy of an open system and of the environment with which it exchanges energy and matter (system + environment) must be positive. This transition from low entropy input to high entropy output describes the evolution of far-from-equilibrium systems as dissipative structures.

2. Prigogine, I., *Introduction to Thermodynamics of Irreversible Processes*, C.C. Thomas: Springfield, 1954.

The irreversibility of this trend underlies Prigogine's concept of the *arrow of time*,[3] which confirms the scientific importance of the historical succession of events.

Similarities between ecosystems and human systems

The planet Earth is a closed thermodynamic system (with negligible exchange of matter with the outside). Its history

> can be regarded as the history of photosynthesis, the green talisman of life [...], a history measured in biological time, a history of relationships and coevolutions, a history that humans are part of and to which humans owe their molecular structure and genes.[4]

Photosynthesis opposes entropic degradation because it orders unordered matter: plants gather unordered matter (low energy molecules of water and CO_2 in disorderly agitation) and organise it into complex structures using solar energy. Photosynthesis is therefore a process that traces the path of evolution through capture of solar energy and lowering of the entropy of the planet. The limits of photosynthesis are not dictated by the energy source, the Sun, which is practically infinite (5.6×10^{24} joules/year of energy, more than 10,000 times the energy that the world population consumes in a year), but by the capacity to exploit the flow of energy in order to absorb negentropy. Morowitz's scheme suggests that any inhibition of the flow of low entropy energy from the source (the Sun) to the intermediate system (the biosphere) and of the flow of heat (high entropy) from the intermediate system to cold sinks (celestial space) could prejudice the capacity of the intermediate system to survive in the long period or to maintain the conditions needed for life.

Thermodynamics can therefore represent the relationships between living systems, the evolution of which is unavoidably limited by physical constraints, and the environment. By virtue of its general descriptive characteristics, thermodynamics provides a key for rigorous study of natural systems, ecosystems and living organisms, and their evolutionary dynamics. At the same time, by affinity of these systems with human systems, certain concepts and definitions may be extended to the study of human behaviour and explain trends and evolutions of social systems, even the economic system.

Nicholas Georgescu-Roegen developed a thermodynamic view of the economic system. Like Schrödinger,[5] who stated that living organisms feed on negentropy (and therefore compete for it), Georgescu-Roegen wrote that the

3. Prigogine, I., The arrow of time. *Ecological Physical Chemistry*, eds C. Rossi & E. Tiezzi, Elsevier: Amsterdam, pp. 1–24, 1991.
4. Tiezzi, E., *The Essence of Time*, WIT Press: Southampton, 2003.
5. Schrödinger, E., *What is Life? The Physical Aspect of the Living Cell*, Cambridge University Press: Cambridge, UK, 1944.

economic struggle is a struggle for new sources of low entropy from the environment.[6] His bioeconomic proposal springs from two questions: (1) infinite economic growth contradicts the basic laws of nature; (2) the reversible and circular representation of production and consumption in the economic system needs to be replaced by an evolutionary version of the economic process within the biophysical context that supports it.[7] In his view, the economic process is irreversible, like all biological processes, and depends on a material base. In other words, the economic system is an open system characterised by input of precious resources (low entropy, scarcity) and output of valueless waste (high entropy).

An economic system (or a society or region in the strict sense) uses relations and exchanges with its environment to survive. According to Mathias Binswanger,[8] the economic system can be likened to a dissipative structure far from thermodynamic equilibrium. The evolution and maintenance of economic systems is possible by virtue of inputs of natural resources from terrestrial ecosystems and output of heat and wastes towards terrestrial ecosystems. If the total entropy balance sheet is considered, it is evident that a system of production creates order from disorder and economic wealth at the expense of the environment.

Georgescu-Roegen observes that the entropy of copper is lower than the entropy of the mineral from which it is refined, but this does not mean that the economic activity of humans does not have to obey the law of entropy. Refining the mineral causes a more than compensatory increase in entropy outside the system.[9]

In entropy terms, any action or process (whether biological or economic) results in a deficit for the overall system: the cost is always greater than the result.[10]

Robert Ayres[11] recognises the resemblance between biological organisms that obtain low entropy at the cost of their surroundings, and industrial processes. From a macrosystemic viewpoint, the limit of survival of human society lies in the efficacy of environmental services and in natural self-organisation. According to Ayres, the supply of environmental services is likely to decrease in the coming

6. Georgescu-Roegen, N., The entropy law and the economic problem. *The Ecologist*, **II(7)**, pp. 13–18, 1972.
7. See also Bonaiuti, M. (ed.), *Nicholas Georgescu-Roegen. Bioeconomia. Verso un'altra Economia Ecologicamente e Socialmente Sostenibile*, Bollati Boringhieri: Torino, 2003.
8. Binswanger, M., From microscopic to macroscopic theories: entropic aspects of ecological and economic processes. *Ecological Economics*, **8(3)**, pp. 209–234, 1993.
9. Georgescu-Roegen, N., 1972, op. cit.
10. Georgescu-Roegen, N., *Energy and Economic Myths*, Pergamon Press: New York, 1976.
11. Ayres, R.U., Eco-thermodynamics: economics and the second law. *Ecological Economics*, **26(2)**, pp. 189–209, 1998.

decades, since demand, generated by demographic increase and economic growth, will grow exponentially.

The greater the system the greater the flows involved in its processes; the bigger the system, the more urgent the need to consume resources (low entropy input) and to get rid of entropic wastes (high entropy output). The basic presupposition for an economic system to survive indefinitely is therefore coherence with the physical limits imposed by thermodynamics and conservation of the ecological basis and ecosystem services on which it rests.

Once the dissipative nature of the economic process and its dependence on natural sources and sinks is recognised, problems and questions for the management of the economic system can be reformulated on a new basis.

Autonomy, dependence, autarchy and globalisation

Thermodynamically, human systems (economic, social, regional, urban) can be considered open systems, with self-organising properties and multiple relations and feedbacks between internal components and between them and the outside. With regard to the society, Edgar Morin[12] sustains that its manner of organisation determines its unity, starting from the multiplicity of its components, and enables the emergence of collective properties, such as culture, language and education, that affect all individuals. Social (and economic) systems are complex in their multi-dimensional structures and relationships. For example, they may simultaneously be acentric (working in an anarchic manner through spontaneous interactions), polycentric (characterised by many centres of control or organisation) and centric (having one centre of decision), and they develop networks of relations and feedbacks with the environment. In this context, Morin defines a concept of autonomy based on environmental dependence. Autonomy and dependence are complementary concepts (though they seem in opposition), because systems need resources in order to self-organise and maintain their individuality and originality. Self-organisation and eco-organisation must therefore be interconnected and this is a complex conceptual problem. There cannot be autonomy without dependence.

Similar reasoning can be developed for the behaviour of human systems and the economic system on the basis of Morin's concepts of autonomy and dependence. The evolution of these systems may occur between the two extremes of autarchy and globalisation.

Autarchy – Autarchic human systems are like forts: they are isolated and survive autonomously on their own resources. Autarchy refers to self-government of political systems and autarky to self-sufficiency of economic systems. The terms autarchy/autarky (from the Greek απολυταρχία: self-rule/

---

12. Morin, E., Le vie della complessità. *La sfida della complessità*, eds G. Bocchi & M. Ceruti, Feltrinelli: Milano, 1995.

αυταρκεια: self-sufficiency), historically concern the concept of State as a self-sufficient organisation, composed of subsystems and interacting elements, such as cities, communities, families, and individuals.

An autarkic economic system is a closed system with its own (non-infinite) resources. It is not subject to outside economic, commercial or cultural influences. This absence of relations and contamination is a rare and unnatural condition, and is easily identified as a dictatorial system in which contact with the outside is prohibited. Isolation is imposed from above and applies to the whole system. In pre-industrial civilisations, autarkic systems may have had some positive aspects (imagine a rural system that lives by agriculture from year to year). The current trend towards progressive integration and globalisation of international markets is incompatible with a condition of autarky, unless economic, political and cultural barriers are imposed.

Globalisation – The process of globalisation is the progressive integration of international markets with the prime aim of stimulating economic growth. The concept of integration, typical of globalisation, goes beyond simple interdependence between national economies, on which the process of internationalisation is based. Daly and Farley[13] define globalisation as economic integration of the planet through the free market, free circulation of capital, and to a lesser extent, facilitated migration. It erodes national boundaries for economic reasons.

Theoretically, perfect globalisation is an arbitrary concept that is to economics as the concept of absolute void is to physics. Though abstract and very remote, the hypothesis of definitive integration of markets, expansion of the economic system to global dimensions, could be interpreted as a process akin to levelling of differences (progressive conformity to rules that hold for everyone) and maximum homologisation of systems (loss of information and disappearance of cultural biodiversity).

A thermodynamic, ...

The definition of these two extreme cases (autarky and globalisation) emphasises the importance of physical limits for the sustainability of the economic system. The thermodynamic theory formulated by Morowitz and Prigogine emphasises the existence of two complementary conditions for the life of far-from-equilibrium systems:

1. a low entropy source is just as necessary for the system as a cold sink for dissipating high entropy;

13. Daly, H. & Farley, J., *Ecological Economics - Principles and Applications*, Island Press: Washington, DC, 2004.

2. throughput, not just availability of resources, enables the system to survive, develop and increase in complexity.

An autarchic system, like isolated systems, is without exchanges of energy, matter or information with the outside. As in the case of biological systems, the ordered state of systems denied all contact with outside is destined to decay into disorder. To avoid this condition of maximum entropy, a system must continuously export the entropy it produces to other systems.[14] Total entropy (system + environment) must increase, according to the second principle, even when the system is in steady state (the case of constant entropy). In a condition of autarchy, the input of negentropy and the output of high entropy are both inhibited, violating conditions 1 and 2 and leading to exhaustion of the system's vital processes.

On the other hand, globalisation is a process in a state of apparently perpetual growth, in which the need for efficiency, competence, capacity, flexibility and competition is combined with the need to maximise certain crucial quantities, first of all consumption and production. Thermodynamics does not envisage infinite growth in a finite planet. On the basis of current trends, technical advances and reduction of inputs per unit product cannot reduce the overall consumption of resources and the production of entropic wastes. A system of production stimulated by global processes, even if increasingly efficient, does not imply a reduction in environmental degradation, in use of natural resources and in emission of pollutants and greenhouse gases.[15] On this topic, Binswanger[16] compared the 25% decrease in energy intensity (energy used per unit economic product) in OECD countries between 1970 and 1988 with the 30% increase in total use of energy in the same period, noting that the saving was insufficient to compensate for the increase. Borghesi and Vercelli[17] pointed out the correlation between globalisation and growth, indicating four causal links, which are technological (increasing exploitation of natural resources), economic (increasing industrial size), demographic (world population increase) and cultural (increasing disinformation: nature is seen as a means to satisfy human needs).

Undoubtedly, globalisation is seen and celebrated today only from an economic point of view, while the ecological and thermodynamic dimension of this collective trend is often neglected. Production of entropy by a globalised industrial society is derived from increasing demand and use of energy and materials,

---

14. Kåberger, T. & Månsson, B., Entropy and economic processes - physics perspectives. *Ecological Economics*, **36(1)**, pp. 165–179, 2001.
15. Tisdell, C., Globalization and sustainability: environmental Kuznets curve and the WTO. *Ecological Economics*, **39**, pp. 185–196, 2001.
16. Binswanger, M., 1993, op. cit.
17. Borghesi, S. & Vercelli, A., Sustainable globalization. *Ecological Economics*, **44**, pp. 77–89, 2003.

solicited by international commerce and the development of communications and information systems. Recent world reports on the state of the environment indicate that the level of exploitation of natural resources, including the capacity of ecosystems to absorb man-made emissions, has already exceeded the carrying capacity of the planet. Many signs confirm the presence of major effects on natural cycles due to human pressure on the environment. Two molecules, ozone and CO_2, whose presence in the atmosphere is related to human activities, play an essential role in the regulation of conditions suitable for life on the planet: thinning of the ozone layer threatens the process of photosynthesis and living species, including humans; increased concentrations of CO_2 in the atmosphere threaten to inhibit the dispersion of degraded energy (heat, high entropy) into space due to the greenhouse effect.[18] The increasing demand for energy and matter to support the global economic system and the presence of an adiabatic membrane around the planet (increase in greenhouse effect) are related processes. In thermodynamic terms, the combined effect of these two phenomena explains why globalisation violates conditions 1 and 2 of Morowitz's entropy diagram.

... *ecological* ...

Alfred Lotka[19] gave a theoretical explanation in an ecological key of the development and evolution of open systems that depend on a certain quantity of available energy. According to his maximum power principle, the maximum use of available energy is possible for as long as resources are abundant and competition is low. When scarcity begins to be felt, organisms that are efficient and economical in implementing parsimonious use of the energy they are able to capture will be favoured. The early phase of development is known as *colonisation*, whereas the phases in which energy use is minimised and of specialisation are known as the *climax*.[20]

With regard to current trends, human behaviour and the struggle for economic growth are processes of a system still in the colonisation phase, whereas environmental emergencies are clear signals of the need for a climax phase. The race towards globalisation amplifies the fight for the inputs needed to fuel the economic system on a global level, sharpening competitivity and increasing the distance between the rich and poor. Our global system runs the risk of triggering exhaustion and collapse that could be fatal for the global economy and for the lives of many people. In short, the economics of globalisation has lost sight of its biophysical foundations.

In the autonomy/dependence terms of Morin, the growing integration of international markets is generating an enormous organism (the global

---

18. Tiezzi, E., 2003, op. cit.
19, Lotka, A.J., Contribution to the energetics of evolution. *Proceedings of the National Academy of Science*, **8**, pp. 147–151, 1922.
20. Rifkin, J., *Entropy: Into the Greenhouse World*, Bantam Books: New York, 1989.

economic system) that is increasingly dependent on the availability of ecosystem goods and services, which are becoming increasingly scarce. This system is therefore becoming less resilient, less able to react to stimuli from outside and to restore the conditions required to survive in time. This trend leads to a paradox: the maximum level of globalisation, which maximises the erosion of ecosystems and their capacity to provide goods and services, amounts to the extreme of economic autarky.

... and socio-political interpretation

In the light of the above, one may well ask if autarchy and globalisation can be achieved from an economic and socio-political viewpoint. Autarchy belongs to the past. It seems anachronistic and contrary to human nature, and cannot be achieved unless imposed by a regime. On the other hand, globalisation dissolves local limits and physical barriers to trade in the name of economic growth, imposing adaptation and conformity to rules and behaviours, which compromises the survival of local economic, social, cultural, political and environmental features. The increasing magnitude of the energy (and heat) and matter (both primary materials and wastes) involved, without any well-defined limits (corresponding to the carrying capacity of the planet), together with the levelling and loss of diversity between distinct systems, makes the global economic model impossible without injustice and iniquity. The process of globalisation harbours certain undeniable contradictions, some of which are already evident:

- the distribution of wealth is grossly skewed, with the annual income of the 225 richest men in the world exceeding the pooled annual income of 47% of the world population;[21]
- the market shows asymmetries: the North exports capital goods, the South exports primary materials and the market is unable to reduce transnational inequality;[22]
- from a merely commercial viewpoint, market protectionism (the opposite of globalisation) by national and supranational economies is an evident contradiction (duties against expansion of the Chinese textile industry are an example);
- an individualistic interpretation of global economics is emerging: proponents view other countries unilaterally, as new consumer markets and as new energy resources and materials to exploit.

Unequal distribution, differences in working conditions, poverty, and absence of democracy make integration of markets even more contradictory

21. Bonaiuti, M. (ed.), 2003, op. cit.
22. Proops, J., The growth and distributional consequences of international trade in natural resources and capital goods: a neo-Austrian analysis. *Ecological Economics*, **48(1)**, pp. 83–91, 2004

with respect to sustainability of the global economic model. Autarchy and globalisation are two extreme configurations of economic and socio-political systems, the manifestations of which are not coherent with the laws of physics, especially the law of entropy. They represent opposite trends that expose society to a double risk of local and global 'entropic drift'. A country or system that makes a political dogma of isolation, rejection of cultural contamination (cross-fertilisation) and self-conservation will go towards thermodynamic equilibrium. The destruction of biological and cultural diversity, together with levelling and globalisation, also lead to thermal death. Excessive defence of diversity and the opposite trend of complete loss of diversity are two aspects of the same thermodynamic folly. Awareness of the existence of thermodynamic limits to the growth of economic systems is the first step to take on the road to a fair and sustainable economy, and away from 'thermodynamic euthanasia'.

Chapter 6

The cube and the living system

The economic system consists of a set of interacting parts. Its aleatory consistency is supported by regulations, laws, decrees, constrictions and codes. Besides this rational system, economics presupposes exchange, action, interaction that can be expressed in money and assumes the existence of a dynamic factor (physical reference system, ecosystem, subjects that exchange) in which humans are the dominant component. An economic system is therefore expressed as the interaction of a contrived rational component (laws, regulations, principles) with a vital dynamic human component (free will, personality, emotions, supply and demand, habits and customs). In the economic system, a set of abstract, mechanical, lifeless structural elements combines with a social component, a community of persons, individuals, groups, companies and other dynamic, vital types of organisms. This conjunction of non-living and living offers an interpretative key for the economic system, which theoretically acquires all the dynamic characteristics of a living organism.

Non-living things (rules, codes)	+	Living agents (society, individuals)	=	Living system (economic system)

A system containing the vitality of its living elements absorbs their properties (rational and emotional) and makes them into a whole. It is difficult to determine because it adapts its behaviour by diffuse and radical structural changes, even in response to very small changes. It is also difficult to control by mechanistic laws. It is evident that the large picture and the ideal of total control upheld by traditional economics are unlikely to obtain complete answers in the increasing complexity of the socio-economic system with its various manifestations, such as globalisation and environmental depletion. The reason why the economy does what it does and why we pay attention to it gets lost along the way. In other words, the instruments of economics are inadequate for the complex socio-economic context in which we live.

To illustrate this concept as a starting point for new foundations for economic disciplines, we were inspired by a fantasy thriller, a cult film for enthusiasts of the genre.

Cube

The first of the seven guests of the *Cube* is sliced up into many small dice. In a flash. In the span of a few frames. Viewers are just allowed a moment of perplexed terror before the blades sink with inexorable indifference and the guest is reduced to a pile of pieces. Good! With such a winsome prologue, spectators are immediately sucked into the vortex of the film.

The plot of *Cube*[1] is simple. Six people and more than a thousand pieces of a seventh (the one who was sliced) are confined to a box full of traps, like a Rubik's cube. According to one of the many reviews, 'All knowable space is represented by the cube; all the time they have to get out of the trap is sanctioned by physiological needs. Three days and three nights without eating and drinking are enough to threaten anyone's survival. A perfect biological deadline.'[2]

The plot of the film can be considered from many viewpoints and lends itself to many interpretations. Six people find themselves in a new and hostile context. It is interesting to observe how they adapt to their aseptic microcosm. Learning by error (as in video games, a maximum of six lives, equal to the number of prisoners) and resorting to mathematical logic: the way out is discovered by deciphering the rules of the game and solving the riddle. The Cube is a system that obeys reducible linear laws, which are therefore determinate and predictable. At the same time, however, there are six personalities, which soon manifest bizarre, unpredictable behaviours under the pressure of a hostile environment. The process of natural selection in a closed box creates unexpected situations. The character who seems the strongest is overcome by emotion, cannot control the situation and adapt – he loses his head. An autistic boy has the qualities necessary to survive aggression by the Cube and to lead the others out, and manages well with their help. From a purely scientific and unromantic viewpoint, the plot of the film revolves around adaptation and selection. The strength of the film is the combination of few essential elements: an aseptic environment and a group of strangers. A box (non-living) that obeys mechanical laws combined with the personalities and emotions of the characters (living) gives rise to an intense sequence of unexpected events and emerging novelties. The Cube can therefore be a metaphor for the system of rules, mechanisms and cogs of the economy, which is assembled on the

1. *Cube*, Directed by Vincenzo Natali, Trimark Pictures: Canada, 1997.
2. Translated from Pirovano, F., http://www.revisioncinema.com/ci_cube.htm, 1999.

basis of rational criteria and acts like a machine. The rooms in the Cube contain different obstacles, as different rules and methods are applied in different states and regions of the world. The characters cannot escape from the Cube because society and local communities cannot escape from the global economic system. Society can only exist inside the Cube. There are no alternatives for anyone, not even for the tiny community of Mapuche in southern Patagonia. The whole story takes place in the Cube and the behaviour of individuals creates understanding or disagreement, separation or conflict. The assembled box follows its inexorable course and the prisoners succumb to the rigidity of its structure. Paradoxically, the autistic boy, who can process information in a linear manner, as required by Cube mechanics, and is helped by the others, is the one who finds the way out. The narrow margins of salvation allowed by the Cube, which represents the rigid schemes of the economy, as we see it, lets few emerge, and the characters' emotions, diversity and thoughts are evidently irreconcilable with cubism. The Cube is a law unto itself and unable to respond to the living component of the society it so rigidly controls. In such a situation, the six prisoners have to learn its rules and take advantage of what they know in order to escape. Faced with an inexorable machine, the instinct to survive leads them into falls, crises, competition, iniquity, disagreement and loss. The result is a complex story, a devastating plot.

Emergence of novelties

The spectator is absorbed by the plot but feels little sympathy for the fate of the characters; rather, he tries to find the solution and to understand why the characters became trapped in the Cube. No answer is offered but there is much food for thought.

The external observer asks who built the Cube and why? A plausible conclusion could be to name the designer, a cynic who exercises power in an arbitrary way. (Let us ignore Martians!) This however would be a pointless conspiracy, a contradiction of terms. Another explanation springs from sharper reasoning and fine logic.[3] When one of the characters comes to the dramatic realisation that he was one of the designers of a section of the Cube, an important clue is revealed. What is the Cube? The Cube is the result of many unrelated processes, small pieces commissioned by an unknown society and conceived by specialists who do not know each other, the overall design, or the final result of their work.

Who built the Cube? A possible answer is everybody and nobody. In other words, the process of formation of the Cube could be a complex process that was activated, ran its course and concluded autonomously by a fatal combination of choices and chance. The characters would therefore be the unfortunate victims of an independent system larger than themselves.

3. A personal speculation by the authors of this book on the basis of little information in the plot of the film.

The process of construction of the Cube that we are discussing simulates the evolution of a complex system having uncontrolled outcomes and may not be science fiction. The construction of a Cube is not an unlikely or improbable event in real life. The honest work of the engineer imprisoned in the Cube (irony of fate!) with the other characters due to his high specialisation, does not necessarily mean that he knows the final aim of the product, whether it be a children's hospital or a war machine (or a cubic prison). His work is merely to exercise his specific skills to perfection. Direct communication between the parts of the process is not required. Certain parts of the process may have interacted and become a spontaneous process or system by a series of expedients and favourable circumstances. This is possible, especially when the immediate task of the parts is to find out how to receive an input from the system, make a transformation and get the system to make an output, at the same time making a profit. This description is familiar in modern economics. The mechanism, uncontrolled by any observer with an overall view of the system, is a possible description of the merely utilitarian cause that generates monsters, such as the Cube. It is not the *sleep* of reason but the *dream* of reason that creates monsters.[4]

To demonstrate this hypothesis, we have to use a specific science that sustains that the system-process exists and can take a recognisable form different from the identity of any of its parts. This concept was clearly expressed by Pascal, 'The whole is more than the sum of its parts', taken up by von Bertalanffy[5] and others, and forms a basis of modern chaos and complex systems theory. In a complex system, when parts become constituents of a whole, they acquire meaning and an aim that they previously did not have. In such cases, the organisation of a system emerges spontaneously as added information that is not available from observation of the single parts.

Atoms tend towards a state of minimum energy by forming chemical bonds and becoming ordered in molecules. Organisms adapt to each other by a process of co-evolution and constitute an ecosystem. These are examples of how groups of agents that seek their own consistency and adapt to each other may transcend themselves and acquire collective properties, such as life and thought, that do not exist at individual level.[6]

This phenomenon is generally explained as the concept of self-organisation. Organisation emerges spontaneously, as if it were the system itself to choose it from many possibilities.[7] Each element of a whole follows its immediate personal interest, adapting its behaviour to that of nearby elements through

4. Tiezzi, E., *Beauty and Science*, WIT Press: Southampton, 2005.
5. Von Bertalanffy, L., *General System Theory*, Penguin Books: Harmondsworth, 1972.
6. Waldrop, M.M., *Complexity. The Emerging Science at the Edge of Order and Chaos*, Simon and Schuster: New York, 1992.
7. Bertuglia, C.S. & Staricco, L., *Complessità Autorganizzazione Città*, Franco Angeli: Milano, 2000.

small adjustments. This phenomenon is indicated as the *law of minimum resistance*. In complex systems, these small processes of adaptation are constantly present and compensate each other through repeated feedbacks, maintaining the system in a steady state in time. The presence of interactions between the parts of the system may, however, also cause sudden changes in the system in response to small perturbations induced by a new situation or by ambient changes. Small reactions to new stimuli may affect much or all of the system, causing non-linear amplifications (positive feedback) and reorganisation of the whole. Nicolis summed up these phenomena: 'Organisation emerges on a macroscopic spatiotemporal scale which is many times greater than the microscopic interactions between the elements'.[8]

Such systems enjoy properties that cannot be predicted from reductive observation of their components. The whole system must be observed in order to apprehend its behaviour, because every part of the system depends on the others by direct and indirect connections. The presence of irreducible systems is coherent with Gödel's theorem, which states that it is impossible to give a detailed, complete and comprehensible description of the world. Most natural systems are irreducible, which places strong restrictions on the intrinsic reductionism of science. According to Gödel's theorem, the properties of order and emergence cannot be observed or known from inside the system, only by an external observer.[9]

The more complex and characterised by interdependence of its parts (often highly specialised) a system is, the more likely it is that effects, which may be due to local phenomena, are felt on a large scale. Collective behaviour with new properties, that elude the control and understanding of individuals, may emerge as an effect of variations in relations between the different (social, economic, technological, physical) components of a system. For example, a variation in the physical environment, adoption of a system of rules, or a slackening market may redefine the behaviour of a community.

Considering the above, we can assume that the Cube is a set of mechanisms produced by the economic system and contemporary society. In the name of growth and progress, the economy and technology advance inexorably, sustained by research and false well-being, on a path that does not envisage any limits. The pursuit of immediate profit promoted by the Western model is increasingly divorced from an overall view of the common good, and thus from the real interests of individuals, from real well-being. This presumed common goal has become ambiguous and not in everyone's interests, but only in the interests of some.

---

8. Nicolis, G., Physics of far-from-equilibrium systems and self-organization. *The New Physics*, ed. P. Davies, Cambridge University Press: New York, 1989.
9. See Tiezzi, E., *Steps Towards an Evolutionary Physics*, WIT Press: Southampton, 2006. Specifically, the first step: on giants' shoulders – a new epistemological insight.

According to the view of Adam Smith, by pursuing their personal interest, individuals automatically and unknowingly act in the interest of all, as if guided by an invisible hand. The theory of complexity shows that this concept is completely untrue. It is difficult to imagine the effects of the work of a Wall Street broker, who operates directly on the cogs of the economic system, when he celebrates a day of high profits in a bar in Greenwich Village. In extreme cases, his action may mean the prosperous survival of a company or the closure of a factory, the ruin of a community and the destitution of factory employees.

The metaphor of the Cube suggests that the consolidated economic system is out of control. Many solid facts suggest the same, by the very mechanism that created the Cube. The disproportionate distribution of planetary wealth, the increasing gulf between rich and poor, the great financial crashes, the economic crises, public debt, global environmental crisis, the effects of global warming and climate change, depletion of water resources and devastating wars are only some of the mechanisms represented by the metaphor of the Cube. They are results of a system that obeys its own laws and eludes all control. We wish that society never built the Cube and we wish there were no wars, but it is not easy to understand which complex mechanisms of the economic system underlie a war, which combinations of personal interest, self-organising phenomena, non-linear amplification, involve thousands of persons, despite themselves, in futureless conflicts. If we could control these complex mechanisms, we could avoid harming ourselves, we could arrest the building of small cubes at any moment, we could dismantle the walls of the global Cube in which we live.

Escher's stairs

The mechanics of traditional economics configures a system that risks being a law unto itself, heedless of community and individual well-being and inclined to let them succumb. The contradictions of the economic system are the basis of the Cube, which represents the set of mechanisms that regulate social behaviour and are not always knowingly determined. The Cube is the unexpected product of a process generated autonomously in a complex system, as are the social and economic systems. In these systems, in turn, interactions between dynamic elements and static normative apparatus generate phenomena that individuals cannot control and that are not easily arrested, such as war or the current environmental crisis. The greenhouse effect and fear of terrorism afflicting the whole human race are results of a system of rules and behaviours adopted by the global village and which in turn impose new constrictions on the village (think of the urgent need to reduce emissions of greenhouse gases in defence against climate change and blanket security measures in defence against the risk of terrorist attacks). The Cube is a set of rules and mechanisms determined by contemporary society but their interactions with living agents are not easy to determine and cause feedbacks, which affect society in many complex plots. As a well-known Italian comedian would say, the Cube is like a lion tamer who opens the lion's jaws, puts in his head, opens his own mouth and puts in the lion's head.

Faced with such striking contradictions, traditional economics is a profoundly inadequate system of thought plagued with evident difficulties. The more power it acquires, the less able it is to govern this power. It denies responsibility for the social, environmental and cultural changes caused by its processes of growth. The economic system rests on unstable foundations as it pursues its one-way course towards infinity, but it always comes back to itself, in the name of deceptive growth, like the famous stairs of Escher, an illusory figure conceived to trick the mind. The architect Renzo Piano has no doubts: 'Modernity, progress and growth are infernal traps and we continue to be cheated in their name'.

Faced with the need to investigate the world and the enormous variety of organisational, regulatory and adaptive solutions encountered in social dynamics, nature and life, economics is forced to change the type of questions it was accustomed to posing. Humankind has to urgently tackle great problems that threaten the survival of the species, problems that transcend the intrinsic utility of the instruments of traditional economics and reductionist science.

The sciences of evolutionary processes clamour to investigate concatenated and non-linear processes that cause novelties to emerge in systems. Economics has to find new, more flexible instruments, more suitable for describing the evolution of the system and its properties.

More in general, the transition from classical deterministic science to complexity theory and evolutionary sciences is revealing a new panorama and new perspectives for disciplines concerned with human systems. As sustained by Marcello Cini:

> The epistemological priority of the categories *simplicity, order, regularity* and *reversibility* is being abandoned in favour of the opposite categories *complexity, disorder, chaos* and *irreversibility*, when it is impossible to reduce the latter to the former, in order to attain a more satisfactory understanding of the world.[10]

10. Cini, M., Scienze naturali e cultura ecologica. *Ecologia e ...*, ed. E. Tiezzi, Laterza: Roma-Bari, 1995.

Chapter 7
Transdisciplinarity

Three economists

François Quesnay (1694–1774) was the surgeon of the King. He earned well and bought a farm that he ran himself. This experience led him to express his ideas on appropriate land use and land yield. The best known of his proposals, *Tableau economique*, was published in 1758 by the Versailles publishing house and became a sort of manifesto for the physiocratic school of economic thought. According to Quesnay, the only source of wealth is land. Empirically he came to realise that good farming practice enables costs to be covered, labour to be paid, peasants to prosper and land to produce rent, whereas he considered industry and commerce to be sterile activities. This was Quesnay's basis for his ideas on free trade, land ownership and other rights he defined as *natural*. His medical training led him to view economic life as a spontaneously functioning organism. From this sprang the dogma that freedom should not be regulated. The physiocrats, followers of Quesnay's school of thought, believed in a natural, essential and absolutely general order that encompassed the fundamental constitutional laws of society.[1]

William Stanley Jevons (1835–1882), son of an industrialist, initially studied chemistry, natural science and mathematics. After various events and traumatic moves for different reasons, he became involved in political economy. He was a major critic of classical economics and the labour theory of value and like Leon Walras and Carl Menger, though independently, propounded ideas that triggered the so-called marginalist revolution. Jevons is remembered for

1. For more details, see Denis, H., *Histoire de la pensee économique*, Presses Universitaires de France: Paris, 1965.

his work *The Theory of Political Economy*[2] and for his practical observations on the state of the economy. In 1865, he published *The Coal Question*,[3] a sort of compendium on Britain's energy status at the time, in which the reader senses a certain anxiety about the fate of industry and the increasing demand for energy (coal). The work is celebrated for Jevons's paradox, according to which an increase in the efficiency of machinery (less coal per unit product) due to continual technological improvement, was leading to an overall increase in coal consumption rather than a decrease. This led him to state that the more efficient use of a resource leads to a widespread consumption of it.[4]

Nicholas Georgescu-Roegen (1906–1994) was a talented mathematician whose scholarly aptitude and various life events led him to study different branches of science. Interested as he was in both theory and its applications, he studied statistics in Paris and then London, where he distinguished himself in other fields as well. His expertise subsequently found him work in economics at Harvard, with Joseph Schumpeter, something he had never contemplated. Once an economist, he made great contributions to acknowledgement of the biophysical foundations of the economic process. He was also interested in the dynamics of nature and was attracted by statistical mechanics, where he learned the law of entropy. This approach made him a reference point for the great interest aroused by environmental questions in the 1960s, leading him to formalise a new discipline known as bioeconomics.[5] Georgescu-Roegen was one of the first to review the Meadows's *Limits to Growth* and was involved in the debut of ecological economics, from which he subsequently disocciated himself, criticising certain of its proponents. His principal revolutionary contributions, however, were the systematic critique of neoclassical economic theory, including its epistemological foundations, and his innovative way of tackling the environmental questions of energy, matter, funds and flows in economics.[6]

Roles and disciplines

In the history of economic thought, there have been many contributions by scholars of other disciplines. Albeit unconsciously, this contamination should have certainly facilitated a wide-angled view of the world.

---

2. Jevons, W.S., *The Theory of Political Economy*, 5th edn, Augustus M. Kelley: New York, 1957.
3. Jevons, W.S., *The Coal Question: An Inquiry Concerning the Progress of the Nation, and the Probable Exhaustion of Our Coal-Mines*, ed. A.W. Flux, 3rd edn, Augustus M. Kelley: New York, 1905.
4. Jevons's paradox is discussed briefly in Chapter 8 from the point of view of efficiency.
5. For example, see Georgescu-Roegen, N., *The Entropy Law and the Economic Process*, Harvard University Press: Cambridge, MA, 1971; Georgescu-Roegen, N., *Energy and Economic Myths*, Pergamon Press: New York, 1976.
6. For more details, see Bonaiuti, M., *La teoria bioeconomica* Carocci: Roma, 2001.

In general, it should come naturally to regard a broad view of science as positive. The human species has the task of managing the planetary situation and of studying its perspectives. This book is concerned with such questions: it describes the state of the planet and what people are trying to do (Chapter 2), proposes foundations (Chapter 3) and paints strong paradoxical images (Chapters 5 and 6), *all based on physical reality rather than on a preconstituted paradigm.*

Economics is much closer to the experimental sciences, to physics, ecology, chemistry, mathematics, environmental sciences and nature (including human nature) than we think. It is much closer to them than to technicalities, business specialisation, the official discount rate and financial law. Economists have to think. They must be concerned with the theory and regulation (*nomos*) of our common house (*oikos*) and must think of them in terms of time, physical limits and relationships. The intermixing of economic theory and technicalities, leading to current confusion of the two, must rigorously observe this hierarchy and chronological order, so that instruments do not rule the process of knowledge. Confusing the role of economics with the role of economic instruments is like confusing the architect with the carpenter or the systems analyst with the computer technician (with due respect to all occupations).

This dichotomy is broken by the relationship between scientific progress and the complexity of nature, giving rise to the so-called *complexity paradox*, as described by Enzo Tiezzi:

> Technology must have a large scientific component because today a fundamental parameter of the productive system is complexity. But this requires increased specialization and consequently loss of understanding and control of reality (which is complex) both by people and by specialists themselves. The more we specialize the less likely we are to be able to predict the effect of technology on Nature. The fragmentation of scientific disciplines should not be regarded as inevitable; to the contrary every effort should be made to recreate the conditions for the unification of science (by favouring interdisciplinary research and scientific–humanistic interaction), so that science can liberate humanity and acquire its true social dimension.[7]

Paradoxically, it is therefore appropriate that economics free itself of its technical instruments and allow itself to be contaminated by other disciplines. This contamination should not be unilateral, or such that the objectives of economic maximisation direct all other choices. It should be multilateral, so that economic behaviour, too, obeys conditions and constraints learnt outside the economic infrastructure. For example, chemistry is now pervaded by economic technicalities. A chemical reaction works if the chemical and physicochemical

7. Tiezzi, E., *The End of Time*, WIT Press: Southampton, 2003.

conditions are right, but it seems that it no longer works if it is not also 'economic'. It would be a good idea to invert the membrane that makes chemistry permeable to economics, so that economics becomes permeable to chemistry and to natural sciences, so that it can receive other stimuli besides those of mere gain and profit!

This illustrates the concept of transdisciplinarity, which is the mutual contamination of different disciplines and viewpoints in order to find something scientifically new. It is the essence of research and more intimately of science. In the words of Mae-Wan Ho:

> Science is a quest for the most intimate understanding of Nature. It is not industry set up for the purpose of validating existing theories and indoctrinating students in the correct ideologies. It is an adventure of the free, enquiring spirit which thrives not so much on answers as on unanswered questions. It is the enigmas, the mysteries and paradoxes that seize the imagination, and making it dance.
>
> If science is this marvellous dance, today's challenge is for a 'thermodynamics of organized complexity', bearing in mind that 'there is as yet no science of organized heterogeneity or complexity such as would apply to living systems'.[8]

This does not mean forging ahead and denying the past, determinism or specialised knowledge. It is an invitation to integrate the particularities of different disciplines in order to understand, study and possibly manage the complex system that is the human species in continuous interaction with its environment.

Transdisciplinarity

Transdisciplinarity is a form of study or research that by its very nature exceeds the often artificial boundaries that separate and distinguish the various disciplines.[9] In their manual of ecological economics, Herman Daly and Joshua Farley give a good description of the concept of transdisciplinarity.

> We think that the disciplinary structure of knowledge is a problem of fragmentation, a difficulty to be overcome rather then a criterion to be met. Real problems do not respect academic boundaries. We certainly believe that thinking should be 'disciplined' in the sense of respecting *logic and facts*, but not 'disciplinary' in the sense of limiting itself to traditional

8. Ho, M.-W., *The Rainbow and the Worm*, World Scientific Publ. Co.: Singapore, 1988, as quoted in: Tiezzi, E., *Steps Towards an Evolutionary Physics*, WIT Press: Southampton, 2006.
9. *Dictionary of the Italian Language*, Treccani, Vol. IV, Istituto della Enciclopedia Italiana: Roma, 1994.

methodologies and tools that have become enshrined in the academic departments of neoclassical economics.[10]

How can the full meaning of transdisciplinarity be understood? The way can be described in stages, beginning at the essence of a single discipline to reach the various ways in which different disciplines communicate with each other and unite. The definitions that follow are rough reference points and may vary from case to case, author to author, discipline to discipline. However, they are useful to clarify our terms.[11]

The concept of *disciplinarity* arose to express monothematic things indicating specialisation in a particular sector. The need for an approach that draws from different points of view for the study of a system led to the concept of *multi-disciplinarity*. Multi-disciplinarity is represented by the sum of the contributions of different disciplines, without any attempt at synthesis or integration. Each discipline works autonomously and independently. In the concept of *pluridisciplinarity*, cooperation between the various disciplines involved is added and the contribution of each reinforces that of the others. Pluridisciplinarity is therefore characterised by a dialogue between the various disciplines for common aims, without modifying their essence or structure. The concept of *interdisciplinarity* envisages the interaction of two or more disciplines in tackling a problem. The type of interaction may vary from simple communication of ideas to complete integration. The concept of *interdisciplinarity* surpasses that of pluridisciplinarity because it not only includes cooperation but also coordination between disciplines. The aim of an interdisciplinary approach is to provide an overall picture. Last of all, we have fusion of disciplines in the concept of *transdisciplinarity*. Integration and merging reach a maximum, which may break down epistemological barriers, creating new disciplines. The fundamental element of the definition of transdisciplinarity is the act of overcoming something. Its essence lies in merging often pre-existing elements in order to create something new.

Without going into any rigorous classification or looking too closely at the above scheme, the evolution of a meeting of disciplines can be described by a four-step example: an engineer meets a medical doctor and they engage in conversation.

1. The engineer confesses that he has pain in his side and the doctor tries to explain what it could be and suggests what to do. The doctor then tells the engineer of a technical problem he had with his computer and the engineer illustrates possible solutions. Both use their disciplines to solve problems (it is therefore good to have at least a doctor and an engineer among one's friends).

---

10. Daly, H. & Farley, J., *Ecological Economics - Principles and Applications*, Island Press: Washington, DC, 2004.
11. See Max-Neef, M.A., *Foundations of transdisciplinarity. Ecological Economics,* **53(1)**, pp. *5–16, 2005; see also* Futures, **36(4)**, 2004, a special issue on transdisciplinarity.

2. Their conversation continues. The doctor tells the engineer that his hospital building has structural problems and that he had to change premises because the paving suddenly came up in his visiting rooms. The doctor asks about building methods, tools, materials and adhesives, and the engineer asks about floor stresses, equipment, trolleys and substances used in medicine, anything that could have a bearing on the problem. Both need information to understand and solve problems.
3. Then it emerges that the doctor is a neonatologist and the engineer specialises in antennas, waves, frequencies. They talk about incubators. Incubators save babies' lives, the neonatologist says, but they also create problems. They are noisy and expose babies to electromagnetic fields. The engineer tells the doctor about progress in mechanics and materials, suggesting positioning of machines in rooms and contemplating acoustic and electromagnetic screens. They discuss the problems from their individual points of view, which partly overlap. They interact with each other, contributing constructively to each other's expertise.
4. It turns out that the neonatologist and the engineer both do research. They eagerly describe their work to each other. The engineer studies time series and the neonatologist studies babies' experience of pain. The engineer makes graphs of animal calls and the doctor records and studies the intensity of babies' crying. The new idea comes in a flash. Why not plot, study and interpret crying with the mathematical and statistical tools of engineering? Signal detection could be developed, insight into human vocalisations could be obtained, pain scales could be validated, and why babies cry in certain ways could be discovered, since crying is a mode of self-expression. Thus something new and unplanned springs from a chance encounter.[12]

The conversation between the doctor and the engineer reflects the different possibilities of interaction between disciplines, going from specialisation and juxtaposition to cooperation, coordination and finally what today is called *cross-fertilisation*. Besides giving rise to major scientific innovations, transdisciplinary approaches have practical implications, especially for the study of environmental dynamics in relation to human activity. Mathis Wackernagel, director of the Global Footprint Network, offers an interpretation of the concept applied to the work of his research group in USA.

> What we are doing is building bridges between cultural perspectives. That is why we are in the United States and operate in Europe, Africa, Australia

12. The example is imaginary but concerns a real study: Facchini, A., Bellieni, C., Marchettini, N., Pulselli, F.M. & Tiezzi, E.B.P., Relating pain intensity of newborns to onset of nonlinear phenomena in cry recordings. *Physics Letters A*, **338(3–5)**, pp. 332–337, 2005. Actually, the idea of combining time series and crying belonged to an economist, but this is more difficult to explain.

and Asia. The overshoot story has to be explained and told in ways that resonate with people from different cultures. We are also building bridges between different disciplines – we are not even implanted in a particular discipline. Perhaps in John Stuart Mills's time, he would have put us in economics, but current economists wouldn't see us in that way. We are not chemists either, even though we work in thermodynamics. We are not earth scientists because we don't study how the Earth works; we are just doing the accounting that brings together human demand and ecological supply. So we are a bridge between the various disciplines, an accounting mechanism to document outcomes so modelling and more sophisticated approaches become possible.

Just as economics uses GDP as a baseline for then testing their models about how they think the economy works, there needs to be some accounting method to test the sustainability models against. Then we can play with scenarios and models to find out what kind of intervention would help to make human enterprise compatible with ecological realities.

Generally, I think disciplines separate us and we need to find ways to be much more problem focused than method driven, and that is why probably rigid academic disciplines are not that useful for the XXI century.[13]

This book was written by an economist, an engineer, a biologist and a chemist who have been working together for many years. The objective of interdisciplinarity has certainly been met in this group. The reader can judge for himself/herself the stage of transdisciplinarity reached.

13. Wackernagel, M. & Galli, A., An overview on ecological footprint and sustainable development: a chat with Mathis Wackernagel. *International Journal of Ecodynamics*, **2(1)**, pp. 1–9, 2007.

Part II

Methods

Chapter 8

'Measuring' sustainability

The number of sustainability indicators grows day by day in response to the need to describe the state of complex systems. Two approaches to the selection of indicators can be taken: selection of existing simple indicators for political or technical–administrative users or selection of indicators based on theoretical premises (similar to those inspiring this book) that have the specific aim of measuring sustainability/unsustainability for scientific purposes and may often be obscure to the technical–political community.

The first approach can be summarised in the words of the report of the United Nations Department for the Coordination of Policy and Sustainable Development, according to which indicators should be:

- based on scientific foundations recognised by the international community;
- relevant – they should cover all crucial aspects of sustainable development;
- transparent – their selection, calculation and meaning should be obvious even to non-experts;
- quantifiable – they must be based on data that are available or easy to obtain and update;
- limited in number, depending on the aim for which they are used; e.g. few are needed for communication, more are needed for monitoring policy and many are needed for experts.

Environmental indicators and the pressure–state–response model[1]

According to the OECD: 'In general, an indicator can be defined as a parameter or value derived directly from parameters that provide information about

1. OECD, *The OECD Core of Indicators for Environmental Performance Reviews*, Organisation for Economic Cooperation and Development: Paris, 1993.

a phenomenon, describing its state, with a meaning that goes beyond that directly associated with the value of the parameter. Indicators summarise a situation and are developed for specific aims.' This underlines the two main functions of indicators:

- They considerably reduce the number of measurements and parameters that would normally be necessary to provide an exact description of the state of the environment. As a result, the width of a set of indicators and the number of details contained in the set must be limited. A set of many indicators would obscure the description. On the other hand, too small a number of indicators, or only a single indicator, may be insufficient. Selection of an appropriate number of indicators is therefore a compromise between clarity and completeness of description;
- They simplify communication of the results of measurements to users. Because of this simplification and adaptation to user needs, indicators do not always meet scientific requirements to demonstrate causal correlations of a phenomenon. Indicators must therefore be considered 'the best knowledge available' (Group on the State of the Environment, 1993).

Indicators can be classified according to how they are constructed (e.g. descriptive, performance, aggregate indicators) and on their dimensions (e.g. environmental, social, economic). Hence there is no structure valid for every purpose and structures may change in time with variations in conditions, such as when the scientific knowledge or the gravity of environmental problems increases, or when social values change.

The first model developed for the large-scale application of indicators was the pressure–state–response (PSR) model developed by the OECD. This model contains the major indicators formulated by international organisations such as the World Bank and European Union. It is based on cause–effect: human activities exert pressure on the environment, changing the quality and quantity of natural resources (state of the environment). Society responds to these changes through environmental, economic and sectoral policy, generally with the aim of restoring lost environmental quality (society response). The PSR model therefore contains:

1. Indicators of environmental pressure describing pressures exerted by human activities on the environment, assessed in terms of degradation of environmental quality or quantitative decrease in natural resources. Pressure indicators may be direct (direct pressure usually expressed in terms of emissions of pollutants and consumption of natural resources) or indirect (linked to human activity and contributing in a secondary way to environmental pressure).
2. Indicators of environmental state, directly linked to environmental quality and quantity of natural resources, and reflecting the aims of environmental policy at a given time.

3. Indicators of environmental response, showing the size of the social response to environmental changes and problems, and concerning individual and collective action to reduce, adapt or prevent negative impact of human activity on the environment and to stop or repair environmental damage already inflicted.

The determinant–pressure–state–impact–response (DPSIR) model evolved from the PSR model and introduces two new elements (determinants and impacts). It is an organisational model of environmental information proposed by the European Environmental Agency and traces the causal sequence between human actions (determinants and pressure), environmental status or quality (state and impact) and solutions (responses).

1. Determinants are sectors of society whose activities have environmental impact. They are generally forms of economic activity, such as industry and transport, with detrimental environmental effects.
2. Pressures are ways in which causes affect the environment, e.g. by emission of contaminants.
3. States are the status of different environmental compartments such as air, water and soil quality.
4. Impacts are the negative effects of environmental degradation, e.g. health problems, loss of biodiversity and economic damage.
5. Responses indicate what can be done to solve the problem, e.g. cleaner production of a product, greater availability of public transport, new regulations or taxes, greater information. They can affect system structure (the determinants), pressures (by regulation) and states (by repair and remediation).

After much debate between statisticians and indicator experts, the DPSIR was accepted by international organisations concerned with the environment as the most suitable to represent environmental information of European member states.

The European Common Indicators Project

The major, established systems of indicators, such as the DPSIR model, were a source of inspiration for the creation of the European Common Indicators (ECI) system (Table 8.1). This project began in May 1999 with the constitution of a Working Group on Sustainability Indicators (supervised by the Group of Urban Experts and coordinated by the French Environment Ministry) and had the task of developing local sustainability indicators in collaboration with local administrations.

The aim of the initiative was to develop and test indicators that could represent local efforts towards sustainability in an integrated manner. In the initial phase, a set of indicators was defined (the final set decided by this commission consisted of 10). They concerned a limited number of aspects, so that methods could be developed through their implementation.

Table 8.1: The 10 European Common Indicators.

European Common Indicators	Main indicator
1. Satisfaction of citizen with local context	General and mean satisfaction with local context (by questionnaire)
2. Local contribution to global climate change	Per capita CO_2 emissions
3. Local mobility and passenger transport	Percentage of movements made by private motor vehicle
4. Access to public parks and local services	Percentage of town dwellers living within 300 metres of public parks > 5000 m^2
5. Local air quality	Exceeded limits of PM10
6. School transport	Percentage of children going to school by car
7. Sustainable management of local authority and firms	Percentage of firms with environmental certification
8. Noise	Percentage of population exposed to $L_{night} > 55$ dB(A)
9. Sustainable land use	Percentage of protected area in total administrative area
10. Sustainable products	Percentage of persons buying sustainable products

The initiative underwent a testing phase, in which the indicators were reviewed and refined to improve their significance and pertinence by monitoring their application to practical experiences and initiatives. This period ended in 2002. The ECI initiative selected the most integrated indicators that could reflect interactions between environmental, economic and social aspects and the general principles defining the idea of local sustainability. However, the indicators only focus on certain aspects of local sustainability of urban systems and cannot therefore be applied to other contexts, despite their misleading name 'European common indicators'.

Measuring sustainability/unsustainability

Sustainability cannot be measured because it is not a physical phenomenon. Sustainability is an ideal, so if we consider a situation we find that it is sustainable or not sustainable. The answer is almost always that the system we are analysing is not sustainable, due to its use of energy and materials and/or due to the wastes it produces. However, if we invert the problem and try to understand more about unsustainability, attempts can be made to measure it as the distance from the ideal of sustainability. Unsustainability is a relative concept.

Our aim is not to know *whether* we are sustainable (we know we are not) but *how* unsustainable we are. This can enable us to understand where we stand in relation to sustainability criteria and to find out what we can do to reduce unsustainability. Since the concept of sustainability is complex and not directly measurable, many indicators are needed to assess how far we have to go to reach this goal.

This is why so many indicators have been created lately and why the scientific community is still far from reaching international agreement on the best indicators to use. Interesting approaches to the problem have sprung from simplifications of general systems theory, giving rise, for example, to indicators based on emergy, the ecological footprint, exergy and extended exergy.[2]

The problems to solve in the construction and selection of sustainability indicators concern their relevance, type (analytical, synthetic) and meaning, or coherence between indicator and 'indicandum'. There is often confusion between environmental indicators and indicators of (environmental) sustainability. The former are monitored continuously by public bodies and are important for public health in certain areas. We are used to seeing the monitoring stations set up in strategic parts of town: usually they sample air to ensure that particulates are below critical levels. They also monitor water quality and quantify emissions at their source (e.g. incinerators). However, these stations only tell us what happens where they are at a given time. It is difficult to extrapolate these data for use as indicators valid for an area. At most, they can represent a set of necessary conditions: if the system exceeds legal limits for air and water it is unlikely to be sustainable. Of course, the fact that all these environmental indicators give positive results is not reassuring about the degree of unsustainability of the area in which they are obtained. Indeed, if an area has banished polluting activities to another area, this is hardly sustainable. If a nation only used electric cars, it would not automatically be sustainable, since it could produce or import electricity generated by carbon, oil or nuclear power plants. In the words of Gabriele Bollini, 'Not all environmental indicators can be assumed to be appropriate and significant measures of sustainability/unsustainability. The many environmental indicators and parameters can often allude, refer indirectly and be interpreted as signs or as more or less meaningful indicators of sustainability/unsustainability trends, but they do not objectively and scientifically measure it *per se*.'[3]

---

2. Emergy and ecological footprint will be discussed later. For analysis based on exergy and extended exergy, see Szargut, J., *Exergy Method: Technical and Ecological Applications*, WIT Press: Southampton, 2005; Sciubba, E., From engineering economics to extended exergy accounting: a possible path from monetary to resource-based costing. *Journal of Industrial Ecology*, **8(4)**, pp. 19–40, 2004.
3. Bollini, G., Gli indicatori ambientali e di sostenibilità. Provincia di Bologna, http://www.provincia.bologna.it/ag21/pdf/indicatori.pdf.

Knowledge of the environmental state of a system is not sufficient to know its sustainability: we need to know in detail how a certain state is reached and the history of the processes necessary to reach it. This type of knowledge can enable an assessment of environmental sustainability, which as we have seen, is much more important than the socio-economic aspects of sustainability. This type of analysis also enables an understanding of the mechanisms leading to unsustainability and what improvements can be undertaken. None of this can be described by DPSIR indicators, because they only concern a local level and miss the global dimension of sustainability, which is what is most threatened by the global phenomena we see today, both at environmental and socio-economic levels.

In the same way, the European Common Indicators of environmental sustainability may also cause confusion. Only two of the 10 indicators are true indicators of environmental sustainability (nos 2 and 9); the others are a set of aspects of the sustainability of social and urban systems (nos 1, 3, 4, 6, 7, 10) or pure environmental indicators (nos 5 and 8). Fortunately, an eleventh *umbrella* indicator, the ecological footprint, has been added. This is one of the most important sustainability indicators on the world scene and certainly the one with the greatest public communication value. It is a synthetic or system indicator that shows system properties, not the microscopic parts. As we shall see, the ecological footprint uses a common denominator, the quantity of land necessary to sustain consumption and absorb the wastes of a population. All consumption can be transformed into land equivalents and this has won appreciation for the ecological footprint throughout the world. It is a true sustainability indicator as it considers resource use and waste production.

The emergy approach is similar. Emergy is the quantity of solar energy directly or indirectly incorporated in a product. Again a common denominator is used to evaluate resource use. Instead of land area, emergy is based on a solar equivalent, or the fundamental energy that feeds all the processes of the biosphere. The relevance of these systemic approaches is certainly greater than that of analytical indicators, which while precise, have little importance for the whole population: indicators related to the ecological footprint or emergy can really tell us if the level of unsustainability of a system is decreasing or not. We will describe these and other methods that provide an overall view of sustainability.

The problem with analytical indicators, besides their relevance, becomes evident when using many independent indicators. If there is no common denominator to clarify relevance, results may disagree and it may be impossible to understand whether the system is coming closer or moving away from sustainability, or whether a system is more or less unsustainable than another. Synthetic indicators are needed because the concept of unsustainability is extremely relative. Analytical indicators only make sense for a closer look at critical points of a system: in such cases, 'microscopic' monitoring of emerging problems is essential.

Sustainability is an 'extensive' problem

As mentioned in Chapter 7, in 1865, the economist William Stanley Jevons observed a sharp increase in coal consumption after Watt's improvements to Newcomen's steam engine. This phenomenon is known as Jevons's paradox. Many thought that more efficient engines would curb coal consumption, but total consumption increased despite the reduction in coal requirements per unit. By making the steam engine more efficient, Watt helped to spread its use throughout the country. Since the industrial process was more economical, firms could increase production without extra cost. Economy of use led to extensive consumption. In everyday life we often encounter this paradox: machines are increasingly powerful, computers increase in speed to support our work, but alas, the quantity of work continues to grow!

George W. Bush was well aware of this when he declared his intention to decrease CO_2 per unit product by 18% in a few years: without a total limit to emissions, his proposal was actually an invitation to even faster growth of consumption and emissions in USA. A widely used indicator, energy intensity, is in this sense useless if total energy consumption is not limited.

In thermodynamics, there are intensive and extensive quantities. Intensive quantities such as temperature, density and pressure are not affected by the size of the system: if the temperature in two equal adjacent rooms is 20°C, it remains the same if the wall between the rooms is removed. Extensive quantities such as mass, volume and energy depend on the size of the system: if the volume of each room is 50 m^3, the volume becomes 100 m^3 when the wall is removed. Thermodynamically, sustainability is an extensive concept because it depends on the total, limited availability of resources and on a finite system's capacity to accept wastes and contaminants. Improvement of intensive parameters (efficiency, CO_2 per unit product or person) is not sufficient to reduce unsustainability. The improvement in efficiency has to be accompanied by a parallel decrease in total consumption, with a consequent decrease in wastes.

Is this impossible? No. The figures on fuel economy of cars in various parts of the world presented by ex-vice-president of USA, Al Gore,[4] show that fuel consumption could have decreased by 30–40% in USA with the technology already used in Europe and Japan. If USA used part of this extra energy for other uses, people would benefit, though perhaps not the oil companies!

In a recent project,[5] we examined the sustainability of tourism and farm stay in Val di Merse, Siena.[6] We found that foreign tourists who spend a week

4. *An Inconvenient Truth*, Documentary by Paramount Pictures, director Davis Guggenheim, based on the book by Al Gore: *An Inconvenient Truth*, Rodale Books: New York, 2006.
5. The project is called SPIn-Eco, *Sostenibilità della Provincia (di Siena) mediante INdicatori ECOdinamici*. The results have been published in a special issue of *Journal of Environmental Management*, **86(2)**, pp. 329–426, 2008.
6. Patterson, T., Niccolucci, V. & Bastianoni, S., Beyond 'more is better': ecological footprint accounting for tourism and consumption in Val di Merse, Italy. *Ecological Economics*, **62(3–4)**, pp. 747–756, 2007.

or two here, consume fewer resources than when they stay at home, despite the fact that they behave 'like tourists' and eat in restaurants. In some cases, the reduction is about 30%, but to judge from answers to the questionnaire they feel that they have been in an earthly paradise. It seems incredible from an economic point of view, but it is possible to live well consuming less.

What makes a sustainability indicator?

Including these considerations among the UN commission's characteristics we can say that a good sustainability indicator should be:

- based on a solid scientific foundation increasingly recognised by the scientific community (the science of sustainability is not yet mature);
- relevant, gathering all aspects of sustainability at all levels (global and local, not just local);
- transparent, communicating clearly even with non-experts, despite its complexity;
- quantifiable, so that statistical organisations can collect the data necessary to calculate it;
- limited in number, though the information should pass correctly at all levels (media, political, administrative, technical).

The ecological footprint

Over the years, there have been many studies aimed at estimating the impact of humans on natural systems. Different approaches have been used, beginning with the so-called IPAT equation introduced by Ehrlich and Holdren,[7] in which human impact (I) is the product of population size (P), its affluence (A) and technology (T). *Affluence* reflects mean consumption of resources whereas *technology* is linked to environmental damage caused by certain technologies related to lifestyle. For example, technology can be expressed as the quantity of contaminants associated with the production and consumption of a unit of material goods.

An interesting way to make this definition operative is embodied by the ecological footprint, which estimates direct and indirect human impact on the environment by quantifying the biologically productive space necessary to sustain humans and all their activities. The choice of this unit is interesting because space gives a good idea of finiteness, facilitating understanding of limits. Conceptual simplicity, together with easy and immediate understanding, have been a great help in spreading this method not only among the

7. Ehrlich, P. & Holdren, J., The impact of population growth. *Science*, **171**, pp. 1212–1217, 1971.

scientific community but also in the political world and among ordinary people. The ecological footprint was recently included in the set of European Common Indicators as number 11, known as an umbrella indicator because it embodies all the information of the other 10. WWF has used it for years in its reports. The most prestigious international journal of sustainability, *Ecological Economics*, dedicated a volume to discussion of the ecological footprint.[8] In 2006, the Global Footprint Network organised a *Footprint Forum* in collaboration with the University of Siena, the first international conference dedicated entirely to this indicator and the launching of a campaign to achieve the standards necessary for rigorous formalisation of the method.

The ecological footprint and biocapacity

The concept of ecological footprint arose in the early 1990s from the ideas of William E. Rees,[9] an ecologist at the University of British Columbia in Canada, and his student Mathis Wackernagel,[10] current director of the Global Footprint Network,[11] an American organisation based in Oakland, California. The aim of the Global Footprint Network is to promote knowledge of the Footprint and to coordinate standardisation of the method. The aim of the method is to quantify human impact through the definition of two parameters: ecological footprint and biocapacity.

The ecological footprint of a population is the quantity of ecologically productive land, aquatic or terrestrial, necessary to sustainably provide all resources of energy and materials consumed by that population and to sustainably absorb all wastes produced by that population. Its units are hectares of ecologically productive land or global hectares (*g*ha).

The ecological footprint (EF) expresses the demand of a population or individual for natural capital, which is the set of natural systems (seas, rivers, lakes, forests, flora, fauna and land) and their products (timber, cereals, fish, etc.) and the ecological services they offer (biodiversity, climate stability, fixation of solar energy and conversion into primary materials, etc.) all of which are fundamental for life. It is based on two assumptions: that it is possible to estimate energy and material resources consumed with substantial accuracy and that it is possible to convert them into the corresponding areas of biologically productive land necessary to renew consumed resources and absorb the wastes created by their use. The consumption categories considered are food and

8. *Ecological Economics*, **32(3)**, pp. 341–394, 2000.
9. Rees, W.E., Ecological footprints and appropriated carrying capacity: what urban economics leaves out. *Environment and Urbanization*, **4(2)**, pp. 121–130, 1992.
10. Wackernagel, M. & Rees, W.E., *Our Ecological Footprint: Reducing Human Impact on the Earth*, New Society Publishers: Gabriola Island, British Columbia, Canada, 1996.
11. www.footprintnetwork.com.

fibre, housing, transport, goods and services, and waste. Each type of good is associated with one or more of the following types of land:[12]

- Cropland: area of cultivated land necessary to produce food and other plant products (cereals, fruit, vegetables, tobacco, cotton, etc.);
- Grazing land: area necessary to produce meat and other animal products (meat, milk, wool, etc.);
- Forest: area of cultivated and natural forest for wood;
- Built-up land: area for roads, houses and other infrastructure;
- Fishing ground: area of seas and lakes to produce fish;
- Energy land: area of forest necessary to absorb CO_2 produced by burning fossil fuels.

The total ecological footprint of a population is obtained by summing the contributions of the various types of land, after normalisation for the different productivity of these lands.[13] The area calculated is not a real area, but an area based on mean productivity for the quantity of biomass used by the population. The ecological footprint is the sum of all these lots of land, irrespective of where they are located. Thus the ecological footprint assigns an 'environmental value' to all resources consumed because it memorises all the effort required upstream, in terms of bioproductive land, to produce and provide that good, and all the effort required downstream to absorb the wastes accompanying its use.

For example, the ecological footprint of a kilogram of bread is about 30 *g*m^2 (global m^2). This value comes from the sum of two contributions: cropland to grow the wheat (75%) and energy land (25%) for the energy necessary for cultivation (e.g. fertilizer), harvest (tractor fuel), transformation into bread and transport to our tables.

The ecological footprint is in line with the so-called principle of responsibility, according to which impacts are distributed on the basis of actual consumption of a good. The ecological footprint is therefore an indicator that links lifestyle and consumption with the natural capital consumed.

The second parameter, biocapacity (BIO), expresses the other side of the coin, namely the potential supply of natural capital of an area. Biocapacity measures the supply of bioproductivity or biological production of an area. It depends on the attributes of local ecosystems (physical area occupied by those ecosystems) and their actual productivity. Biocapacity does not depend solely on natural conditions but also on dominant agricultural and forestry methods.[14]

12. This classification reflects that used by the International Union for the Conservation of Nature (IUCN).
13. Equivalence factors that reflect the different productivity of various types of land are used. This is necessary in order to sum terms that would otherwise be heterogeneous.
14. Monfreda, C., Wackernagel, M. & Deumling, D., Establishing national natural capital accounts based on detailed Ecological Footprint and biological capacity assessment. *Land Use Policy*, **21**, pp. 231–246, 2004.

To account for the different productivity of various types of land, two conversion factors are used: an equivalence and a yield factor. The former considers the difference in productivity of a certain type of land with respect to global average productivity of primary biomass in a given year. Its units are *g*ha/ha. A hectare with global mean productivity has an equivalence factor of one. The equivalence factor of a certain type of land is the same for all nations and may change from year to year in relation to management practices, productivity and prevalent technologies.

The yield factor indicates by how much local productivity of a particular type of land differs from global mean productivity of the same type of land. For example, this factor expresses how many times more productive Brazilian forests are than global mean forest productivity. Each nation has its own set of yield factors that may change from year to year. These factors are checked yearly by Global Footprint Network researchers and are based on potential land productivity established for Global Agro-Ecological Zones (GAEZ) by the International Institute for Applied Systems Analysis (IIASA) and the Food and Agriculture Organization (FAO).

The planet Earth is populated by millions of species of animals and plants, though humans are by far the species with the highest impact and occupying the most space. The presence of all other species is fundamental to maintain biodiversity and sustain life. A percentage of total biocapacity (12%) is therefore subtracted to ensure a minimum of vital space for other species. Complete agreement has not been found about the most appropriate percentage to assign to wild life. Although the authors of the method recognise that 12% is not enough, this decision is in line with the UN convention on biodiversity.

If the total productive area of the Earth is about 11.3 billion *g*ha (about a quarter of the area of the globe), each person is assigned 1.8 *g*ha. Since the two indicators, EF and BIO, are expressed in global hectares of global mean productivity, comparisons are possible. To do so, human demand for natural capital (EF) is compared with the potential availability of land to supply environmental goods and services (BIO). An 'ecological balance' of this type shows whether the attitude and lifestyle adopted by a population is correct (i.e. observes biological tempos and natural limits), towards other populations (intragenerational equity) and towards future generations (intergenerational equity).

This comparison can give rise to two situations: ecological surplus or ecological deficit. The former occurs when biocapacity exceeds the ecological footprint: BIO > EF. This is the optimum situation because it means that limits have not yet been exceeded: less natural capital is used than is available every year. Ecological deficit occurs when biocapacity is less than ecological footprint: BIO < EF. It sounds an alarm that indicates that limits have been exceeded: more natural capital has been used than is annually available. This deficit is possible in two ways: import of the missing biocapacity from outside the system, e.g. through markets, and/or use of stocks of resources that ought to be left for future generations. The former clearly depends on the type of system analysed: the system must be open (able to exchange materials with its surroundings), as in the case of nations, whereas the Earth is a closed system and cannot exchange matter with other planets of the solar system. The second way, as we shall see, is currently being used by humans to maintain their present lifestyles.

Historical trend of the ecological footprint and biocapacity

Figure 8.1 shows the growth of the ecological footprint while biocapacity, one planet Earth, remains constant. In the last 40 years, the weight of humans on the Earth has almost tripled. In the early 1980s (left part of graph), the Earth was in ideal condition known as ecological surplus. Herman Daly[15] describes this situation as 'empty world economy' in which resources and natural capital were abundant. The imbalance between demand and supply of natural capital began in the early 1980s and has continued to grow. Today we are in ecological deficit or 'full-world economy', and natural capital has become the limiting factor for development. It has been estimated that the demand for natural capital, now 2.2 *g*ha/person, exceeds supply (1.8 *g*ha/person) by almost 20%. In other words, our ecological deficit is –0.4 *g*ha/person. This means that 1.2 planets are necessary to sustain the yearly consumption of the world population. This is

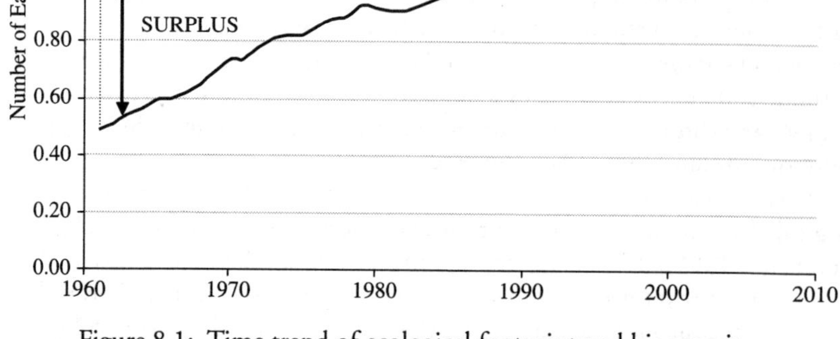

Figure 8.1: Time trend of ecological footprint and biocapacity.

15. Daly, H., Toward some operational principles of sustainable development. *Ecological Economics*, **2**, pp. 1–6, 1990.

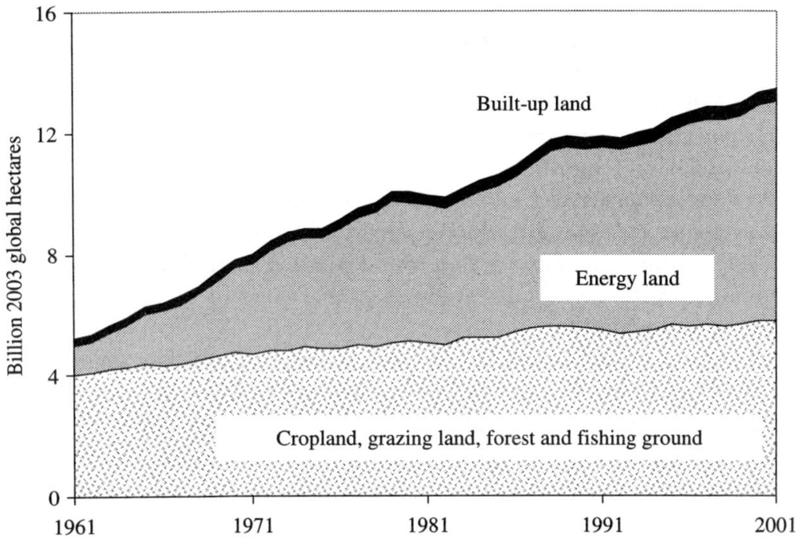

Figure 8.2: Time trend of ecological footprint according to land category.[16]

only possible because of increasingly intensive exploitation of the stock of natural capital that would otherwise maintain Earth's bio-geo-chemical equilibria for future generations.

If we break down the Footprint by land categories, we can see what factors have caused this type of growth. Figure 8.2 shows that demand for energy land, directly and indirectly related to energy consumption, is the main cause for the increase. Today, more than 60% of the ecological footprint is due to energy land and its contribution in the last 40 years has grown from 0.3 to 1.2 gha/person. The demand for cropland and forest has also increased.

Footprint depth

The ecological footprint refers to the impression humans leave on nature by virtue of their consumption. Comparison of footprint size, and therefore of the space occupied, gives a feeling of the various impacts. In a world in which the lack of space increases with the consumption of non-renewable resources and production of wastes and long-living emissions, this two-dimensional representation may no longer be enough to describe the dynamics of impact. We therefore made a three-dimensional model, which includes footprint depth.[17]

16. UNEP-WCMC, WWF, *Living Planet Report 2006*, ed. World Wildlife Fund, 2006.
17. Bastianoni, S., Niccolucci, V. & Tiezzi, E., Implication of a flow-stock distinction on ecological footprint analysis. *Communication at the XXII National Conference of the Italian Chemical Society, Florence*, 10–15 September 2006.

The deeper the footprint, the greater the impact. The need for this third dimension sprang from the difference between the concept of stock and flow. The size of the ecological footprint regards the use of flows, namely resources regenerated each year, while its depth regards the use of the stock of resources. These two components are technically incommensurable.

The ecological footprint was thus redesigned as a three-dimensional model with two components: base and height. The base is the spatial component that on our planet corresponds to biocapacity, or the quantity of natural capital available, whereas the height or footprint depth is ecological deficit. The deficit diminishes the capital that produces annual flows of goods and services necessary to support life.

An important difference between the two components lies in the fact that the former is consumed each year and regenerated the following year, whereas the latter is the irreversible erosion of natural stocks that adds up from year to year, inexorably accumulating 'environmental debt'. In Fig. 8.1, we see that when the world was in ecological surplus (left side of graph), the increase in consumption led to an increase in the base or area component, as demand for resources and space was still within the carrying capacity of the globe. From the mid-1980s (right side), this trend changed. The area component of the ecological footprint remained constant and equal to the carrying capacity of the planet, whereas the depth began to increase from year to year, memorising past years, as does the public debt of a nation.

The *Living Planet Report*

The *Living Planet Report* is published every two years by the WWF. Its aim is to assess the health status of ecosystems and the rate of consumption of resources through two indicators, the living planet index and the ecological footprint. The former shows that in the last 30 years, there have been 31%, 28% and 27% reductions in the number of terrestrial, freshwater and marine species, respectively, on the Earth. The ecological footprint shows the demand for natural capital induced by human consumption. This is the only document that shows the ecological footprint of 156 nations, analysing the time trend of the ecological footprint and scenarios for the future. The rich database created enables comparisons between different lifestyles.

A first major consideration emerging from these numbers is that a small minority of persons consumes almost all the natural capital available to the whole population of the Earth. More detailed information at national level is shown in Table 8.2: an American consumes twice as much as is available every year, an Englishman about 3.5 times and an Italian four times as much, whereas a Brazilian only exploits 20% of what Brazil has to offer on a yearly basis. Clearly, the other 80% of land is used to produce environmental goods and services that are exploited by other countries. If all the Earth's inhabitants copied the American lifestyle, more than five planets like the Earth would be necessary.

Table 8.2: Ecological footprint and biocapacity of various nations in 2003.

	Ecological footprint (gha/person)	Biocapacity (gha/person)	Surplus (+)/ deficit (–) (gha/person)
Brazil	2.1	9.9	+7.8
Canada	7.6	14.5	+6.9
China	1.6	0.8	–0.9
France	5.6	3.0	–2.6
Germany	4.5	1.7	–2.8
Japan	4.4	0.7	–3.6
India	0.8	0.4	–0.4
Italy	4.2	1.0	–3.1
Mexico	2.6	1.7	–0.9
United Kingdom	5.6	1.6	–4.0
Russian republics	4.4	6.9	+2.5
USA	9.6	4.7	–4.8
World	**2.2**	**1.8**	**–0.4**

Source: *Living Planet Report 2006*.

The numbers published in the *Living Planet Report* should make us reflect about the aleatory nature of the link between consumption and well-being. The ecological footprint of an American citizen is very different from that of an Italian or European citizen, showing how different are our levels of consumption and lifestyles. What can be said about the level of well-being perceived by the population? Does it increase in proportion to consumption or are its dynamics different? In 1974, Richard Easterlin formulated the so-called *happiness paradox*,[18] according to which economic well-being and wealth were not always accompanied by an increase in subjective well-being. This paradox is echoed by a line of economic research known as 'economics of happiness', which studies the material condition of individuals and their subjective perception of satisfaction.

Emergy evaluation

Emergy evaluation was introduced in the 1980s by H.T. Odum[19] of the University of Florida and is based on the laws of thermodynamics and sustainability. Emergy was conceived as an instrument for assigning an environmental value

18. Easterlin, R., Does economic growth improve human lot? Some empirical evidence. *Nation and Households in Economic Growth: Essays in Honour of Moses Abromowitz*, eds P.A. Davis & M.W. Reder, Academic Press: New York-London, 1974.
19. See Odum, H.T., *Environmental Accounting. Emergy and Environmental Decision Making*, John Wiley & Sons: New York, 1996.

to resources, as coherently as possible with the real processes underlying human and natural systems.[20] The innovation of this method was to provide qualitative and quantitative factors for assessing the 'real value' of natural resources, assuming that everything has an energy content and requires flows of energy and matter for its production. In this way it is possible to consider a system's economic and environmental aspects simultaneously (the latter have been largely disregarded by economists), expressing all inputs, flows and outputs in the same terms, namely solar energy equivalent.

By definition, solar emergy, or simply emergy, is the quantity of solar energy necessary directly and indirectly to obtain a product by a certain process. It is an extensive quantity (depending on the size of the system) and its unit is solar emergy joules (seJ). All resources, i, used in a process have an energy content, E_i, and an environmental cost per unit energy which can be expressed in terms of the solar energy used directly or indirectly in time to produce it. This environmental cost varies from resource to resource and is called *transformity*, *Tr*. The total emergy, *Em*, of a product produced by a process is the sum of the energy content (E_i) of the i inputs supporting the process multiplied by their transformities (Tr_i):

$$Em = (E_1 \times Tr_1) + (E_2 \times Tr_2) + (E_3 \times Tr_3) + \cdots + (E_n \times Tr_n) = \sum_{i=1}^{n} E_i \times Tr_i.$$

For example, to calculate the emergy of a kilogram of coal, we measure all the solar energy required for the photosynthesis of a certain amount of plants, all the energy contained in those plants, all the energy involved in compressing and fossilising the plant mass and all the energy necessary to mine it and transport it to where it is burnt. Emergy therefore discriminates the different forms of energy and materials on the basis of their different 'content' of solar energy equivalent. The common denominator was not a chance choice: solar energy is the most elementary form of energy available, and together with geothermal heat, underlies all processes occurring on the Earth.

Emergy can be considered an energy memory, or the memory of all the solar energy necessary to support a system, including the energy inputs upstream of transformation processes in the system and those involved in all steps of the processes themselves. Emergy can also be viewed as the solar energy directly and indirectly necessary to renew a resource once the resource has been consumed. The greater the overall emergy flow necessary to support a process, the greater the quantity of solar energy the process 'consumed' or the greater the present and past environmental costs necessary to maintain or reproduce it. This means that a large flow of emergy may indicate a high level of organisation of an element of a system or inefficient use of resources. Thus the quantity 'emergy' is not sufficient *per se* to characterise a system. Emergy is best used to obtain more specific indicators.

---

20. For more information visit the website of the newborn Intenational Society for the Advancement of Emergy Research (ISAER): www.isaer.org.

Comparison of emergy evaluation with traditional analyses

Traditional energy and economic analyses usually ignore inputs that they cannot evaluate in terms of energy and money, respectively. Since different inputs have different units (grams of mineral, kWh of electricity, hours of work, etc.), a complete balance is impossible. However, when a product is attributed a *transformity* or emergy content, all inputs of whatever unit can be measured in the common unit of emergy.

Figure 8.3 summarises the differences between conventional economic analysis and emergy analysis, showing that the latter succeeds in accounting a greater number of factors, including natural factors. Models of emergy evaluation are radically different from traditional economic models. The main criterion for decisions in political economy is the market, and therefore things that are not evaluated in money are considered externalities of the system: the environment and social needs are generally relegated to the status of externality requiring corrective mechanisms of economic decision making. A change in perspective through environment-centric models, in which the environment is finally attributed its primary role, provides precious insights into regional systems and their dynamics, completing economic analysis. Emergy evaluation

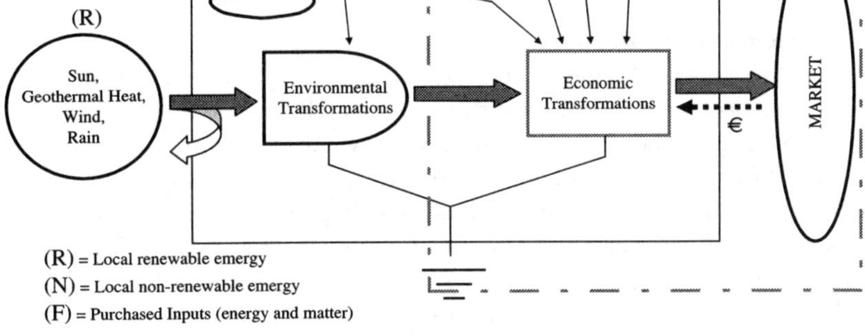

Figure 8.3: Flow diagram comparing emergy and conventional economic approaches. Thermodynamic analysis based on the emergy function provides more concrete answers than traditional energy and economic analyses because it considers the environmental components of a system (natural capital) as well as purely economic ones. Economic accounting is concerned with the monetary flows within the dashed box.

considers the different inputs contributing to system development, besides providing important indicators for development models and for economically and environmentally correct use of natural and man-made capital. Emergy evaluation also differentiates between economically similar but not necessarily equally sustainable systems. Indeed, emergy does not depend solely on the initial and final conditions of a process, but above all on the path between the two (i.e. it is not a thermodynamic *state function*). For example, if we consider different ways of producing electricity, we obtain different transformities according to whether we generate it directly from the sun (with photovoltaic panels), from biomass, or from a coal-fired power station.

Emergy evaluation of regional systems

Figure 8.4 is a block diagram showing the main steps of a regional analysis. The different steps are interrelated and interacting. The first step is to define the boundaries of the geographical area to be analysed. Then information on the region is gathered, pin-pointing the natural and artificial constituents and the different relations between them in the various processes and systems of production. The data makes it possible to construct an energy diagram showing the parts of the system and all flows of energy and materials involved. Emergy evaluation is normally done on the time scale of a solar year to avoid errors due to seasonal fluctuations. The next step is the analysis itself. All flows of energy and materials are quantified and classified as renewable, non-renewable, local or imported. The emergy indicators, explained below, are elaborated on the basis of these categories. Finally, the values of the different indicators, which constitute a sustainability map, are obtained.

The system and the flows

Regional systems are thermodynamically open, meaning that they can exchange matter, energy and information with the outside. Regions can receive energy to fuel their processes from the sun, rain or wind and from resources such as unfinished products and high quality energy, in order to sustain and feed natural, agricultural and industrial processes. Regions export their products, emissions of degraded energy and wastes. Continuous exchanges with the outside sustain and enable regional *metabolism*.

The study of a regional system requires definition of its borders, which may have a physical basis or may simply be an administrative convention. In general, the smaller a system, the more flows of energy and matter tend to come from outside rather than inside.

At conceptual level, resources can be classified in at least two ways:

1. On the basis of provenance, it is possible to distinguish local and non-local (or imported) resources, showing what is typical of the system and what the system has to import. Examples of local resources are direct solar energy,

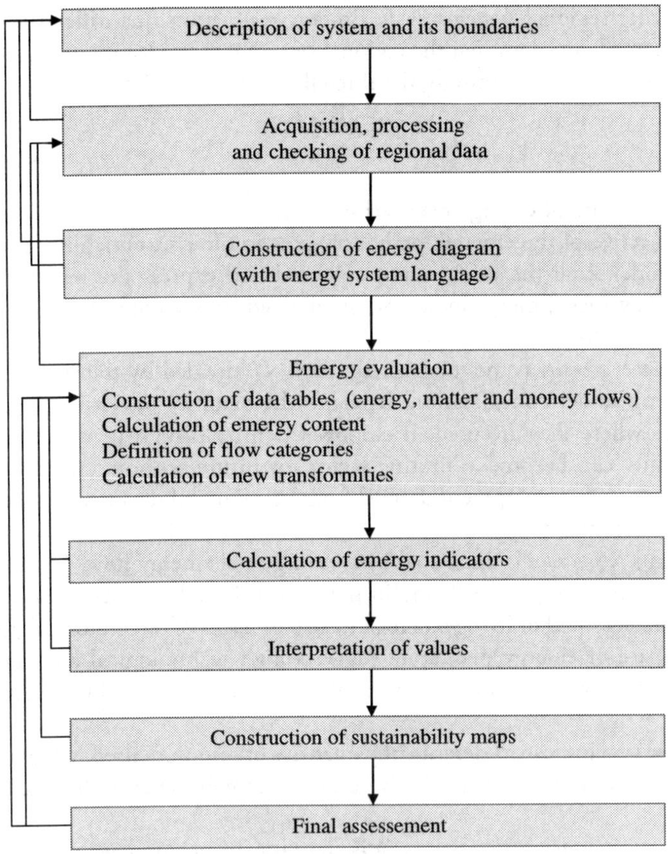

Figure 8.4: Steps of a regional emergy analysis.

rain, wind, geothermal heat and minerals, whereas electricity, fuels and commercially imported goods are generally non-local.

2. On the basis of regeneration time, resources can be distinguished as renewable or non-renewable. In the long run, all natural resources are renewable but the discriminant is the rate at which they form, compared to the rate at which they are used. Humans should incentivate the use of natural resources with their renewal time in mind; this means using them in a renewable way. For example, river water is a renewable resource only if less water is taken than rain and other sources bring to the river. Otherwise, water should be considered non-renewable or very slowly renewable.

The flow of solar emergy derived from the use of local renewable resources is indicated as *R*, local non-renewables as *N* and all goods and services imported from other regional systems as *F*. Emergy evaluation quantifies the flow of solar energy equivalent that the regional system receives for maintenance of its development, *U*, by summing the three flows *R*, *N* and *F*.

$$U = R + N + F.$$

The indicators of emergy evaluation

The objective of the emergy methodology is to offer sustainability indicators that condense all the information collected and express the results through aggregate values. Emergy indicators are derived from a combination of different types of flow.

Empower density is the total emergy flow, *U*, divided by the surface area of the region under consideration. It relates the quantity of resources used and the area where they are used. If empower density is high it means that land availability can become a limiting factor for future economic growth of the system, though development derived from better use of resources and available space is not impeded.

Emergy per person is calculated by dividing total emergy flow, *U*, of a region by the number of persons living in the region. Broadly, it can be regarded as the mean standard of living of a region, also in terms of technological progress. A high use of emergy per capita suggests high technological and industrial development with high environmental stress, unless renewable resources are used.

These two indicators describe the quantity of resources used, while the next two are concerned with qualitative aspects, namely renewability and provenance.

The *environmental loading ratio* is the ratio of non-renewable ($N + F$) to renewable (*R*) emergy. If the ratio equals 10 it means that the system consumes 10 times more non-renewable than renewable resources. If this indicator is monitored in time it provides a measure of the trend towards or away from sustainability. A decreasing trend of the environmental loading ratio indicates careful regional planning; for example, incentivation of electricity generation from renewable resources may lead to such a reduction. Rigorous observation of Daly's first principle (see Chapter 2), which underlies the idea of sustainability, would cause this indicator to approach its limit value of zero, because resources would not be used unsustainably.

The *emergy investment ratio* is the ratio of resources from outside the system (*F*) to local resources ($R + N$) and indicates to what degree the system depends on the outside, namely to what extent it exploits its own resources without making its unsustainability weigh on other regions. If this ratio equals 4 it means that the system requires 4 imported units for every local unit of emergy exploited. Although a region that exchanges materials and energy with the outside is not isolated, a decreasing trend of this index is desirable.

It is worth repeating that these indicators analyse flows of emergy (i.e. resources derived from solar energy or solar equivalent through self-organisation of ecosystems) and not energy in the traditional sense. The prospect of political economy based on emergy is offered as an instrument for assessing planning of regional systems and production. Emergy analysis is a good starting point for increasing the integration of humans with their environment, in other words of economics and ecology. These indicators have the advantage of providing a rigorous and immediate assessment of the sustainability of a system, reconciling the need for easy interpretation with scientific rigour. Translating impacts into a single value that represents a situation makes it possible to compare the situation with others in space and time.

Climate change and the IPCC greenhouse gas inventory

The increase in the greenhouse effect is recognised as the main environmental problem on a global scale. Human responsibility for the increase in atmospheric concentrations of certain gases that change the chemico-physical characteristics of the atmosphere and cause climate change all over the planet was stressed with great scientific certainty (>90%) in the Fourth Assessment Report of the IPCC, published in February 2007.

Awareness that certain gaseous emissions produced by human activities could affect climate on a planetary scale has been known since the end of the 19th century, but re-emerged towards the end of the 1960s with the first climate conference organised by the World Meteorological Organisation (WMO). In 1988, the WMO in collaboration with the United Nations Environment Programme (UNEP) instituted the *Intergovernmental Panel on Climate Change* (IPCC), an intergovernmental commission charged with assessing and broadcasting scientific information about climate change.[21] In 1990, two years after its establishment, the IPCC published its first climate report, in which the greenhouse effect emerged as the main threat to climate stability.

On the basis of this report, the United Nations Framework Convention on Climate Change (UNFCCC) was presented in New York on 9 May 1992 and at the summit on environment and development in Rio de Janeiro on 4 June 1992. The aim of the agreement was to stabilise concentrations of greenhouse gases at a level that would exclude any effect on global climate. The convention also established the Conference of the Parties as its governing body, with the main task of examining actuation of agreements and legal instruments to implement the agreements.

21. In 2007 the IPCC received (together with former Vice-President of the United States Al Gore) the Nobel Peace Prize *for their efforts to build up and disseminate greater knowledge about man-made climate change, and to lay the foundations for the measures that are needed to counteract such change.*

In 1997, the Conference of the Parties met in Kyoto to update the basic convention. Since the non-binding objectives decided in Rio had not been achieved, adoption of a more rigorous protocol was deemed necessary. On that occasion, the Kyoto Protocol, the only working agreement, was ratified. It established specific binding objectives of reduction of emissions for all signatory countries. For industrialised countries and transition economies, identified in the protocol as Annex 1 countries, the document imposes 5.2% mean reductions of greenhouse gas emissions with respect to 1990 levels in the period 2008–2012. Single mean reductions range from 8% for the European Union to a tolerated increase of up to 10% for Iceland. Australia and Norway can also increase emissions by 8% and 1%, respectively, whereas New Zealand, the Russian Federation and Ukraine should maintain 1990 levels of emissions. For other eastern European countries converting to market economies, reductions range from 5% to 8%; Canada and Japan 6%, and USA 7%.

The protocol indicates the policies and measures that each country should adopt to achieve these reductions: energy efficiency, development of renewable resources, protection of forests and an increase in forest area, development of sustainable agriculture, and so forth. Three mechanisms based on reduction of emissions outside national limits are also envisaged. They are known as flexible mechanisms: (1) emissions trading; (2) joint implementation; (3) clean development mechanisms.

After ratification by Russia, a country responsible for 17% of world emissions, the protocol finally came into effect on 16th February 2005, since the quota of man-made emissions necessary for the aims to have a result (55% of emissions of industrialised and transition economy countries) had been reached. The protocol then became law in ratifying countries. In Italy, six lines of action with the following aims were defined by CIPE no. 137 *Guidelines for national policy and measures for the reduction of greenhouse gas emissions* on 19 November 1998 (G.U. n. 33, 10 February 1999):

1. increased efficiency of the electrical grid;
2. reduced energy consumption in transport sector;
3. production of energy from renewable resources;
4. reduction of energy consumption in industrial, domestic and tertiary sectors;
5. reduction of emissions by non-energy sectors;
6. absorption of carbon emissions by forests.

The first check of emission trends in Italy after 1990 gave alarming results. In January 2006, APAT published the data of national inventories sent annually to the UNFCCC secretary. The latest data (2004) show that emissions increased by 12.2% in the period 1990–2004. According to the Ministry for the Environment, this means that the reduction for Italy in 2008–2012 rises to 18.7% with respect to 1990 levels, requiring an overall reduction of 93 million tons of CO_2 equivalent (instead of the 43 million tons initially envisaged).

Greenhouse gas inventory

The greenhouse gas inventory is a monitoring instrument for detecting sectors to regulate, to reduce greenhouse gas emissions under the Kyoto Protocol. The 2006 IPCC Guidelines for National Greenhouse Gas Inventories (2006 Guidelines) were solicited by the UNFCCC to update the previous guidelines and include two recent manuals: *The Good Practice Guidance and Uncertainty Management in National Greenhouse Gas Inventories* and *The Good Practice Guidance for Land Use, Land-Use Change and Forestry*. The new guidelines were designed to be used in national inventories of greenhouse gas emissions, to send each year to the IPCC secretariat. The inventory requires countries to pin-point a few key sources and sinks of man-made emissions of greenhouse gases and to plot them on national spatial and annual temporal scales. All emissions and removals of greenhouse gases on national territory and in areas of national jurisdiction are included.

Emissions of the following gases are accounted in the 2006 Guidelines: carbon dioxide (CO_2), methane (CH_4), nitrous oxide (N_2O), hydrofluorocarbons (HFCs), perfluorocarbons (PFCs), sulphur hexafluoride (SF_6), nitrogen trifluoride (NF_3), trifluoromethyl sulphur pentafluoride (SF_5CF_3), halogenated ethers ($C_4F_9OC_2H_5$, $CHF_2OCF_2OC_2F_4OCHF_2$, CHF_2OCF_2O-CHF_2) and other halocarbons not included in the Montreal Protocol (CF_3I, CH_2Br_2 $CHCl_3$, CH_3Cl, CH_2Cl_2). Halocarbons are not derived from natural processes; their presence in the atmosphere is largely due to human activities. Halogenated gases are emitted in much smaller quantities than CO_2, CH_4 and N_2O but may have long lives and radiative forcing 3000–13,000 times more than CO_2. The mathematical combination of the two factors, radiative forcing and persistence, is known as global warming potential (GWP) and is the conversion factor used to calculate emissions of all greenhouse gases in CO_2 equivalent. From the chemico-physical viewpoint, GWP is the long-period contribution of a gas to global warming. This index is weighted in relation to the atmospheric life of the gas and its capacity to absorb infrared radiation emitted by the Earth. A GWP was assigned to the above gases in the IPCC Third Assessment Report (Table 8.3).

Although they do not have a GWP, gases with indirect effects on climate, such as oxides of nitrogen (NO_x), carbon monoxide (CO), volatile organic compounds not included in the Montreal Protocol (NMVOCs), and sulphur dioxide (SO_2), are also counted. In the presence of sunlight, carbon dioxide, nitrogen oxides and NMVOCs contribute to the formation of tropospheric ozone and are called ozone precursors. Oxides of nitrogen are also involved in the nitrogen cycle and can lead to indirect emissions of nitrous oxide. Emissions of sulphur dioxide lead to the formation of sulphate particles in atmospheric aerosol that play a role in climate change.

Table 8.3: GWPs established by the IPCC in the Third Assessment Report (2001).

Greenhouse gas	GWP at 100 years
CO_2	1
CH_4	23
N_2O	296
HFC-23	12,000
HFC-125	3,400
HFC-134a	1,300
HFC-143a	4,300
HFC-152a	120
HFC-227ea	3,500
HFC-236fa	9,400
Perfluoromethane (CF_4)	5,700
Perfluoroethane (C_2F_6)	11,900
Sulphur hexafluoride (SF_6)	22,200

Emissions and absorptions of greenhouse gases are divided into emission macrosectors, as indicated in the 2006 Guidelines:

1. energy;
2. industrial processes and product use;
3. agriculture, forestry and other land uses;
4. wastes.

The methodological approach for the calculation of emissions requires data on human activities to be combined with coefficients that quantify emissions or absorptions per unit activity. These coefficients are called emission factors and the equation for the general calculation of emissions produced by a certain activity is:

$$\text{Emissions} = \text{Activity data} \times \text{Emission factor.}$$

Besides this simple equation, which holds in most cases, the method also includes a mass balance method for certain sectors, e.g. for changes in the carbon stock in living biomass and in reservoirs of dead organic matter.

The basic concept of the IPCC methodology is to promote the development of a high quality greenhouse gas inventory through good practices: as far as the state of the art enables us to tell, an inventory drawn up according to good practices does not overestimate emissions, and uncertainties are reduced to a minimum. The categories and emission sources and sinks for each sector are reported below.

Energy

Energy is usually the major sector of the greenhouse gas inventory and may contribute up to 90% of CO_2 emissions and 75% of total greenhouse gas emissions in developed countries. Combustion of fossil fuels produces mostly CO_2 and water.

Categories
Stationary combustion
Mobile combustion
Leakage
Transport, injection and geological storage of CO_2

For the first time, capture and storage of CO_2 was introduced in the guidelines as a possibility for CO_2 removal at large energy plants. All emissions due to transport, injection and geological storage should be included in the sector.

Industrial processes and product use

Greenhouse gases are produced by a wide variety of industrial activities. The energy sector is excluded from this macrosector. The main emissions come from industrial processes in which materials undergo physical or chemical transformation. These processes may release greenhouse gases, such as CO_2, CH_4, N_2O and PFCs. Emissions due to processes are produced at the same time as emissions due to combustion of fuels, making attribution difficult and creating situations of double accounting.

Categories
Mineral industry emissions
Chemical industry emissions
Metal industry emissions
Non-energy products from fuels and solvent use
Electronics industry emissions
Emissions of fluorinated substitutes for ozone depleting substances

Agriculture, forestry and other land uses

This macrosector unifies the macrosectors Agriculture and Forestry and other land uses of the *Revised 1996 Guideline.* It now includes greenhouse gas emissions due to changes in land use and variations in the stock of organic carbon in living and dead biomass. Six types of land are recognised and changes in land use can involve all types. Absorption of CO_2 during growth of forest ecosystems is accounted in this macrosector. Emissions of greenhouse gases in agriculture can be divided into two large categories: those due to livestock, a major source of methane, and those due to fertilizers, the main source of nitrous oxide emissions.

Categories
Changes in surface area of forest land
Changes in cropland
Changes in pastures and meadows lands
Changes in wetlands
Changes in area of settlements
Emissions by livestock and manure
Emissions from ploughed soil and CO_2 emissions due to application of lime and urea
Harvested wood products

Wastes
This macrosector concerns methane emissions from landfills and methane and nitrous oxide emissions from wastewater. Anaerobic decomposition of organic matter by methanogenic bacteria in landfills releases methane to the atmosphere. This source is estimated to constitute 5–20% of all man-made emissions of methane. Liquid wastes with a high content of organic matter (domestic, industrial and from livestock) are responsible for 8–11% of world methane emissions.

Categories
Waste generation, composition and management
Solid waste disposal
Biological treatment of solid urban waste
Incinerators and open burning of waste
Wastewater treatment and discharge

Once all emissions of greenhouse gases and absorption of CO_2 in the four macrosectors have been entered in the inventory, it is possible to compare man-made CO_2 emissions with the absorption capacity of forest ecosystems and the quantity of CO_2 captured and stored, to obtain a figure for net emissions and assess a nation's capacity to absorb its own emissions.

Responsibility for greenhouse gas emissions: a proposal
Mitigation of the greenhouse effect and the spiralling use of fossil fuels call for technological research and political compromises. Research is necessary into the major sources of greenhouse gas emissions: it is important not only to identify fuel consumption as the main source of these emissions, but also to localise where these gases are emitted, why they are emitted and which economic sectors are involved in the emission.

The method proposed by the IPCC is a standardised, internationally recognised accounting method; however, it has problems, some of which are related to the estimation of GWPs: the dynamics of greenhouse gas emissions and impact on climate are described by mechanical relations of cause and effect; basal static atmospheric conditions are assumed; numerically equivalent emissions may not be equivalent in their long-term effect on climate.

The IPCC model attributes responsibility for emissions on the basis of a geographical criterion (territorial responsibility): it considers emissions of sectors within the geographic boundaries of the system. The contribution to global emissions of greenhouse gases is evaluated for all direct emission sources at the local level, without including indirect emissions, e.g. fuel used for transport. This has the following consequences:

- a nation that imports finished goods has a high standard of living and low emissions;
- a nation that produces and exports pays for CO_2 emissions that regard products it does not enjoy directly;
- a nation crossed by heavy transport of goods pays for the CO_2 emissions of a service associated with goods that it neither produces nor consumes.

Let us consider three systems, the emissions attributed to which are in fact those occurring within their boundaries. For example, system A, a producer, has most of the industry and emits 50 units of CO_2; system B is an intermediate system, which does intermediate processing or transporting and emits 30 units; system C is a consumer and emits 20 units.

An alternative method could be that of consumer responsibility, based on the concept of the ecological footprint: if a good is produced in nation X and consumed in nation Y, the land requirements associated with its consumption are attributed totally to nation Y. As final consumer, nation Y is therefore responsible for the entire ecological impact of the process underlying availability of the good, and is ascribed all the emissions connected with the process. Systems A and B are ascribed zero emissions, and system C is ascribed 100 units of emissions. This method of calculation would attribute low levels of emission to developing countries and high levels to rich nations. The final user of the goods pays the tax for high emissions, whereas the producer is less motivated to reduce emissions. This could be partly compensated if consumers choose producers who reduce their emissions. However, consumer sensitivity is rarely evident in the absence of immediate economic incentives.

A compromise can be reached, exploiting the philosophy underlying emergy analysis. A subject is considered responsible for its direct emissions and co-responsible for emissions generated to make and market the goods and services it uses. In this accounting system, greenhouse gas emissions accumulate and are memorised artificially, so that the total emissions calculated are divided in new proportions based on a system of added emissions for each phase. The following scheme should help understand the procedure. True emissions are shown in brackets and those for which a system is considered co-responsible are shown in italics. The artificial sum of all contributions comes to 230.

(50)	(30)	(20)
A	B	C
50	30+*50*	20+*30+50*

The three systems A, B and C are therefore cumulatively co-responsible for 230 units of emissions that are divided percentage-wise according to the responsibility/co-responsibility of each: system A is ascribed 50/230 (= 22%), system B 80/230 (= 35%) and system C 100/230 (= 43%). The new proportions deduced by the criterion of added emissions, or *carbon emission added*,[22] makes it possible to divide responsibility for total emissions in a way that is intermediate between the geographic principle (IPCC) and that of final consumer (ecological footprint), eliciting virtuous behaviour from consumers (choice of environmentally friendly products) and producers (environmentally friendly technology). The approach therefore decreases but does not cancel the responsibility of countries providing primary materials and incentivates importers to select production methods that emit fewer greenhouse gases.

22. Bastianoni, S., Pulselli, F.M. & Tiezzi, E., The problem of assigning responsibility for greenhouse gas emissions. *Ecological Economics*, **49**, pp. 253–257, 2004.

Chapter 9

Plus and minus of sustainability: the index of sustainable economic welfare

The small wooden statue of a figure in ancient costume in front of the cathedral of Chester in Cheshire carries an inscription from Ecclesiastes: *The king himself is served by the field.* It is curious to think that even the supreme authority of the kingdom, who does not have to answer to anyone, has to adapt to something, namely what the field gives him. The message is a bud of environmental sensibility aspiring to a harmonious relationship between humans and nature. Even the king is served by the field, he who could go to the moon or own mines, water, everything through his wealth. He still has to adapt to what the field produces naturally: no field, no king.

Growth or well-being?

The main test of human activities in a region is the economic measure of these activities. This calculation is done by special instruments of economic statistics, such as added value or gross domestic product, GDP. However, it is now well known that these instruments do not provide an exhaustive picture of the complexity of human relationships on a region, since economic assessments completely ignore certain fundamental components of life, such as environmental and many social components.

The GDP represents the dynamics of an economic system. It is commonly believed that growth of GDP brings opulence, occupation, security and widespread well-being. Growth is considered a necessary condition for implementing projects of importance to society, such as health schemes, education, environment and energy, and it is also considered a goal by governments, an index of good administration and supreme judge of political and economic management. This is why society seeks growth of GDP, neglecting what this instrument neglects. As Daly wrote in the Preface to this book, 'when the economy's expansion encroaches too much on its surrounding ecosystem, we will begin to sacrifice natural capital (such as fish, minerals and fossil fuels) that is worth more than the man-made capital (such as roads, factories and appliances) added by the growth. We will then have what I call uneconomic growth, producing 'bads' faster than goods – making us poorer, not richer.'

The scientific literature concerned with sustainability, such as the journal Ecological Economics, does not share the view that all decisions should be based on the predictions of economic growth and the trend of GDP. Economic growth does not follow the path of quality of life and sustainability, indeed it is often antithetic.

We owe a first critique of the economic product as index of the welfare of a nation to Simon Kuznets, Nobel Laureate in Economics (1971), who also made a big contribution to standardisation of national accounting systems. He sustained that the welfare of a nation can scarcely be inferred from a measurement of national income.

The association between growth of GDP and welfare seemed to hold for as long as the material dimension of the economy was far from the limits imposed by the biosphere. Proponents of dominant economic theory seem to have difficulty understanding the blatant thermodynamic fact that infinite growth is impossible in a finite planet.

In 1972, William Nordaus and James Tobin[1] investigated the existence of links between economic growth and people's perception of welfare, developing a corrective index for GDP that they called *measure of economic welfare* (MEW). MEW highlighted elements correlated with economic welfare. The results were encouraging for economists, since GDP and MEW seemed correlated in the period 1929–1965, extended to the 1980s by Samuelson and Nordhaus. Economic growth (a concept that was not yet obsolete) could therefore continue to be an objective, since for high levels of welfare the economic system first had to increase production of wealth. However, it did not pass unobserved that MEW ignored certain components affecting welfare, such as unequal distribution of wealth, environmental degradation and certain social problems, that further growth would have aggravated.

An important contribution in this direction was made by Xenophon Zolotas,[2] former prime minister of Greece, who formulated the index called *economic aspects of welfare* (EAW), which counted costs of pollution and depletion of resources among economic aspects. He was aware that beyond certain levels of GDP, welfare calculated by EAW and economic growth could diverge.

1. Nordhaus, W. & Tobin, J., Is growth obsolete? *Economic Growth*, General Series No. 96, National Bureau of Economic Research: New York, 1972.
2. Zolotas, X., *Economic Growth and Declining Social Welfare*, Bank of Greece: Athens, 1981.

There is a risk of value judgements in considering more qualitative aspects of economic growth and of formulating instruments that are not entirely neutral with respect to different cultural and ideological models. However, choice of a purely quantitative index such as GDP as a measure of the 'economic success' of a society is hardly free of value judgements either.

In any case, there is a pressing need for something more, in terms of information, than a simple measure of a country's productive capacity. This need has probably become more evident in recent years, prompting certain economists to diverge from conventional theory and sustain heterodox or innovative positions.

In order to complement information provided by GDP, which indicates the wealth of a country, other indices such as the *genuine progress indicator* (GPI), *human development index* (HDI), *index of economic freedom* (IEF) and *index of sustainable economic welfare* (ISEW) have been proposed.

The index of sustainable economic welfare

The theoretical framework of ISEW was proposed in 1989 for the US economy by Herman Daly and John Cobb.[3] The method integrates traditional economic accounting, placing it in its environmental and social context. For example, Daly and Cobb entered damage to the finite natural heritage (environmental degradation and depletion of resources) as negative entries in their new accounting system that considers environmental quality as an essential condition for human welfare. The creation of ISEW is an attempt to highlight quality of life rather than economic wealth, a short-sighted measure. To provide a more complete image of economic progress towards welfare of the population, ISEW corrects certain aspects of the calculation of GDP. It subtracts:

- Social costs due to air and water pollution;
- Long-term environmental damage;
- Defensive private expenditures on health and education;
- Deterioration of renewable, and depletion of non-renewable natural resources.

It adds, as a component of welfare, the value of unpaid domestic work in families. ISEW also considers the distribution of wealth (more equable distribution that increases poor people's share of national income increases ISEW). It considers services of durable goods and public infrastructure as benefits, but their cost as a negative value, so that spending for durable goods decreases ISEW but increases GDP.

---

3. Daly, H. & Cobb, J., *For the Common Good: Redirecting the Economy Towards Community, the Environment and a Sustainable Future*, Beacon Press: Boston, 1989.

Studies based on this index have only recently become popular. They have been undertaken for USA, UK, Germany, Italy, Sweden, Austria, Chile, the Netherlands, Poland, Scotland, Belgium and other countries are being added. These studies show that a country's ISEW increased much more slowly than GDP after the Second World War and began to decrease in the early 1980s. Figure 9.1 shows the trend of GDP and ISEW in various countries. In two

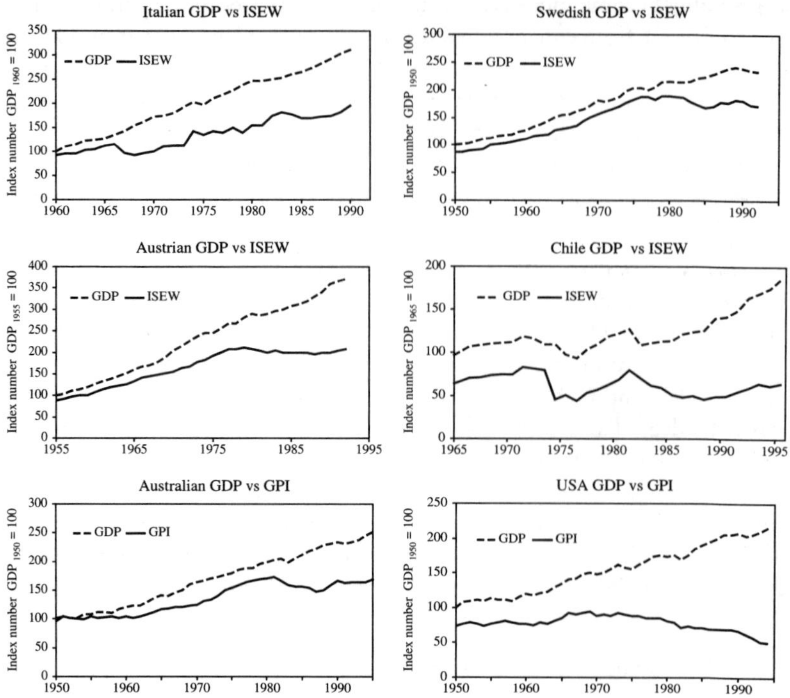

Figure 9.1: Comparison of trends of GDP and ISEW (or GPI) of several national economies.[4]

4. Guenno, G. & Tiezzi, S., The Index of Sustainable Economic Welfare (ISEW) for Italy, Wor-knote 5.98, Fondazione Enrico Mattei, Milano, 1998; Jackson, T. & Stymne, S., *Sustainable Economic Welfare in Sweden: A Pilot Index 1950–1992*, Stockholm Environment Institute, The New Economics Foundation, 1996; Stockhammer, E., Hochreiter, H., Hobermayr, B. & Steiner, K., The index of sustainable economic welfare (ISEW) as an alternative to GDP in measuring economic welfare. The result of the Austrian (revised) ISEW calculation, 1955–1992. *Ecological Economics*, **21(1)**, pp. 19–34, 1997; Castañeda, B.E., An index of sustainable economic welfare (ISEW) for Chile. *Ecological Economics*, **28**, pp. 231–244, 1999; Hamilton, C., The genuine progress indicator: methodological developments and results from Australia. *Ecological Economics*, **30(1)**, pp. 13–28, 1999; Anielski, M. & Rowe, M., The Genuine Progress Indicator – 1998 Update, Redefining Progress: San Francisco, 1999.

cases (USA and Australia), GPIs are shown; GPI is similar to ISEW except for minor differences in components.

In this book, we present the first cases of calculation of ISEW at local level. Although difficulties are involved, particularly the difficulty of obtaining reliable information, this calculation is important, primarily because it shows that it is possible and appropriate for local government to apply different instruments in order to obtain insights into its region and regional dynamics. It is also possible to detect particularities and critical elements that do not emerge from indices applied at national scale. Moreover, it can reveal features on which to build local development of a kind that is not based exclusively on economic results of the period but also considers the living conditions of the population, environmental quality and availability of resources. The political–administrative process of implementation is complex, involving acquisition of the data necessary to calculate various indices and translation of the results into procedures, regulations and laws to orientate the community in the direction of sustainability.

Items composing ISEW

ISEW is an aggregate indicator of development that integrates information contained in GDP by correcting aspects such as inequable distribution of wealth, environmental damage and some social variables. It is composed of a number of variables that are indicated with letters of the alphabet. The final series of items is somewhat arbitrary but is largely based on the postulates of Daly and Cobb. The letter *A* refers to the year of the historical series; *B* represents private consumption, as in GDP, and *D*, weighted consumption. The weighting is based on Gini's index of income distribution, indicated by the letter *C*. Variables *E*, *F*, *G* and *H* are positive values, representing services that contribute to people's welfare, not considered in traditional economic accounting. Variables *I*–*Q* are negative items that correct overestimation of economic welfare linked to the level of private consumption. Variables indicated by the letters *R*, *S*, *T* and *U* are usually negative, estimating consumption of natural capital without any real return in economic welfare.

A – year of reference

Though some pilot studies have been conducted on a single year, ISEW becomes meaningful when used on historical series, so that its trend can be compared with that of GDP.

B – private consumption

Private consumption is directly linked to economic welfare. Assuming that individual welfare depends largely on the quantity of goods and services consumed, consumption will reflect individual preferences, given a certain amount of economic resources. However, the aggregate has limits as an indicator of welfare and is not used as such but weighted by means of the inequality index.

C – inequality index
As suggested by Daly and Cobb, the Gini index is used to weight consumption on the basis of the distribution of economic resources among the population. The question is important for calculation of general welfare, because €10 in the pocket of a rich man is worth less than in the pocket of a poor man. The value of this index may vary from zero to one: zero indicates perfect equal distribution and one indicates that wealth is concentrated in few hands.

D – weighted private consumption (+)
This variable is the starting item for the calculation of ISEW. Potential welfare from a given level of consumption decreases with increasing inequity of distribution. The value is obtained correcting aggregate private consumption with the Gini inequality index.

E – domestic labour (+)
Domestic labour (work that contributes to home and family stability) is part of the so-called invisible economy because it is unpaid: although it produces direct benefit, it does not involve market exchange at a documented price. Because this item does not reflect a true movement of economic resources and represents a service that has no market, it is excluded from GDP. In the calculation of ISEW, it is added to weighted consumption. The final value is obtained multiplying mean market price of domestic help by the male and female population over the age of 14 years. This category is distinguished into three groups (students, unemployed and retired persons, and housewives), associating a type-package of working hours with each: 8 hours a day for housewives, 4 hours for unemployed and retired persons, 2 hours for students.

F – services of consumer durables (+)
Money spent for durable goods, such as cars and appliances, (this item also includes houses), is not a good measure of welfare because these goods have lasting utility. ISEW counts services from durable goods among benefits (positive sign), but subtracts the initial capital used to buy them as a cost (see item *I*). The calculation considers the mean life of durables. Houses are ascribed 5% of the total stock, assuming 20-year home loans on average. Services from other durable goods are 10% of the total stock because we assume that such goods have a lifespan of 10 years. A large proportion of so-called durable goods are replaced too often with respect to their lifetime, increasing levels of consumption and GDP without significantly increasing welfare.

G – services from public infrastructure (road system) (+)
Road maintenance increases the welfare of users. This part of public spending brings benefits without any corresponding expenditure by the population (or

at least nothing under the item consumption). The monetary value of this variable is therefore the sum of money that would have to be paid, were road infrastructure not conceded publicly. To calculate it, a mean road maintenance cost of non-tollways is attributed.

H – public expenditure on health and education (+)
The correlation between increase in public spending and welfare is weak, because much of this item is defensive. The final value attributed to this item is derived from the percentage of public spending regarded as being related to welfare: 100% of education costs and 50% of health costs are assumed, the other 50% being regarded as defensive and not affecting welfare of the population. In evaluating welfare, defensive expenditures (environmental, social or economic) are always linked to negative externalities resulting from production and consumption, and has the purpose avoiding, reducing or compensating damage caused by those externalities and external diseconomies.

I – expenditure on consumer durables (–)
As we have seen (item *F*), a person's welfare is not related to how much he/she spends to buy goods but to lasting satisfaction resulting from their purchase. While spending for consumer durables increases levels of consumption, there is no correspondence with sustainable welfare and this item is therefore subtracted.

J – private defensive expenditure on education and health (–)
This item is negative for the purposes of ISEW because it is defensive. The whole sum is already accounted in the starting variable (private consumption). That part of expenditure sustained solely because the context requires it, but which does not increase welfare, is therefore subtracted. The amount to subtract is 50% of private spending for education and health and could be avoided if our behaviour was globally more sustainable.

K – national expenditure for advertising (–)
The cost of advertising, paid in the end by consumers, is subtracted from aggregate private consumption because it induces demand rather than satisfying needs related to welfare. Actually, part of advertising has a real purpose of informing real and potential clients of the existence of goods and services; according to Daly, however, this only occurs locally, so most of this expenditure can be considered a result of market distortion.

L – commuting costs (–)
Being a commuter, namely living in a different place from where one works and having to travel back and forth each day, is synonymous with inconvenience.

Commuting costs money and is therefore subtracted from consumption for the purposes of ISEW because it expresses a need rather than a level of welfare. We estimate that 30% of private and public vehicle use is for commuting. The item is calculated using the formula: $L = 0.3\alpha + 0.3\beta + 0.3\gamma$, where L is direct cost of commuting, α the value of the services of the stock of vehicles in a year, β costs sustained for tickets on public transport and γ maintenance costs of public and private vehicles; 0.3 is the portion of private vehicle use and of kilometres travelled on public transport to go to work.

M – costs of urbanisation (–)
Part of private costs for housing is due to increased urbanisation, which creates environmental externalities of various types. With increasing population of urban areas, the cost of land and houses increases without any compensating increase in welfare. This item should therefore be subtracted from private consumption. However, buying a house is associated with a high level of satisfaction and the monetary value of the investment tends to be maintained in time, except in rare contingencies. The concentration of population in cities stimulates the supply of homes, which at least partly compensates the increase in price due to urbanisation and is regulated by local town planning authorities. In the studies of Part 3, the costs of urbanisation are therefore not subtracted from private consumption.

N – costs of road accidents (–)
In all developed countries, the cost of road accidents amounts to 2% of GDP. In Italy, 6,600 persons die in road accidents each year and 240,000 are wounded, making it the principal cause of death in the 15–30-year age group in the European Union. Road accidents are one of the highest costs of road transport. A third of the victims are under 25 years of age. In calculating ISEW, the costs of road accidents are subtracted from private consumption as they represent a decrease in welfare. Although the cascade of economic activity generated by road accidents (vehicle repair, health costs, insurance premiums, etc.) creates flows of money representing productive capacity (as measured by GDP), it does not lead to welfare. The value of this item is obtained by multiplying the revenue of insurance premiums due to car accidents by the number of accidents occurring in the period in consideration.

O – costs of water pollution (–)
The economic definition of pollution includes two orders of factors, one physical, related to the direct effects of emissions, discharges and wastes released into the environment, the other biological or chemical, manifesting as loss of welfare, e.g. threats to health, damage to ecosystems and acid rain. In economic terms, pollution is seen as an external cost when an activity undertaken

by one agent causes loss of welfare to another agent, and when loss of welfare is not compensated.

Both conditions are essential for a cost to be considered external. If loss of welfare is compensated, the external effect is internalised. This item can be estimated in various ways because there are various indicators of water quality. One can choose to use the costs of treatment of drinking water sustained by local authorities, or alternatively biological oxygen demand (BOD) and chemical oxygen demand (COD). A further method is to calculate *equivalent inhabitants*, namely the biodegradable load in waste water having a five-day BOD (BOD_5) of 60 g O_2/day. There are conversion tables for calculating equivalent inhabitants for different activities that affect water quality, and water treatment costs associated with equivalent inhabitants to express the value of man-made water pollution in monetary terms.

P – costs of air pollution (–)

Atmospheric contaminants can be classified as:

- primary contaminants, released into the atmosphere directly by the process that produced them and persisting unmodified in the atmosphere. They include carbon monoxide, carbon dioxide, oxides of nitrogen, oxides of sulphur, particulate and unburned hydrocarbons.
- secondary contaminants, formed from primary contaminants by chemical processes that generally involve atmospheric oxygen and light. They include ozone, various aldehydes, peroxides and other chemical species that may be more toxic than the primary contaminants.

Traffic, home heating and industrial processes are the three main causes of air pollution. When high-pressure conditions in winter prevent air turnover, emergency measures may be taken in cities but are often ineffective. Structural policies are necessary to stably reduce sources of pollution in cities.

The final monetary value of air pollution is subtracted from local private consumption as an imaginary tax to compensate for the negative effects of human behaviour. The value is obtained multiplying total tons of contaminants produced by the cost per ton of abatement.

Q – costs of noise pollution (–)

Noise affects quality of life and human welfare. Recognised as a major environmental problem, though often regarded as less important than other forms of pollution, noise causes increasing discontent in exposed populations. Eurispes estimated total direct and indirect costs due to noise at 1.5% of GDP in 2004, about 20 billion Euro. Seven million Italians suffer from hearing problems and 7/10 are exposed to noise levels above legal limits. Loss of working days per year due to hearing-related pathologies is estimated at 35 million. The monetary value of this type of pollution is obtained by multiplying the abatement cost of noise caused by one car by the number of cars in the region.

R – loss of wetlands (–)

Land provides food, water and energy for many biological systems and is fundamental for all human activities. One of the main tasks in the construction of sustainable infrastructure is to direct the development of urban areas towards harmony with the natural environment, though up to now cities have usually destroyed it. Hydrogeologically, chemically, physically, biologically, environmentally, culturally and scientifically, as well as for biodiversity, industrial production, leisure and education, wetlands are of vital importance, even if they cover only 3% of the Earth's surface. Loss of wetlands is therefore directly correlated with loss of welfare and is subtracted from private consumption using different economic criteria.

S – loss of agricultural land (–)

In developed countries, agricultural land has progressively decreased in area under pressure from urbanisation, infrastructures and fragmentation. This reduction has been accompanied by intensification of agricultural practices and heavy pressure on soil resources, leading to exhaustion. Less land is cultivated but production has increased, maintaining food production but depleting the organic matter and fertility of soils. As in the case of wetlands, loss of agricultural land to other types of settlement involves an often irreversible loss of welfare. The various policies of land planning and management therefore have the task of integrating agricultural use of land in the wider objective of conserving nature from the effects of human behaviour. Development of rural areas must safeguard local culture, promoting multifunctionality of farming and forestry activities, favouring the typical quality and cultural content of production, and also making the countryside available for leisure purposes. The monetary value of this item is calculated by counting the decrement in agricultural surface area and multiplying it by the economic value of farmland.

T – depletion of non-renewable resources (–)

It is not necessary to be an economist to understand that a person or a community that draws most of its resources from its capital rather than from its income is headed for bankruptcy. Mining and quarrying, in particular, are major causes of irreversible modification of the environment and regional profile, often in areas of high natural value. The close and delicate relationship between economic and employment questions and regional conservation, as well as the non-renewable nature of mineral deposits, means that this activity must be governed by laws, planning and procedures of authorisation and control with sustainability in view.

For the calculation of ISEW, this item is accounted as a cost for future generations that is subtracted from the capital balance of the current generation. The quantity to subtract is obtained by an estimation method proposed by Salah El Serafy,[5] modified by Cobb and Daly. El Serafy indicates the sum to set aside, after liquidation of an activity (such as a mineral deposit), in order to generate a permanent flow of future income equal to the part of earnings derived from non-renewable goods consumed in the present.

U – long-term environmental damage (–)

In the past, climate was regarded as something that humans could not modify and climate change in terms of rare, unpredictable events. In the last decades of the 20th century, however, it became evident that not only does climate affect human activity, but that human activity may also change climate, with dramatic repercussions. Large-scale industrial activity tends to modify climate by a gradual increase in atmospheric temperature: this phenomenon is determined by the increase in greenhouse effect caused by the use of fossil fuels. The greenhouse gases released affect climate for many years, as in some cases their lifetime in the atmosphere can be measured in decades. For this item, an attempt is made to assign a monetary cost to the increasing use of fossil fuels, summing the monetary value of yearly consumption with that accumulating from previous years (Daly and Cobb calculate back to the year 1900). This is a sort of set-aside, calculated in the form of a tax (like a carbon tax), subtracted from current consumption in order to compensate future generations for damages they will incur as a result of the behaviour of the present generation. The calculation envisages application of a tax (the minimum estimate of 0.5 dollars of 1972 proposed by Daly and Cobb has been maintained), which is multiplied by barrels of oil equivalent consumed in the current year and previous years.

V – net capital growth (+)

For economic welfare to be sustainable in time, the supply of capital must grow or at least remain constant to satisfy the needs of a growing population. In this case the merely economic aspect of sustainability is considered; it can be regarded as capacity to generate income, profits and work indefinitely in time. ISEW calculates net capital growth as the difference between the quantity of new capital and the need for capital, namely the quantity necessary to maintain the same level of capital per worker. This item concerns net investments as for GDP, except for a correction for employment dynamics.

5. El Serafy, S., The proper calculation of income from depletable natural resources. *Environmental Accounting for Sustainable Development*, eds Y.J. Ahmad, S. El Serafy & E. Lutz, An UNDP-World Bank Symposium, World Bank, Washington, 1988.

W and X – ISEW (absolute and per capita)
ISEW is derived from additions to and subtractions from weighted private consumption, *D*, according to whether the items represent economic, social or environmental costs or benefits.

Y and Z – gross domestic product (absolute and per capita)
Values of GDP and per capita GDP are presented at the end of the calculation tables to show the difference with respect to ISEW.

Part III

Applications

Chapter 10

ISEW in the Province of Modena

The index of sustainable economic welfare (ISEW) for the Province of Modena is one of the first examples of application at the local level. It represents a starting point for a new political–administrative approach that is useful at the local level for two reasons: (1) administrative decentralisation implies greater responsibility for local government in many fields, including legislative power in land and resource management; (2) administrators require regional knowledge that can no longer be based on approximate data and traditional indicators. The aim of the study was to also demonstrate the adaptability of the ISEW methodology at the local scale.

The Province of Modena has a dynamic and varied industrial sector including ceramics at Sassuolo, widespread food production and processing, Ferrari motor cars at Maranello and certain world-famous agricultural products, such as Vignola cherries. Modena plays an important role in the economies of Emilia-Romagna and Italy, being situated strategically for transport in the Po plain.

District-type organisation and links with international markets are typical of provincial productivity. This model of development has now been questioned, not only because of a long period of economic down-turn but also due to the social and environmental pressures it has generated in time.

Obviously, absolute sustainability of production and of the Modena area is an impossible aim, however what a sustainable path for this area could be is a good question, since the present situation is only partly due to economic problems and industrial structure. Economic profile and certain conditions have been determined by centuries of history and various economic, political and social premises and cannot be modified, though strategic choices could be important for sustainability in a general sense. In formulating a sustainability project that all have to agree to, caution is necessary. To ensure this development, all the instruments of regional management and government (such as planning laws and regional, urban, infrastructural and economic development programmes) must be brought into line with their environment. In various sectors, the economy of the province is on the verge of uneconomic growth; this is growth that does not lead to an increase in social welfare and quality of life of the population. It is therefore important to favour sectors that contribute less to material growth of the local economy. A path of sustainability should favour and enhance the biological support basis of the system, with targeted investments in natural capital to create 'economic biodiversity'. The health status of the Province of Modena with its main problems and characteristics was analysed for this purpose. The case study proposed here is divided as follows:

- brief description of the provincial system;
- analysis of the main items of ISEW;
- discussion of the results.

The Province of Modena

The Province of Modena in the Region Emilia-Romagna is composed of 47 municipalities and has an area of 2,690 km^2, extending from the Appenine divide into the Po plain. The mountain belt occupies 948 km^2 (about 37% of the total) and consists of high (about 3%), middle (about 14%) and low mountains (about 20%). The hill belt occupies 464 km^2 (about 17%) and includes the foothills. The rest of the province, 1,278 km^2 (48%) is plain (high, middle and low). The Province of Modena has a dense network (3,641 km) of rivers and canals. The Secchia and Panaro are major affluents of the Po, flowing from south to north, with a combined length of more than 100 km.

Modena has a population of 651,996 (31 December 2003), which increased by 18,003 with respect to 2001, the year of the last ISTAT census. The most populated municipalities are Modena (178,874), Carpi (63,316) and Sassuolo (41,393). The demographic density of the province is 242 persons/km^2, with peaks in the municipalities of Sassuolo (1,070 persons/km^2), Modena (979 persons/km^2) and Vignola (965 persons/km^2). Demographic changes in the last 12 years have been characterised by increasing immigration,[1] immigrants reaching 41,639 (6.4% of the population) in 2003, compared to 8,610 in 1992.

Entrepreneurship is varied. The primary sector is important and the tertiary sector is increasing. The main sector, however, is industrial, including mechanical, ceramic, textile, clothing, agriculture, food processing and biomedical sectors.

1. See http://demo.istat.it/.

Analysis of a historical series (1971–2003) of the items composing ISEW

The following sections describe the outcome of calculating the different items according to the method described in Chapter 9.

A – years of the historical series

Application of ISEW to the Province of Modena covers a long time series from the early 1970s to 2003, in five-year intervals from 1971 to 2001 and analysis of 2003 as the most recent year for which there are data. The tables show values in euro (current value and 2003 value), adjusted by means of coefficients published by ISTAT.[2]

B – private consumption

As illustrated in Table 10.1, population and family spending show quite different trends. Population increased from 565,862 in 1971 to 651,996 in 2003 (an increase of 95,144 or 17%), whereas at 2003 prices, family spending almost doubled from €3,731,184,372 in 1971 to €8,166,895,038 in 2003.

C – Gini index

In the absence of abundant literature or documents with systematic calculation of this index for the province, we used different sources to complete the historical series. In 1971 we attributed the same value as in 1976 (0.656). For 1976, 1981 and 1986, data were obtained from a document of the Bank of

Table 10.1: Private consumption in euro (current and 2003) and population of the Province of Modena.

	Population	Consumption at current prices (€)	Consumption at constant prices (€, 2003 value) *B*
1971	556,852	271,331,237	3,731,184,372
1976	580,237	577,644,877	4,178,683,040
1981	596,025	1,402,636,409	4,590,828,967
1986	595,345	2,545,082,596	4,886,813,093
1991	604,680	4,392,782,396	6,382,273,543
1996	613,625	5,631,808,313	6,548,103,526
2001	633,993	8,108,537,328	8,509,909,926
2003	651,996	8,166,895,038	8,166,895,038

2. ISTAT, Il valore della moneta in Italia dal 1861 al 2005, 2006.

Table 10.2: Gini index.

	Gini index C
1971	0.656
1976	0.656
1981	0.628
1986	0.593
1991	0.383
1996	0.427
2001	0.425
2003	0.314

Italy for northern Italy;[3] for 1991, 1996 and 2001 from a document edited by the province administration;[4] for 2003 from a document of the Ministry of Social Solidarity.[5]

D – weighted private consumption (+)
Application of the Gini index to private consumption gives weighted private consumption (private consumption corrected by the index of inequality), which is the starting item for calculation of ISEW (Table 10.3).

Table 10.3: Actual private consumption and private consumption weighted by the Gini index.

	Private consumption (€, 2003 value) *B*	Gini index *C*	Weighted private consumption (€, 2003 value) *D*
1971	3,731,184,372	0.656	2,253,130,660
1976	4,178,683,040	0.656	2,523,359,324
1981	4,590,828,967	0.628	2,819,919,513
1986	4,886,813,093	0.593	3,067,679,280
1991	6,382,273,543	0.383	4,614,803,718
1996	6,548,103,526	0.427	4,588,720,060
2001	8,509,909,926	0.425	5,971,866,615
2003	8,166,895,038	0.314	6,215,293,027

3. D'Alessio, G. & Signorini, L.F., Disuguaglianza dei redditi individuali e ruolo della famiglia in Italia, Tema di Discussione n. 390, Banca d'Italia, Roma, 2000.
4. Osservatorio Economico e Sociale, Verso un sistema di indicatori economici e sociali per la Provincia di Modena, Provincia di Modena, Modena, 2004.
5. Ministry of Social Solidarity, Rapporto sulle politiche contro la povertà e l'esclusione sociale, Roma, 2004.

Weighted private consumption in euro (2003 value) increased from €2,253,130,660 in 1971 to €6,215,293,027 in 2003. This is the starting variable for ISEW, to which the other items are added or subtracted.

E – services of domestic labour (+)

Domestic labour contributes to the welfare of society but is not counted in the calculation of GDP. Table 10.4 shows that the monetary value of this unpaid service undergoes a constant decline throughout the period, from almost 4 billion euro in 1971 to just over 1.3 billion in 2003. The trend of this variable in the study period depends on the number of persons belonging to the ISTAT category 'inactive', that includes housewives, students and all persons who for various reasons no longer work. We also included people seeking their first job, which ISTAT classifies as 'active'. The pay of a person working at home was assumed equal to the mean pay of domestic help, namely €7 per hour.[6]

F – services of consumer durables (+)

Here we provide the values of services of consumer durables, namely cars, appliances and houses.

Services derived from car ownership (10% of total) – To calculate this value we obtained data on the number of cars in the province (provided by the Italian Automobile Club[7]) and the mean price of cars (obtained from a document of the Bank of Italy[8]).

Services derived from ownership of domestic appliances (10% of total) – Domestic appliances were classified as white goods (refrigerators, dishwashers, washing machines, etc.) and black goods (TVs, radios, personal computers, cassette players, etc.). Family ownership of appliances was obtained for the study period from an ISTAT document entitled *Family consumption*, for different geographical areas. We attributed mean market prices to the stock of goods.

Services derived from home ownership (5% of total value) – Clearly home ownership has a major effect on the economic and social welfare of a population. To calculate this item we counted a service worth 5% of the overall monetary

6. Pulselli, F.M., Ciampalini, F., Tiezzi, E. & Zappia, C., The index of sustainable economic welfare (ISEW) for a local authority: a case study in Italy. *Ecological Economics*, **60**, pp. 271–281, 2006.
7. ACI, Serie storiche sullo sviluppo della motorizzazione e sull'incidentalità stradale in Italia negli anni 1921–2003, Direzione centrale studi e ricerche – Automobile Club Italia, Area statistica, 2005.
8. Tomat, G.M., Beni durevoli, indici di prezzo e cambiamenti di qualità: un'applicazione ai prezzi delle automobili in Italia, 1988–1998, Tema di discussione n. 439, Banca d'Italia, Roma, 2002.

Table 10.4: Inactive population (including people seeking their first job) and value of services of domestic labour.

	Inactive population	Resident population	Percentage of total population	Services of domestic labour (€, 2003 value) +*E*
1971	206,995	556,852	37	3,908,179,556
1976	214,688	580,237	37	2,342,835,580
1981	213,696	596,025	36	2,460,566,533
1986	213,452	595,345	36	2,329,046,016
1991	119,240	604,680	20	1,301,079,747
1996	144,000	613,625	23	1,571,306,053
2001	127,000	633,993	20	1,385,761,801
2003	123,500	651,996	19	1,347,536,827

Table 10.5: Number of cars in the Province of Modena and price of cars.

	Number of cars	Mean price (€, current value)
1971	145,855	1,438
1976	195,290	2,732
1981	253,355	6,039
1986	306,193	11,303
1991	370,343	15,852
1996	381,204	26,598
2001	405,497	29,465
2003	413,669	30,925

value of all houses occupied by residents, since we assumed a 20-year mean period to pay off home loans. Table 10.6 shows the increasing trend of this value except in the five-year period 1981–1986.

G – services of the road system (+)

To calculate this item we had to consider all roads in the province (state, provincial and municipal) freely available to the population. We considered the mean cost of maintenance of the three types of road which we obtained from provincial records and interviews.

H – public expenditure on health and education (+)

As shown in Table 10.8, spending for education reached a peak in the early 1980s, decreasing until the mid-1990s and then increasing again. The trend

Table 10.6: Monetary value of services derived from ownership of consumer durables from 1971 to 2003.

	Services of cars (10%) (€, 2003 value)	Services of appliances (10%) (€, 2003 value)	Services of home ownership (5%) (€, 2003 value)	Services of consumer durables(€, 2003 value) +*F*
1971	288,373,817	45,658,204	529,246,012	863,278,033
1976	385,954,082	31,742,908	991,350,070	1,409,047,060
1981	500,796,330	71,253,738	1,495,915,793	2,067,965,861
1986	664,537,638	79,971,916	1,170,937,902	1,915,447,455
1991	852,929,797	88,758,742	2,302,618,783	3,244,307,322
1996	1,178,871,406	97,110,983	2,981,811,896	4,257,794,285
2001	1,253,928,466	116,496,688	2,929,903,974	4,300,329,129
2003	1,279,269,251	121,091,987	3,702,920,003	5,103,281,241

Table 10.7: Monetary value of services provided by the road system.

	Road system services (€, 2003 value)+*G*
1971	82,500,946
1976	85,429,297
1981	87,418,284
1986	58,964,293
1991	51,251,213
1996	51,900,492
2001	53,374,920
2003	54,683,800

of the item as a whole closely follows the peak and trough of spending for education, because spending for health has had a much more linear increasing trend, being linked to population: health spending increased from about €989 to more than €1,500 per capita in 2003. The number of students was obtained from the planning department of Modena Provincial Administration.[9]

I – expenditure on consumer durables (–)
Annual spending of resident families for consumer durables was subtracted from aggregate private consumption (item *B*), except the costs of house purchase (it

9. Osservatorio Economico e Sociale, 2004, op. cit.

Table 10.8: Public spending for health (50%) and education, and number of students.

	Public expenditure on health (50%) (€, 2003 value)	No. of students	Public expenditure on education (€, 2003 value)	Total (€, 2003 value) +*H*
1971	320,201,094	78,569	501,978,249	822,179,342
1976	333,597,126	90,606	578,727,336	912,324,462
1981	342,693,557	102,642	655,715,144	998,408,701
1986	342,317,582	89,338	570,773,678	913,091,260
1991	347,682,135	69,270	442,579,781	790,261,915
1996	352,852,515	62,571	399,781,418	752,633,934
2001	418,482,445	65,018	415,384,881	833,867,326
2003	497,681,098	74,491	475,922,999	973,604,097

is not included in consumption). Table 10.9 shows a trend typical of Western societies, which are the victims as well as perpetrators of consumerism. Note the rise in spending for cars from about €300,000,000 in the 1970s to more than €500,000,000 in the 1980s, peaking at almost €1,000,000,000 in 2001.

J – private defensive expenditures on education and health (–)
Defensive expenditures on education depend on the number of scholars. In the five-year period 1971–1976 the province had a high percentage of school children, following an increase in birth rate. In subsequent years, a decrease in birth rate of the autochthonous population was compensated by an influx of immigrants, increasing the birth rate of the province. The first results of this phenomenon were evident in 1996 when 1.6% of children in kindergartens

Table 10.9: Expenditure on consumer durables (cars and appliances).

	Spending for appliances (€, 2003 value)	Spending for cars (€, 2003 value)	Total expenditure (€, 2003 value) –*I*
1971	3,956,746	339,808,769	343,765,514
1976	52,742,988	281,683,831	334,426,819
1981	62,575,109	537,769,728	600,344,837
1986	37,561,905	559,552,615	597,114,520
1991	77,776,184	759,924,491	837,700,675
1996	53,175,598	831,417,240	884,592,838
2001	57,501,122	984,441,629	1,041,942,751
2003	53,859,258	899,730,451	953,589,709

Table 10.10: Private defensive expenditures for health and education.

	Private defensive expenditures for education (50%) (€, 2003 value)	Private dDefensive expenditures for health (50%) (€, 2003 value)	Total (€, 2003 value)–*J*
1971	20,887,503	67,128,389	88,015,892
1976	55,315,137	83,122,206	138,437,344
1981	23,264,676	34,555,837	57,820,513
1986	25,637,900	53,569,943	79,207,843
1991	36,523,156	30,980,973	67,504,129
1996	34,602,196	111,376,907	145,979,103
2001	35,650,055	167,941,055	203,591,111
2003	35,978,605	177,331,995	213,310,600

were from foreign families, which was higher than the figure for all of Emilia-Romagna (1%). In elementary schools the figures were 2.5% in the Province of Modena and 2.1% in the rest of the Region.

The figures for the first part of secondary school were 1.3% of foreigners compared to 1.5% in the whole region. The 2001 data confirm this growth with 5.64% of foreign students, exceeding the regional figure of 4.8% and the national one of 2%.

Private spending for health grew in the last 10–15 years, possibly due to ageing of the population. Defensive spending was particularly high in the last decade of the historical series.

K – national spending for advertising (–)
Since it was not possible to obtain this data at local level, the item was eliminated from the ISEW calculation.

L – commuting costs (–)
The cost of commuting is calculated from services of motor vehicles, spending for maintenance of private cars and spending for services of the urban and extraurban transport network. Since 1971, the cost of commuting has increased. This is not surprising since there is a close relationship between loss of economic, social and/or environmental welfare and exaggerated use of cars.

N – cost of road accidents (–)
A study by the Province of Modena indicates that urban areas have a higher frequency of accidents[10] accounting for 76% of the total and 42% of deaths.

10. See also ACI, 2005, op. cit.

Table 10.11: Cost of commuting, maintenance of private vehicles, tickets for public transport and value of the services of the car pool.

	Number of cars	0.3α (€, 2003 value)	0.3β (€, 2003 value)	0.3γ (€, 2003 value)	Cost of commuting (€, 2003 value) –*L*
1971	145,855	86,512,145	3,052,019	25,337,786	114,901,949
1976	195,290	115,786,225	3,703,066	35,899,719	155,389,009
1981	253,355	150,238,899	4,644,843	45,988,152	200,871,894
1986	306,193	199,361,292	6,571,562	55,162,226	261,095,080
1991	370,343	255,878,939	7,765,916	66,309,623	329,954,479
1996	381,204	353,661,422	8,694,362	68,109,536	430,465,320
2001	405,497	376,178,540	5,551,612	71,757,897	453,488,048
2003	413,669	383,780,775	4,772,831	51,383,904	439,937,510

α = monetary value of services provided by all cars in the province; β = spending for tickets on public transport in province; γ = spending for maintenance of public and private motor vehicles.

Management of urban transport by the local administrations is good, since the frequency of accidents has decreased significantly in recent years. This item has relatively low values compared to other areas. The number of accidents was obtained from the Automobile Club of Italy ACI (2005) and the social cost from the document *L' assicurazione italiana 2003–2004* of the Italian Insurance Association ANIA.

Table 10.12: Car accidents in the Province of Modena, social cost per accident and total cost of road accidents.

	Number of road accidents	Social cost/ accident (€, current value)	Cost of road accidents (€, 2003 value) –*N*
1971	3839	140	7,387,428
1976	2891	266	5,562,170
1981	1917	588	3,688,469
1986	1839	1002	3,538,668
1991	2636	1325	5,072,675
1996	2941	1842	6,298,720
2001	4184	3068	13,471,919
2003	3799	3489	13,254,711

O – cost of water pollution (–)
Two types of data are necessary to calculate this item: organic load of effluent (estimated equivalent inhabitants of the province) and cost of water treatment per equivalent inhabitant (€14.56 in 2001). [11] Equivalent inhabitants may be civil (the level of pollution ascribed to the population), industrial or due to livestock. Conversion coefficients are used to obtain the latter two (Table 10.13).[12] Table 10.14 shows estimates and the final value of the item, which is relatively constant.

Table 10.13: Equivalent inhabitants according to sector.

	Civil	Industrial	Livestock
1971	556,852	1,533,627	2,262,503
1976	580,237	1,682,763	2,594,754
1981	596,025	1,831,898	2,927,005
1986	595,345	1,830,609	2,672,051
1991	604,680	1,829,320	2,417,097
1996	613,625	1,814,148	2,153,181
2001	633,993	1,798,976	1,889,265
2003	651,996	1,798,976	1,889,265

Table 10.14: Equivalent inhabitants and cost of water pollution.

	Equivalent inhabitants treated	€/equivalent inhabitants (€, current prices)	Cost of water pollution (€, 2003 value) –*O*
1971	4,352,982	1.11	66,517,134
1976	4,857,754	2.11	74,240,822
1981	5,354,928	4.67	81,838,938
1986	5,098,005	7.96	77,903,166
1991	4,851,097	10.52	74,133,547
1996	4,580,954	13.14	70,004,892
2001	4,322,234	14.56	66,046,840
2003	4,340,237	15.28	66,321,939

P – cost of air pollution (–)
Table 10.15 indicates a major presence of contaminants due largely to the combustion of fossil fuels. Carbon dioxide emissions have increased and oxides of sulphur have decreased since 1980 due to conversion to methane,

11. Pulselli, F.M., Ciampalini, F., Tiezzi, E. & Zappia, C., 2006, op. cit.
12. ARPA Emilia-Romagna, *Annuario Regionale dei dati ambientali*, Bologna, 2003.

after which coal and fuel oil were phased out. The final figure is of the same order as certain economic variables.[13]

Table 10.15: Emissions of various air pollutants in the Province of Modena (in tons).

	Total CO_2	Total NO_x	Total SO_x	Total PM10
1971	2,266,228	2,926	13,342	803
1976	2,266,228	2,926	13,342	803
1981	4,703,997	6,691	12,710	1,331
1986	4,400,745	5,893	6,940	1,077
1991	5,170,838	16,929	11,740	2,201
1996	5,112,522	16,184	8,602	2,217
2001	4,815,321	13,207	6,634	2,212
2003	5,007,203	6,844	3,196	1,222

Table 10.16: Unit cost of abatement of pollutants in euro (current value) per ton.

	CO_2	NO_x	SO_x	PM10
1971	1.03	90.56	232.87	12.94
1976	1.97	172.17	442.73	24.60
1981	4.35	380.59	978.66	54.37
1986	7.41	648.75	1,668.21	92.68
1991	9.80	857.43	2,204.83	122.49
1996	12.25	1,071.45	2,755.17	153.06
2001	13.57	1,186.96	3,052.18	169.57
2003	14.24	1,245.71	3,203.25	177.96

Table 10.17: Total cost of air pollution.

	Cost of air pollution (€, 2003 value)–*P*
1971	78,765,144
1976	78,775,817
1981	116,252,167
1986	92,412,299
1991	132,709,333
1996	120,901,929
2001	106,650,005
2003	90,267,750

13. Emissions and abatement costs are from APAT and DGERM data and from Pulselli *et al.*, 2006, op. cit.

Q – cost of noise pollution (–)
Since no information is available on noise levels in the Province of Modena, only traffic noise was considered. Since the cost (€120 in 2000) is related to the number of motor vehicles[14] in the province, it has increased.

Table 10.18: Cost of noise calculated on the basis of number of motor vehicles in the Province of Modena.

	Number of motor vehicles	Cost of noise (€, 2003 value) –*Q*
1971	145,855	18,893,102
1976	195,290	25,303,778
1981	253,355	32,815,264
1986	306,193	39,662,252
1991	370,343	47,974,310
1996	381,204	49,385,403
2001	405,497	52,528,687
2003	413,669	53,585,977

R – loss of wetlands (–)
The data acquired only regards wetlands in the plain because this is where the largest ones are concentrated. The following criteria were used to choose them:

- only the biggest wetlands (>5 ha) were considered;
- areas on the floodplains of the Secchia and Panaro were counted;
- running water, water courses and their beds were not considered, except floodplains of the Secchia and Panaro;
- rice fields were not considered;
- fish farms and sedimentation ponds of sugar factories were considered.

To obtain data on annual variations in wetland area during the study period (that was divided into intervals depending on the availability of data), a constant rate of variation was assumed (during each interval), dividing total variation in wetland among different years and associating a monetary value each year with a hectare of wetland, about €1,033 in 1990.[15] The provincial administration's special concern for conservation of environmentally vulnerable areas, such as wetlands, has had excellent results, leading to an increase in wetland area. This trend is different from that at world level and in fact the item had a positive value.

14. Provincia di Bologna, Il Mobility Management della Provincia di Bologna, www.provincia.bologna.it/mobility/, 1999.
15. Guenno, G. & Tiezzi, S., The Index of Sustainable Economic Welfare (ISEW) for Italy, Worknote 5.98, Fondazione Enrico Mattei, Milano, 1998.

Table 10.19: Area and monetary value of wetlands in the Province of Modena.

	Wetland area (ha)	Annual increase (ha)	Monetary value of change in wetland area (€, 2003 value)+*R*
1971	500	4	6,386
1976	520	4	6,387
1981	610	18	28,741
1986	730	24	38,327
1991	900	34	54,295
1996	1,250	70	111,785
2001	1,320	14	22,357
2003	1,470	75	119,766

S – loss of agricultural land (–)
Official sources of data on area of agricultural land used (ALU) and total area of agricultural land (TAL) in the province are ISTAT and the agriculture census (Table 10.20). Since data were only available for census years, the total variation was divided between the years of the period (Table 10.21).

Table 10.20: Trend of total area of agricultural land (TAL) and area of agricultural land used (ALU) in the study period.

	TAL (ha)	ALU (ha)
1970	231,727.67	174,191.44
1982	221,530.68	162,256.60
1990	206,275.28	153,423.26
2000	179,029.53	136,813.40

T – depletion of non-renewable resources (–)
Table 10.22 shows that the Province of Modena has been very parsimonious with quarrying in the last 30 years. Material quarried in the first two years was mainly gravel (>2 million m^3/year), clay and limestone (about 1 million m^3/year). Subsequently gravel and sand continued to be quarried in smaller quantities, ornamental stone increased and the first clay quarries for bricks were authorised in the plain.

U – long-term environmental damage (–)
In order to attribute a monetary value to the damage that the present generation is bequeathing to future generations, it is necessary to consider total consumption of all fossil fuels over the study period. The monetary value of this

Table 10.21: Monetary value of agricultural land lost.

	Hectares of agricultural land lost	Monetary value of agricultural land (€/ha, 2003 value)	Loss of agricultural land (€, 2003 value) –*S*
1971	1560	593.13	12,724,351
1976	995	1,922.16	13,829,371
1981	995	4,248.80	13,830,801
1986	1104	4,757.90	10,087,286
1991	1661	6,745.55	16,278,683
1996	1661	8,075.45	15,595,534
2001	1661	12,904.24	22,494,737
2003	1661	13,738.48	22,819,431

Table 10.22: Quantities of material quarried, cost of extraction, sales proceeds and economic value of depletion of non-renewable resources.

	Extracted quantities (m^3)	Total extraction costs (€, current value)	Proceeds of the sale of material (€, current value)	Economic value of resource depletion (€, 2003 value) –*T*
1971	3,251,061	167,149	5,051,713	67,169,598
1976	3,251,061	317,736	9,602,086	67,162,987
1981	1,314,000	644,451	17,729,868	55,920,569
1986	1,314,000	1,098,593	30,223,702	55,923,121
1991	1,270,300	1,360,855	35,840,930	50,096,102
1996	1,251,941	3,227,523	80,278,895	89,587,631
2001	1,650,147	5,615,429	136,639,987	137,510,274
2003	1,640,118	4,636,169	116,324,440	111,688,271

item is obtained by applying a tax of €1.96/barrel equivalent of oil consumed, obtained by energy conversion coefficients. Note that €1.96 equals $US 0.50 (1972 value) used by Cobb and Daly.

V – net capital growth (+)

This item is based on gross fixed investments of industry in Emilia-Romagna, weighted on the basis of the number of employees in different sectors calculated at regional (645,648) and provincial levels (149,330) in 2001 (from ISTAT). Production dynamics in the province are largely represented by the increasing trend of investments.

Table 10.23: Trend in oil consumption and monetary value of the lasting environmental damage caused.

	Annual consumption in barrel equivalents	Sum of consumption over 10 previous years in barrel equivalents	Long-term environmental damage (€, 2003 value) $-U$
1971	5,766,946	57,872,284	124,786,919
1976	5,766,946	70,317,675	149,190,451
1981	13,310,097	85,439,437	193,632,923
1986	12,492,708	103,813,123	228,058,170
1991	14,010,794	126,138,057	274,810,730
1996	14,619,069	135,330,187	294,027,844
2001	15,419,483	146,127,882	316,769,985
2003	16,042,388	149,242,960	324,099,604

Table 10.24: Gross fixed investments in the Province of Modena.

	Gross fixed investments (€, current value)	Gross fixed investments (€, 2003 value)$+V$
1971	30,880,828	424,654,624
1976	137,729,131	996,332,532
1981	258,407,059	845,766,303
1986	386,688,260	742,480,128
1991	615,138,639	893,734,928
1996	889,948,417	1,034,743,025
2001	1,163,244,073	1,220,824,654
2003	1,244,312,216	1,244,312,216

W – index of sustainable economic welfare

ISEW consists of the algebraic sum of the above items. Although the economic elements are still relevant, ISEW is also greatly affected by social and environmental variables. This demonstrates the importance of these items for assessing the welfare of a population.

Y–Z – gross domestic product

Hereafter, for the sake of clarity, we will use the acronym GRP (*gross regional product*) to refer to the economic product of the Province of Modena. The trends of ISEW and GRP for the Province of Modena are now compared over the period.

Comparison of ISEW and GRP of the Province of Modena (1971–2003)

The items of ISEW are economic, social and environmental. Besides providing all major information clearly and concisely, this division enables an overall view of the system of the Province of Modena.

Economic dynamics

Consumption and investments are the main items of provincial demand for goods and services, through which the interaction between production, income and life-styles can be seen.

The level of consumption reflects changes in the life-style of Modenese families. The achievement of welfare by families, prevalently represented by how much they consume, depends largely on their capacity to generate income in the system of production. The capacity to ensure oneself a source of income also depends on many social and demographic factors, such as age, education, family composition and other economic factors. The trend of consumption reflects available income, average levels of which have increased in Modenese families, especially in the recent part of the historical series. The increase in income is in turn linked to higher education levels in the population, greater emancipation of women in the work force, and greater accessibility of luxury goods. More specifically:

- Recent university reform has increased the number of graduates in the population. Net family income increases with increasing level of education of the main provider.
- The increase in mean income in the population of Modena is also a result of better access to employment and therefore greater production of family income, on which changes in life-style depend.
- The increase in private consumption is also due to greater accessibility to certain types of goods, hitherto regarded as luxury items (e.g. cell phones, organisers, PCs, global positioning technology) but now regarded as essential.

The real estate market accounts for a large part of item *F*, *services of consumer durables*. This market is in rapid expansion and one of the few that has not seen periods of stagnation that could impair investment value. In 2003, services of real estate in the Province of Modena amounted to 72% of total services of durables. The construction of new buildings and urban renewal never seem to saturate the demand for real estate or to lower prices and rents. A further aspect of the increasing trend of services of durables is the tendency to accumulate a great variety of goods, suggesting dependence of our society on material possessions. This phenomenon is clearly linked to levels of consumption.

The quantity of investments directly affects internal demand and therefore gross product. It is related to private and public net capital stock derived from the income-generating capacity and entrepreneurship of the whole production

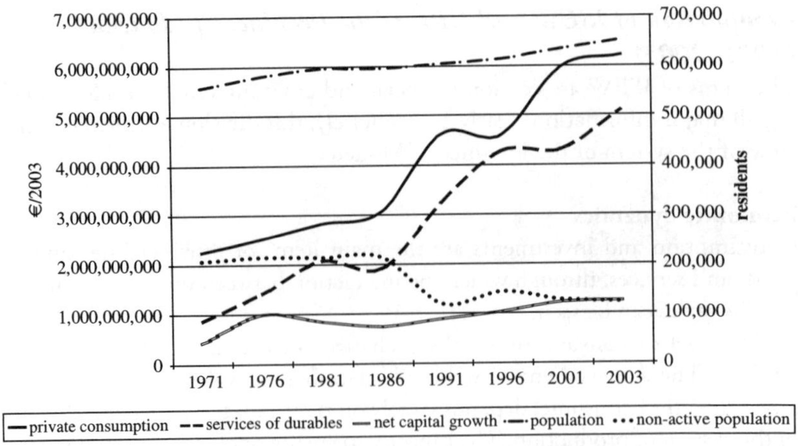

Figure 10.1: Trend of population (total and non-active), private consumption, services of durables and net capital growth in the Province of Modena (1971–2003).

system of Modena. Increasing attention towards analysis of investments and capital growth at regional level goes back only a few years. The first studies of this kind were national studies by ISTAT, which produced estimates of private capital in the three main sectors (agriculture, industry and services) in three geographical areas over the period 1951–1963. Only at the end of the 1970s was a research programme established to estimate fixed capital according to sector and region.[16]

This item was calculated using rather disconnected historical data, references of different types and estimates on information of varied origin. Although not completely in line with Daly's calculation of *net capital growth*, it provides an overall view of the dynamics of the manufacturing sector of the province. The long industrial tradition of Modena and its high level of internationalisation determine an increasing trend in fixed investments in this area. These help to maintain industrial infrastructure and are also considered important from the viewpoint of purely economic sustainability. Clearly, investments orientated to meet the needs of environmental sustainability (such as clean technologies, renewable energy, resource productivity, reduction of emissions and wastes) are more likely to produce fruit in the medium to long period. Fig. 10.1 shows the main economic items of ISEW.

Social dynamics

Social aspects of importance for calculating welfare are not considered in traditional accounting. An item of ISEW regards the weight of equality of

16. Rosa, G. & Siesto, V., Il *capitale fisso industriale. Stime settoriali e verifiche dirette*, Il Mulino: Bologna, 1985.

income distribution among families by means of the Gini index. As well, the monetary value of commuting due to progressive urbanisation is considered a factor contributing substantially to air pollution and creating a series of diseconomies and inconvenience for the community. ISEW also considers services provided by domestic work and private and public defensive spending for health and education, two basic services for a modern society seeking to ensure a good living standard for its members.

Equality is a key concept for sustainable development; the economic literature includes a series of studies and very interesting critiques of this concept. ISEW concentrates mainly on equality of income distribution within a territorial system, in our case the Province of Modena. This concept is important because it links the socio-demographic characteristics of a region with economic characteristics.

The trend of the Gini index shows that at the beginning of the study period, income distribution was unequal. The situation improved in the early 1990s and was sustained to the end of the period. Emancipation of women in the labour market has certainly favoured a more equal distribution of income. Indeed, in recent years, families with more than one income have increased. On the negative side, this emancipation has accompanied a constant fall in birth rates, reflected by a sharp decrease in two items: *services of domestic labour* and *public spending for education* (Fig. 10.2). The birth rate in the first part of the time series was high and the recent increase is certainly due to immigrant families, since Italy had almost zero population growth in the 1990s.

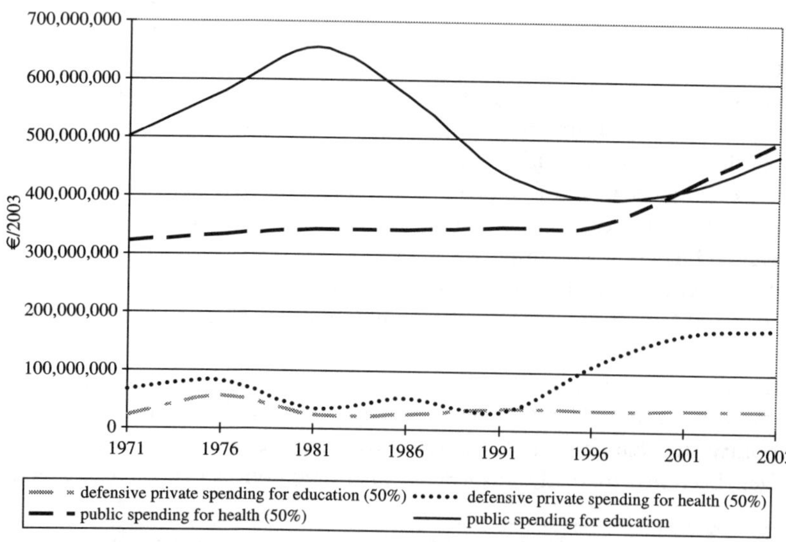

Figure 10.2: Public spending and private defensive expenditures for health and education in the Province of Modena (1971–2003).

The birth rate went from 13.6% in 1971 to 9.5% in 2003 with a minimum of 7% in 1986. That of the foreign residents of the Province of Modena was first calculated in the 1990s and is about 25%, with a maximum of 26.8% in 2001.

Since the 1990s, Modena has become a multi-cultural province. One of the main tasks of the administration has been to redefine the community on the basis of its variegated cultural profile. The administration of the city of Modena and the community have worked hard to formulate concrete policies of integration. In fact, the present flow of immigrants into Italy, and in this case Modena, interacts with other factors, such as expansion of markets, increase in forms of exclusion and poverty, transformation of employment profiles, union contracts and models of social stratification, stressing the welfare systems of central and local governments. The crisis of welfare systems is redefining the criterion of equality: access to resources no longer depends solely on essential needs such as jobs, houses and other types of services but also on the capacity to be an active member society. Immigration, in such a context, is an important impulse for improving the quality of social fabric, acting as a catalyst of integration.

Hence a slight increase in private spending for education beginning in the 1990s is due partly to structural changes in the sector and partly to progressive integration of immigrants in the younger age groups of the population, which is also growing as a result of family reunions.

The number of families enjoying health services increased considerably, especially in the last years of the historical series. This is due to ageing of the population and increased demand for medical services and basic consultations, which weigh on the financial budgets of local health authorities. The increase in private defensive spending for health is due to irresponsible consumption (often abuse) of medicinal products due to excessive prescription and taking of drugs, increasing hypochondria and demand for 'health' created by marketing. Deterioration of environmental conditions (effects of pollution on health) also seems to inflate this item.

An essential element of progressive environmental deterioration is the constant increase in vehicle traffic in the Province of Modena, which generates overcrowding and commuting.

Commuting in the Province of Modena, especially by private car, is related to the problem of road accidents, a complex phenomenon with social–demographic, cultural and economic aspects.[18] Indeed, road safety and the rationalisation of transport and of road infrastructure have long been subjects of discussion. The demand for safety is closely linked to the need for mobility that has increased dramatically. Extra demand for transport has largely been met by road transport, as a national political choice (see invest-

17. ISTAT, *Statistica degli incidenti stradali*, Volume Informazioni, Settori: Sanità e previdenza – Giustizia – Servizi, 2006.

ment in roads and incentives to wreck old cars and buy new ones). The number of cars and trucks on the road has increased, together with mean distances travelled. This is an important item of ISEW, particularly in a province crossed by two very congested motorways (the A1 Autosole and A22 Brennero).

Environmental dynamics

The paradigm of 'sustainable development' has revolutionised the conceptual framework in which public policy and private investments in the environmental field are assessed, offering a theory to integrate the contributions of different disciplines for a long-period view. The 'economic' intangibility of environmental goods, caused by the absence of market valuation, makes it difficult to formulate criteria for monetisation of the environment. Criteria of monetisation are, however, necessary to assign a value to environmental deterioration so that damage can be quantified (negative externality, e.g. air pollution) and to provide an economic reason for the decision of firms to invest in ecocompatibility, which is soon likely to become competitive. For environmental goods not traded on the market, it is difficult to quantify damage and the economic equivalent of the resulting environmental deterioration. However an indication of the cost of environmental damage is useful for local administrations, and has major socio-economic implications.

We now list the items of ISEW concerned with decline in welfare due to pollution (water, air, noise), irreversible environmental damage and loss of resources such as wetlands, agricultural land and non-renewable resources (especially mineral resources).

Local administrations have shown much interest in monitoring environmental damage (air, water and noise pollution). With regard to noise, the Modena Council and 10 other smaller councils undertook research that revealed that most complaints regarded improper use of cars and acoustic signals. The increased number of private cars has greatly raised noise levels, especially in towns. It has also influenced air pollution, intensifying emissions due to increased traffic in residential areas. Overexploitation of fossil fuels is responsible for a large proportion of loss of welfare also due to long-term environmental damage. The monetary value calculated for this item of ISEW is represented numerically by a value that increases and cumulates in time, because contaminants emitted into the atmosphere have long residence times. The item therefore translates environmental degradation into sums of money to compensate future generations for the damage done by the present generation. Residence times of greenhouse gases mean that the extra greenhouse effect manifests for a long time, affecting future generations.

Much effluent discharged directly and indirectly by industry and normal human activities (domestic waste water) reaches rivers, lakes, seas and groundwater without appropriate treatment. The effects may be chemical or bacterial

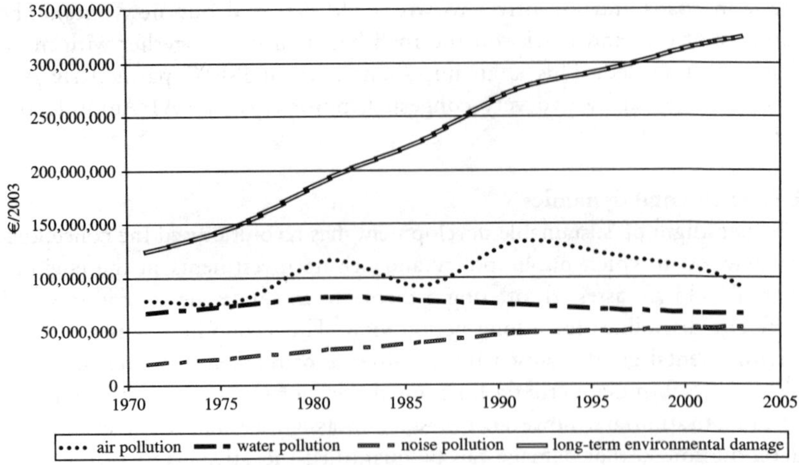

Figure 10.3: Trend of the monetary value of air, water and noise pollution, and long-term environmental damage (1971–2003).

and the consequences can threaten the health of flora, fauna and humans, damaging ecosystems, contaminating drinking water, fouling tourist resorts and preventing other legitimate uses of water. Hot water discharged by cooling systems of industrial processes is another form of water pollution because it upsets the thermal balance of ecosystems. Loss of welfare due to water pollution has decreased in recent years as a result of stricter legislation (Fig. 10.3).

Comments in the previous chapter about developed countries are also valid for Modena, where increasing urbanisation has consumed agricultural land and resources. To maintain agricultural productivity from a reduced area of arable land, soils have been exploited intensively using large quantities of chemical fertilisers and pesticides. Traditional rotations and natural fertilisation have been abandoned in favour of short rotations and high-income crops. Although the impact is much less than in arid areas of Africa, loss of land productivity (or potential productivity) in the Po plain is becoming economically, socially and environmentally significant. The problem is aggravated by the fact that loss of fertility is associated with soil contamination, salinisation of groundwater and erosion. Loss of agricultural land is therefore a major factor in the decline in agricultural production and consequently the autonomy and food self-sufficiency of a region. Loss of agricultural land due to urbanisation and infrastructures also damages landscape diversity, biodiversity, drainage and water filtration, which amounts to irreversible environmental deterioration. In the Province of Modena, loss of agricultural land has been constant in time, with a slight increase in recent years. Conservation of this precious natural resource must remain a priority for the administration of the province.

Quarrying is an activity that modifies the environment and landscape permanently and is often authorised in areas of high naturalistic value. Laws, planning instruments, authorisation procedures and policing are absolutely essential because quarry materials are non-renewable resources. Regions need to manage quarrying very closely to avoid compromising their sustainability. The experience of Modena showed that it is possible to improve ISEW through sensitivity to environmental problems, e.g. by reducing the volume of material quarried, use of low-sulphur fuels and by wetland management (Fig. 10.4).

Environmental problems associated with well-regulated quarrying may be temporary or permanent; the impact on landscape is acutely perceived by the population. Temporary impacts include noise, dust, air and water pollution, energy consumption for extraction and transport, all of which are related to the volumes of material moved. Permanent impacts include depletion of non-renewable resources, modification of landscape and alteration of hydrogeological and hydrographic profiles.

In order to control the damage caused by quarrying, Italian regions normally pass laws to limit volumes of material and quarry sites, and safeguard against contamination of groundwater and erosion. The provinces formulate planning regulations for application of the laws, through which demand for materials can be assessed in relation to environmental compatibility. They

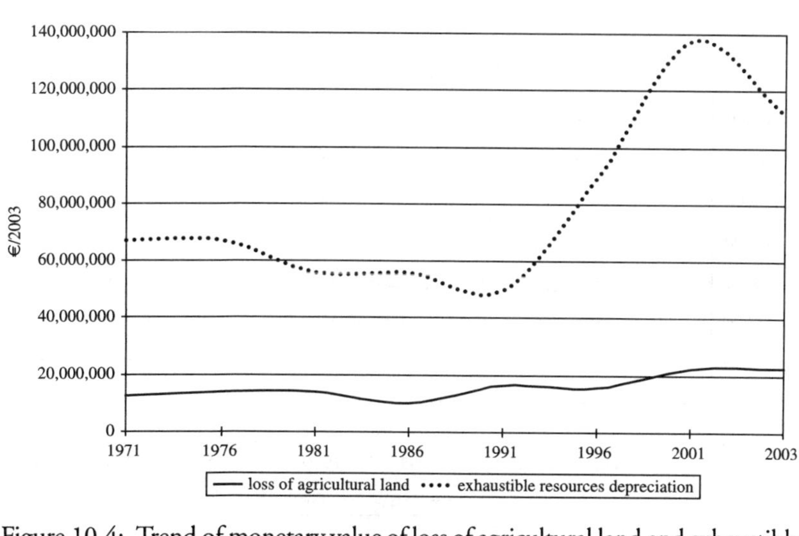

Figure 10.4: Trend of monetary value of loss of agricultural land and exhaustible resources depreciation in the Province of Modena (1971–2003).

define rates of exploitation in relation to the size of the province and guidelines for environmental remediation after quarry termination. The provincial plans are conceived in a framework of sustainable management of mineral resources, in which it is necessary to reconcile quarrying and the three dimensions of sustainable development: environment, economy and society. The effects of application of these planning instruments in the Province of Modena since the 1970s are evident. Since 1976, the total quantities of material extracted decreased drastically from over 3 million m^3 per year to just over 1.3 million m^3/year in 1981/1986, to rise slightly in the early 2000s to just over 1.6 m^3/ year. Modena, with its strong ceramics sector, expresses a high demand for mineral resources, which is largely met by importing materials from outside the province. This amounts to exporting unsustainability, not to reducing it.

Conclusions

The trend of ISEW in relation to GRP of the Province of Modena (1971–2003) is similar to that calculated for Italy in the period 1960–1991.[18] It increases almost parallel to gross product, seemingly belying the different approach of ISEW. However, it is important to note that the divergence between gross product and ISEW occurring at the end of the 1970s remains to this day. This significant gap reached about 40% of gross product in the 1990s. Between 1981 and 2001, mean annual growth of GRP was 2.26%, whereas that of ISEW was only 1.89% (Fig. 10.5). Today this difference seems to have narrowed, due possibly

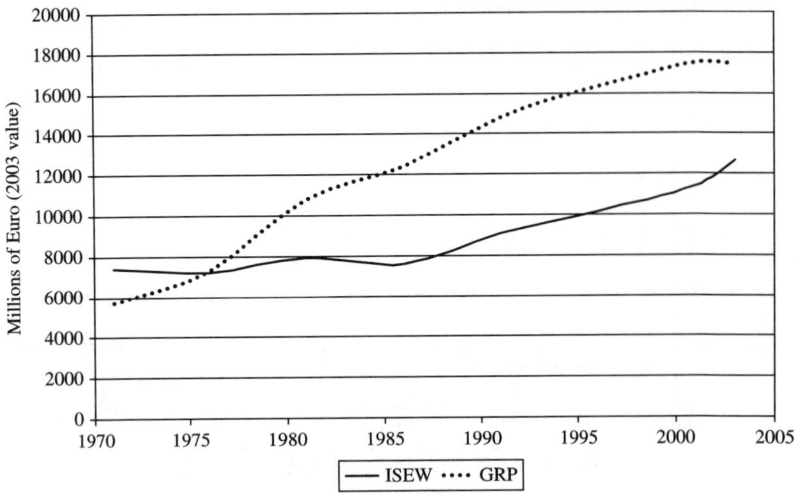

Figure 10.5: ISEW and GRP of the Province of Modena (1971–2003).

18. Guenno, G. & Tiezzi, S., 1998, op. cit.

to improved social conditions more than to less environmental degradation, a problem that is far from being solved. Table 10.26 and Figures 10.6–10.13 show the trend of ISEW item by item. In general, the interaction between society and environment is reflected by a worsening of ecosystem health, not only at the local level, which affects the welfare of the population. Evidence of this kind is not measured by traditional economic accounting, which is greatly in need of revision from this point of view. This need is expressed by the decision of the Modena administration to use environmental and sustainability indices (emergy analysis, ecological footprint, greenhouse gas inventory and ISEW) to analyse the overall situation of the province.

Table 10.25: ISEW and GRP of the Province of Modena in millions of euro (2003 value).

	ISEW	GRP
1971	7,431	5,740
1976	7,227	7,264
1981	7,923	10,750
1986	7,582	12,392
1991	9,059	14,801
1996	10,150	16,293
2001	11,352	17,445
2003	12,650	17,459

Table 10.26: Summary of monetary values of the items composing ISEW: Province of Modena, 1971–2003.

A	1971	1976	1981	1986	1991	1996	2001	2003
B	3,731,184,372	4,178,683,040	4,590,828,967	4,886,813,093	6,382,273,543	6,548,103,526	8,509,909,926	8,166,895,038
C	0.656	0.656	0.628	0.593	0.383	0.427	0.425	0.314
D	2,253,130,660	2,523,359,324	2,819,919,513	3,067,679,280	4,614,803,718	4,588,720,060	5,971,866,615	6,215,293,027
E (+)	3,908,179,556	2,342,835,580	2,460,566,533	2,329,046,016	1,301,079,747	1,571,306,053	1,385,761,801	1,347,536,827
F (+)	863,278,033	1,409,047,060	2,067,965,861	1,915,447,455	3,244,307,322	4,257,794,285	4,300,329,129	5,103,281,241
G (+)	82,500,946	85,429,297	87,418,284	58,964,293	51,251,213	51,900,492	53,374,920	54,683,800
H (+)	822,179,342	912,324,462	998,408,701	913,091,260	790,261,915	752,633,934	833,867,326	973,604,097
I (–)	343,765,514	334,426,819	600,344,837	597,114,520	837,700,675	884,592,838	1,041,942,751	953,589,709
J (–)	88,015,892	138,437,344	57,820,513	79,207,843	67,504,129	145,979,103	203,591,111	213,310,600
L (–)	114,901,949	155,389,009	200,871,894	261,095,080	329,954,479	430,465,320	453,488,048	439,937,510
N (–)	7,387,428	5,562,170	3,688,469	3,538,668	5,072,675	6,298,720	13,471,919	13,254,711
O (–)	66,517,134	74,240,822	81,838,938	77,903,166	74,133,547	70,004,892	66,046,840	66,321,939
P (–)	78,765,144	78,775,817	116,252,167	92,412,299	132,709,333	120,901,929	106,650,005	90,267,750

Q (–)	18,893,102	25,303,778	32,815,264	39,662,252	47,974,310	49,385,403	52,528,687	53,585,977
R* (+)	6,386	6,387	28,741	38,327	54,295	111,785	22,357	119,766
S (–)	12,724,351	13,829,371	13,830,801	10,087,286	16,278,683	15,595,534	22,494,737	22,819,431
T (–)	67,169,598	67,162,987	55,920,569	55,923,121	50,096,102	89,587,631	137,510,274	111,688,271
U (–)	124,786,919	149,190,451	193,632,923	228,058,170	274,810,730	294,027,844	316,769,985	324,099,604
V (+)	424,654,624	996,332,532	845,766,303	742,480,128	893,734,928	1,034,743,025	1,220,824,654	1,244,312,216
W	7,431,002,516	7,227,016,074	7,923,057,560	7,581,744,356	9,059,258,475	10,150,370,420	11,351,552,443	12,649,955,472
X	13,344	12,455	13,293	12,735	14,982	16,541	17,905	19,402
Y	5,739,868,150	7,264,364,353	10,749,563,864	12,392,325,400	14,800,692,300	16,292,915,100	17,445,484,259	17,458,496,892
Z	10,308	12,520	18,035	20,815	24,477	26,552	27,517	26,777
Population	556,852	580,237	596,025	595,345	604,680	613,625	633,993	651,996

A: Year; B: Private consumption; C: Gini index; D: Weighted private consumption; E (+): Services of domestic labour; F (+): Services of consumer durables; G (+): Road system services; H (+): Public expenditure on education and health; I (–): Expenditure on durables; J (–): Private expenditure on education and health; L (–): Commuting costs; N (–): Road accident costs; O (–): Water pollution costs; P (–): Air pollution costs; Q (–): Cost of noise pollution; R* (+): Increase in wetlands; S (–): Loss of agricultural land; T (–): Depletion of non-renewable resources; U (–): Long-term environmental damage; V (+): Net capital growth; W: ISEW; X: ISEW per capita; Y: GRP; Z: GRP per capita.

*Over the study period, wetland area has increased.

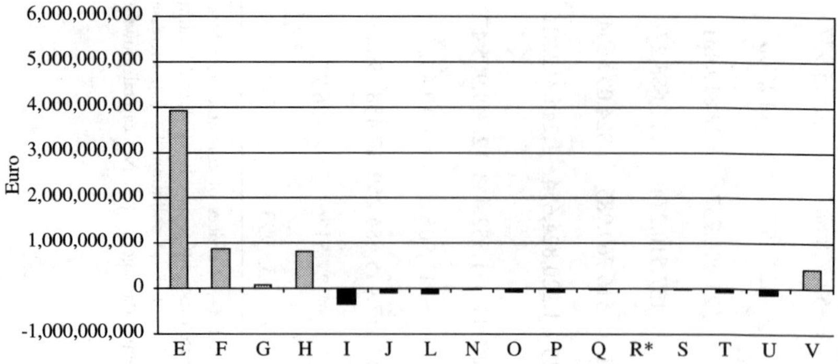

Figure 10.6: Positive and negative items of ISEW in 1971.

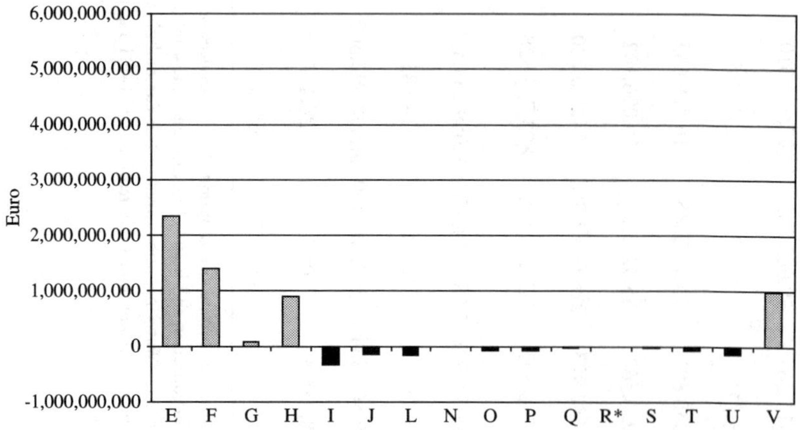

Figure 10.7: Positive and negative items of ISEW in 1976.

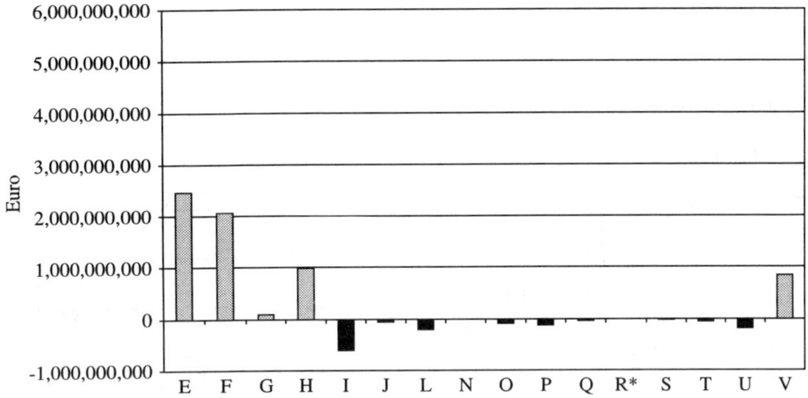

Figure 10.8: Positive and negative items of ISEW in 1981.

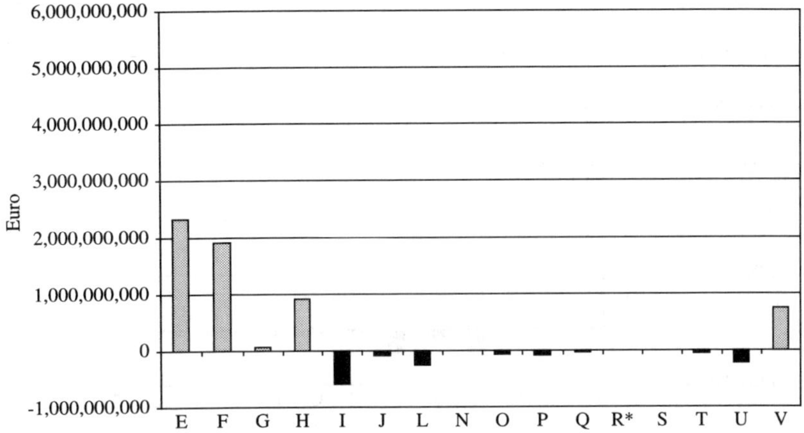

Figure 10.9: Positive and negative items of ISEW in 1986.

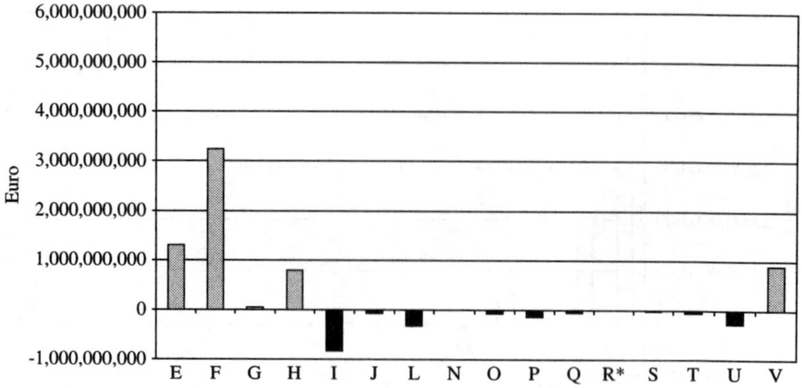

Figure 10.10: Positive and negative items of ISEW in 1991.

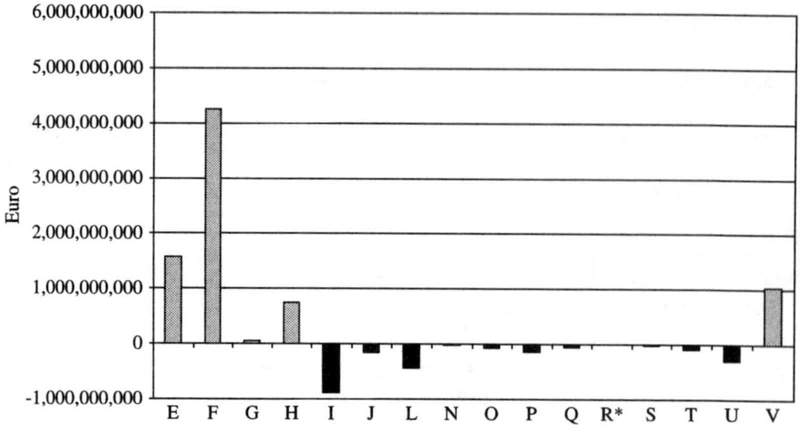

Figure 10.11: Positive and negative items of ISEW in 1996.

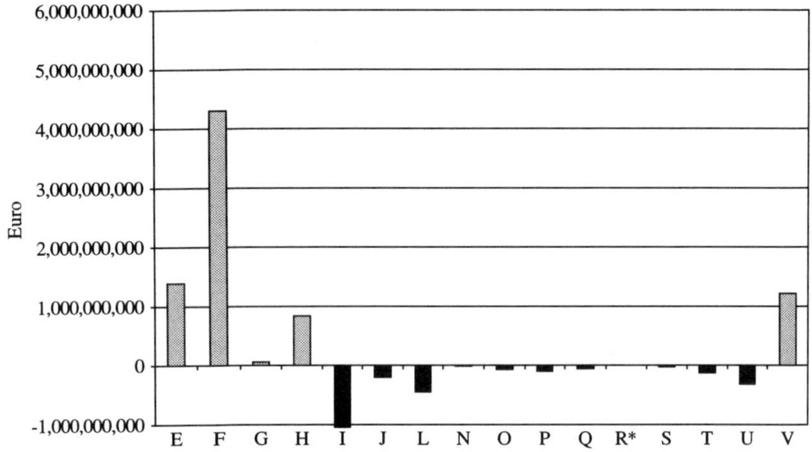

Figure 10.12: Positive and negative items of ISEW in 2001.

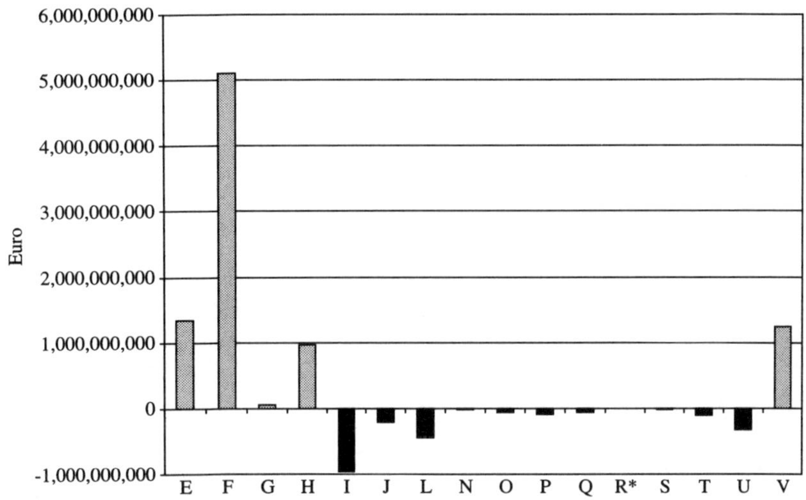

Figure 10.13: Positive and negative items of ISEW in 2003.

Chapter 11

ISEW in the Province of Rimini

The Province of Rimini

The Province of Rimini has an area of 534.8 km^2 and a population density of 544 persons/km^2, the highest of all the provinces of Emilia-Romagna and double that of the Province of Bologna, which is in second place with 245 persons/km^2. The municipalities with the highest densities are Cattolica and Riccione with 2,683 and 2,035 persons/km^2, respectively. After Bologna (2714 persons/km^2), they are the most densely populated municipalities in Emilia-Romagna. The Municipality of Rimini has a density of 1,008 persons/km^2 whereas that of Torriana and Gemmano is only 58 persons/km^2.

The forested area of the province increased from 291 to 942 ha between 1970 and 1998. In the same period, the forested area of Italy increased by only 10%. Despite this, the forested area of the Province of Rimini is only 1.7% of the total area, compared to regional, national and European averages of 18%, 23% and 30%, respectively.

Despite intense processes of urbanisation, agricultural land still occupies 71.6% of the area of the province. This percentage is stable but not homogeneous: in municipalities such as Riccione, Cattolica and Torriana the percentage is as low as 24%, 31% and 42%, respectively, for different reasons.

The productive structure of Rimini differs from that of other provinces due to the preponderance of commerce and tourism (28.3% and 24.6%, respectively), which bring in a higher income than industry.

The main environmental problems of the Province of Rimini are due to tourism, namely hospitality and leisure facilities stretching from Bellaria-Igea Marina to Cattolica. The range of these categories includes more than 5,000 firms. The area is known as the major holiday resort of Europe in terms of supply of accommodation and bathing facilities, entertainment, events, and opportunities. Firms are small to very small, two-thirds being individual firms and 80/100 having less than three employees.

With regard to industry of high environmental impact, the province is well below the regional average for metal-working and mechanical firms, textiles and clothing. Chemical firms reach the regional average and exceed the national average.

Environmental impact, accentuated by millions of tourists in summer, stresses water supply and waste treatment, energy supply, disposal of solid wastes and air quality. Noise increases due to vehicle, railway, air, and sea traffic.

Analysis of a historical series (1971–2003) of the items composing ISEW

A – years of the historical series

The items of ISEW were calculated over the period 1971–2003. In some cases it was necessary to use data sources that were not directly from the province, but from municipalities within the province. When this was not possible we used data from the Province of Forlì. This was necessary because the Province of Rimini was only established in 1992, previously being part of the Province of Forlì. In some cases, older data had been lost or cancelled from databases or removed from archives to make room for new data. The availability of databases in which the information is separated into categories is important for pursuing sustainability and is the only way to know a regional system. A shortage of statistical data, especially environmental, is a common problem throughout Italy and is the result of decisions made by the central data processing organisation. In discussing the items of ISEW in this chapter, we refer to Chapter 9 and 10, where they have already been illustrated.

B – private consumption

This starting variable is considered a determinant of welfare. It is also a key for GDP because spending for goods and services is a sign of a healthy

Table 11.1: Private consumption in euro (current and 2003 value) of the population of the Province of Rimini.

	Population	Consumption in € (current value)	Consumption at constant prices (€, 2003 value) *B*	Consumption per capita at constant prices (€, 2003 value)
1971	231,010	114,264,465	1,571,296,357	6,802
1981	250,328	592,654,202	1,939,757,202	7,749
1991	258,718	1,880,129,616	2,731,640,319	10,558
1996	265,158	2,446,413,575	2,844,445,063	10,727
2001	272,676	3,451,051,512	3,621,878,562	13,283
2003	279,774	3,458,777,235	3,458,777,235	12,363

Table 11.2: Weighting of private consumption using the Gini index.

	Private consumption (€, 2003 value) *B*	Gini index *C*	Weighted private consumption (€, 2003 value) *D*
1971	1,571,296,357	0.656	948,850,457
1981	1,939,757,202	0.628	1,191,497,053
1991	2,731,640,319	0.523	1,793,591,805
1996	2,844,445,063	0.427	1,993,304,179
2001	3,621,878,562	0.390	2,605,668,030
2003	3,458,777,235	0.293	2,675,208,628

economy in an affluent society. This variable was obtained from ISTAT (1973–1996).[1]

C – Gini index
The Gini index, which ranges from 0 (perfect equal distribution of income) to 1 (complete inequality), decreased from 0.656 in 1971 to 0.293 in 2003 (Table 11.2). It is lower than the national value for 2003, which was over 0.30, collocating Italy among the European countries with the highest inequality index with Greece, Portugal, Spain and Ireland. Since data on this index were not available for the province, we used different sources to complete the historical series. For 1971, 1981 and 1991 we used the Gini index for northern Italy calculated by the Bank of Italy.[2] For 1996 and 2001 the figure was extrapolated from a series of documents on social and regional indicators by the method of Milanovic.[3] For 2003 it was obtained from a report of the Centre for Public Political Analysis.[4]

D – weighted private consumption (+)
This is the starting variable for the calculation of ISEW. Private consumption is corrected for unequal distribution of income because the welfare deriving from given level of consumption decreases with increasing inequality, due to the diminishing marginal utility of income.

1. ISTAT, I consumi delle famiglie italiane (dal 1973 al 1996). *Collana d'informazione*, Roma, 1973–1996.
2. D'Alessio, G. & Signorini, L.F., Disuguaglianza dei redditi individuali e ruolo della famiglia in Italia, Tema di Discussione n. 390, Banca d'Italia, Roma, 2000.
3. Milanovic, B., A simple way to calculate the Gini coefficient, and some implications. *Economics Letters*, **56**, pp. 45–49, 1997.
4. CAPP, *Tributi locali e distribuzione del reddito nei comuni dell'Emilia Romagna*, Dip. di Economia Polilitica, Università di Modena e Reggio Emilia, Modena, 2004.

E – services of domestic labour (+)

Unpaid work in the home is part of the invisible economy. It is not traded on markets and does not have a documented price, but it contributes directly to welfare. This item was accounted as in Chapter 10, with the exception of data sources (mean pay of domestic help[5] and inactive population[6]).

Table 11.3: Inactive population (including people seeking their first job) and value of services of domestic labour.

	Inactive population	Resident population	% total population	Services of domestic labour (€, 2003 value) +*E*
1971	131,675	231,010	57.0%	1,375,598,442
1981	146,165	250,328	58.4%	1,527,101,563
1991	103,487	258,718	40.0%	1,081,141,162
1996	121,000	265,158	45.6%	1,263,964,484
2001	113,000	272,676	41.4%	1,180,532,545
2003	120,000	279,774	42.9%	1,255,845,356

F – services of consumer durables (+)

Services derived from car ownership (10% of total) – To calculate this value we obtained data on the number of cars in the province from the Italian Automobile Club[7] until 1992. For the preceding years, data were estimated from the number of cars in the Province of Forlì;[8] the mean price of cars was obtained from a document of the Bank of Italy.[9] For the missing years we calculated the price of cars using monetary correction coefficients provided by ISTAT[10] (Table 11.4).

5. Pulselli, F.M., Ciampalini, F., Tiezzi, E. & Zappia, C., The index of sustainable economic welfare (ISEW) for a local authority: a case study in Italy. *Ecological Economics*, **60**, pp. 271–281, 2006.
6. Ufficio Statistica Province of Rimini. www.provincia.rimini.it/informa/osservatori/index.htm, 2006.
7. ACI, Serie storiche sullo sviluppo della motorizzazione e sull'incidentalità stradale in Italia negli anni 1921–2003, 2005.
8. Ibid.
9. Tomat, G.M., Beni durevoli, indici di prezzo e cambiamenti di qualità: un'applicazione ai prezzi delle automobili in Italia, 1988–1998, Tema di discussione n. 439, Banca d'Italia, Roma, 2002.
10. ISTAT (Istituto Nazionale di Statistica), Il Valore della moneta in Italia dal 1861 al 2003, Rome, 2004.

Table 11.4: Trend of services of consumer durables.

	Services of cars (10%) (€, 2003 value)	Services of home ownership (5%) (€, 2003 value)	Services of appliances (10%) (€, 2003 value)	Services of consumer durables +*F*
1971	119,573,532	196,476,765	17,761,314	333,811,610
1981	204,303,787	562,230,897	28,849,062	795,383,746
1991	341,320,079	881,628,644	36,344,507	1,259,293,230
1996	473,365,094	1,153,040,443	42,184,253	1,668,589,790
2001	519,216,811	1,127,660,703	49,581,824	1,696,459,338
2003	533,903,773	1,308,985,328	52,454,471	1,895,343,572

Services of appliances (10% of total value) – The data were obtained from ISTAT in various documents presenting disaggregated consumption data for north-eastern Italy. Prices of appliances were obtained from a previous study.[11]

Services derived from house ownership (5% of total value) – Using house areas in square metres from ISTAT population censuses[12] and prices per square metre[13] in the Province of Rimini we calculated the value of this variable.

In the study period, *services of consumer durables* mostly reflected services of houses (60–70% of the total), followed by services of cars (25–30%) and services of appliances (3–5%). Table 11.4 shows the trend of this item.

G – services of the road system (+)

To calculate this item we multiplied kilometres of state, provincial and municipal roads in the Province of Rimini by the mean cost of maintenance per km each year. Data source was the roads office of the Province of Rimini. Prices were obtained from the balances of the province for the years 1996, 2001 and 2003[14] as well as estimates we made based on information obtained in other north-eastern provinces of Italy.

H – public expenditure on health and education (+)

According to Guenno and Tiezzi,[15] this item was calculated adding 100% of public spending for education to 50% of spending for health. Sources were

11. Pulselli, F.M., Ciampalini, F., Tiezzi, E. & Zappia, C., 2006, op. cit.
12. ISTAT, *Censimento della popolazione e delle abitazioni*, Roma, Various years.
13. Il Sole 24 Ore, Dossier – Il mercato immobiliare, 19 January 1998; Provincia di Rimini, Rapporto Statistico, 2003; O.R.S.A (Osservatorio Regionale del Sistema Abitativo), *Rapporto Provinciale di Rimini*, a cura di Nuova Quasco, 30 June 2004.
14. Provincia di Rimini, Bilanci Consuntivi, Ufficio Economato, 1996, 2001 e 2003.
15. Guenno, G. & Tiezzi, S., The Index of Sustainable Economic Welfare (ISEW) for Italy, Worknote 5.98, Fondazione Enrico Mattei, Milan, Italy, 1998.

Table 11.5: Trend of monetary value of road services.

	Services of the road system (€, 2003 value) +*G*
1971	5,997,605
1981	5,900,913
1991	7,510,689
1996	6,994,118
2001	8,697,463
2003	8,040,736

Table 11.6: Public expenditure for health and education in the Province of Rimini.

	Public spending for health (50%) (€, 2003 value)	Public spending for education (€, 2003 value)	Total (€, 2003 value) +*H*
1971	132,835,394	189,371,778	322,207,172
1981	143,929,856	205,187,236	349,117,092
1991	148,759,057	212,583,745	361,342,802
1996	152,473,689	230,087,320	382,561,008
2001	179,986,402	253,827,493	433,813,896
2003	213,491,539	285,965,251	499,456,790

the regional health service agency,[16] the Ministry for Education,[17] the Istituto Nazionale per la Valutazione del Sistema dell'Istruzione[18] and ISTAT.[19]

I – expenditure on consumer durables (–)
Data on spending for black and white goods per family are from ISTAT[20] and the number of resident families was the sum of families in the 20 municipalities of the province. Spending to purchase cars was obtained multiplying mean price of cars (Bank of Italy document[21]) by the number of cars registered

16. ASSR, Evoluzione della spesa sanitaria nel decennio dal 1995 al 2004, 2004.
17. Ministero della Pubblica Istruzione, Indicatori della spesa pubblica per l'istruzione scolastica. Ufficio Sistan, Settembre 1999.
18. INVALSI, www.invalsi.it, 2002.
19. ISTAT, I conti della protezione sociale: sanità, previdenza e assistenza anni 1960–1982. Supplemento al bollettino statistica n. 28, Rome, 1983.
20. ISTAT, Consumi delle famiglie 1997–1999 e 2003, Roma, 1999, 2003.
21. Tomat, G.M., 2002, op. cit.

Table 11.7: Expenditure on consumer durables in the Province of Rimini.

	Sivapending for appliances (€, 2003 value)	Sivapending for cars (€, 2003 value)	Total expenditure (€, 2003 value) –*I*
1971	11,307,346	114,622,338	125,929,684
1981	10,358,424	175,091,824	185,450,248
1991	14,418,326	253,134,604	267,552,930
1996	24,990,582	313,115,103	338,105,685
2001	25,346,428	342,258,519	367,604,947
2003	23,330,684	321,310,215	344,640,899

Table 11.8: Private defensive expenditures for education and health.

	Private defensive expenditures on education (50%)	Private defensive expenditures on health (50%)	Total (€, 2003 value) –*J*
1971	8,125,363	26,113,344	34,238,707
1981	7,490,707	11,126,209	18,616,917
1991	10,561,081	8,958,497	19,519,578
1996	9,429,469	30,351,401	39,780,870
2001	9,112,137	42,925,654	52,037,791
2003	9,037,140	44,542,419	53,579,559

annually (data from ACI for Province of Rimini 1996, 2001 and 2003; data from ACI[22] for Province of Forlì, 1971, 1981 and 1991). See item *F* for data on spending for appliances.

J – private defensive expenditures on education and health (–)
The value of private defensive expenditures to subtract from private consumption was 50% of costs sustained for education and health.[23]

K – national spending for advertising (–)
Since it was not possible to obtain significant data at local level, the item was omitted.

L – commuting costs (–)
The 30% of the services of private and public vehicles is a good estimate of the cost of commuting, provided without any real increase in welfare of

22. ACI, 2005, op. cit.
23. ASSR, 2004, op. cit.

Table 11.9: Cost of commuting, maintenance of private vehicles, tickets for public transport.

	Number of cars	0.3α (€, 2003 value)	0.3β (€, 2003 value)	0.3γ (€, 2003 value)	Cost of commuting (€, 2003 value) –*L*
1971	60,478	35,872,060	2,386,920	17,528,295	38,788,981
1981	103,358	61,291,136	3,000,761	24,972,275	64,821,836
1991	148,202	102,396,024	1,439,663	32,614,881	104,365,708
1996	153,069	142,009,528	4,086,032	31,630,659	146,602,276
2001	167,905	155,765,043	2,447,144	31,404,833	158,566,235
2003	172,645	160,171,132	2,067,489	22,016,888	162,634,620

α = monetary value of services provided by all cars in the province; β = spending for tickets on public transport in province; γ = spending for maintenance of public and private motor vehicles.

the population. Table 11.9 shows the trend of spending for maintenance of private cars, part of the services of cars for commuting and part of spending for services of public transport.

Since 1971, the cost of commuting has increased, indicating that public transport is used less than private cars. The trend seems to level off in 2001. Presumably commuting costs will decrease in time with increasing use of technology. Telework and electronic commerce are destined to spread, modifying traditional criteria of centralisation and regional hierarchy.

N – cost of road accidents (–)

According to the Centre for Research and Services of Rome, Emilia-Romagna is the region of Italy with the highest rate of road deaths. Heavy traffic on roads of the region increases the risk of accidents. Public transport needs to be improved for this and other reasons.

The final value of this item was obtained by multiplying the number of road accidents[24] by their social cost each year.[25] Data on social cost of road accidents were not available before 1996 and were therefore estimated using monetary conversion coefficients provided by ISTAT.[26]

24. ACI, 2005, op. cit.
25. Ania, L'assicurazione italiana, e ISVAP, circolari 544/S del 2004, 516/S del 2003 e 395/S del 2000 e ISVAP, Istituto per la Vigilanza sulle Assicurazioni Private e di Interesse collettivo, www.isvap.it, 2003–2004.
26. ISTAT, 2004, op. cit.

Table 11.10: Trend of social costs of road accidents.

	Number of road accidents	Social cost/accident (€, current value)	Cost of road accidents (€, 2003 value) –*N*
1971	1,688	140	3,247,551
1981	1,756	588	3,379,091
1991	1,941	1,325	3,734,920
1996	2,301	1,842	4,928,037
2001	2,547	3,068	8,200,999
2003	2,891	3,489	10,086,699

Table 11.11: Trend of equivalent inhabitants (EI) and cost of water pollution in the Province of Rimini.

	Civil EI	Industrial EI	Livestock EI	Tourism EI	Total EI	€/EI (€, current value)	Cost of water pollution (€, 2003 value)
1971	231,010	216,518	66,218	38,942	700,239	1.11	10,688,487
1981	250,328	259,754	253,883	42,680	806,646	4.67	12,329,511
1991	258,718	266,464	357,756	37,451	920,389	10.52	14,067,696
1996	265,158	288,266	253,883	39,563	846,870	13.14	12,938,377
2001	272,676	310,389	308,654	43,957	935,676	14.56	14,297,806
2003	279,774	325,222	1,000,280	42,052	1,647,328	15.28	25,171,170

O – cost of water pollution (–)

Equivalent inhabitants were multiplied by unit treatment cost (from Pulselli *et al.*[27]) to obtain a monetary value of man-made water pollution. Table 11.11 lists equivalent inhabitants for industrial, civil, tourist, and farming sectors. Tourist population was considered in relation to mean stay (total number of tourist presences divided by 365 days).[28]

P – cost of air pollution (–)

Air pollution was calculated as suggested by the IPCC, assessing emissions of contaminants in relation to inputs of fossil fuels into the system of

27. Pulselli, F.M., Ciampalini, F., Tiezzi, E. & Zappia, C., 2006, op. cit.
28. IRSA-CNR, Istituto di ricerca sulle acque del CNR, quaderno 90, 1991; ISTAT, 8° Censimento dell'industria e dei servizi, Rome, http://www.istat.it/censimenti/industria/, 2001; ISTAT, 5° Censimento dell'Agricoltura, Rome, 2000; Ufficio Statistica Province of Rimini, www.provincia.rimini.it, 2006.

Table 11.12: Abatement cost per ton of contaminant and cost of air pollution in the Province of Rimini.

	Abatement cost per ton (€, current value)/ton				Cost of air pollution (€, 2003 value) –*P*
	CO_2	NO_x	SO_x	PM10	
1971	1.03	90.56	232.87	12.94	16,576,729
1981	4.35	380.59	978.66	54.37	18,674,888
1991	9.8	857.43	2,204.83	122.49	19,704,743
1996	12.25	1,071.45	2,755.17	153.06	22,163,132
2001	13.57	1,186.96	3,052.18	169.57	24,707,082
2003	14.24	1,245.71	3,203.25	177.96	27,302,173

the province.[29] A monetary value was determined in relation to abatement costs.[30] Expression in monetary terms enables decision makers to formulate environmental remediation policies.

Though the values may be inaccurate due to the variety of sources and the estimation procedures, Table 11.12 shows that quantities of CO_2 and NO_x have been increasing since 1970, while SO_x has decreased since 1980 due to construction of the methane distribution network of Italy.

Q – cost of noise pollution (–)
Since no information is available on noise levels in the Province of Rimini, only traffic noise was considered. The noise of one car[31] was multiplied by the number of motor vehicles in the province.[32]

R – loss of wetlands
According to the provincial administration, there are no wetlands in the Province of Rimini. We therefore considered areas of naturalistic value. Emilia-Romagna is a good example of regional conservation. The 25 protected areas are in first position for visitors' facilities and management services.

29. IRSE (Inventario Regionale delle Emissioni), Rapporto: Qualità dell'aria, inquinamento acustico, industrie a rischio, inquinamento elettromagnetico, 2000; DGERM (Direzione Generale dell'Energia e delle Risorse Minerarie), Combustibles consumption: time series. https://dgerm.attivitaproduttive.gov.it/dgerm/venditeprovinciali.asp, 2003; GRTN (Gestore della Rete di Trasmissione Nazionale), Disponibile on-line all'indirizzo, http://www.grtn.it, 2003; Società Gas Rimini, http://www.gasrimini.it/; Gruppo Hera, http://www.gruppohera.it/.
30. Pulselli, F.M., Ciampalini, F., Tiezzi, E. & Zappia, C., 2006, op. cit.
31. Provincia di Bologna, Il Mobility Management della Provincia di Bologna, www.provincia.bologna.it/mobility/, 1999.
32. ACI, 2005, op. cit.

Table 11.13: Cost of noise calculated on the basis of number of motor vehicles in the Province of Rimini.

	Number of cars	Social cost/Car (€, current value)	Cost of noise (€, 2003 value) –*Q*
1971	60,478	9.42	7,833,981
1981	103,358	39.57	13,387,244
1991	148,202	89.16	19,198,058
1996	153,069	111.42	19,830,259
2001	167,905	123.43	21,750,664
2003	172,645	129.54	22,364,139

Table 11.14: Area and increment in value of reserves.

	Area of reserves in hectares	Increase in hectares	Monetary value of increase in area of reserves (€, 2003 value) –*R*
1971	4,492	0	0
1981	4,492	0	0
1991	5,448	156	249,119
1996	5,448	0	0
2001	5,448	0	0
2003	5,448	0	0

Parks and reserves are not left to fate but form part of local socio-economic life, are open to visitors and have educational facilities. This region was one of the first to adopt a landscape plan that attributed value to natural areas; the regional parks in the Apennine montane belt are an example. The economic value of reserves was calculated attributing a value of €1,033 (1990 value[33]) to each hectare added since 1971; this figure was adjusted using correction coefficients obtained from ISTAT.[34] Actually, only the Ornano Reserve in the Municipality of Gemmano (156 ha) was instituted during the study period.

S – loss of agricultural land (–)

Loss of agricultural land is difficult to measure and can be approached in different ways. The monetary value of this item was obtained by counting changes in area

33. Guenno, G. & Tiezzi, S., 1998, op. cit.
34. ISTAT, 2004, op. cit.

Table 11.15: Monetary value of loss of agricultural land.

	Area of agricultural land (ha)	Loss of agricultural land (ha)	Monetary value of agricultural land (€, current value)/ha	Value of loss of agricultural land (€, 2003 value) –*S*
1971	33,772	197	593	1,607,465
1981	31,801	197	4,249	2,740,660
1991	31,126	–66	6,746	–642,529
1996	32,456	135	8,075	1,583,623
2001	29,252	641	12,904	9,615,820
2003	28,581	224	13,738	3,222,581

of agricultural land from one census to the next.[35,36] Since this information is only available in census years, the total variation was divided evenly between years.

T – depletion of non-renewable resources (–)

The monetary value of this item was obtained by counting the quantities of materials quarried (source *Ufficio Difesa del Suolo*, Province of Rimini and *Ufficio Difesa del Suolo e della Costa della Regione Emilia Romagna*, only for 1996, 2001 and 2003) and multiplying them by the cost of extraction.[37] The data show a decrease in quantities from the mid-1990s due to closure of a number of quarries of clay (for roof tiles), limestone and sand in the Conca valley.

Table 11.16: Quantities of material quarried in the Province of Rimini (1971–2003), cost of quarrying, proceeds and economic value of depletion of non-renewable resources.

	Volume quarried (m^3)	Total quarrying costs (€, current value)	Proceeds of sale of material (€, current value)	Depletion of non-renewable resources (€, 2003 value) – *T*
1971	986,500	50,720	1,532,889	20,381,901
1981	986,500	483,829	13,310,894	41,982,985
1991	986,500	1,056,824	27,833,644	38,904,041
1996	986,500	2,543,212	63,257,877	70,592,941
2001	235,000	799,702	19,459,113	19,583,052
2003	90,500	255,819	6,418,661	6,162,842

35. ISTAT (Istituto Nazionale di Statistica), 5° Censimento dell'Agricoltura, Ufficio Statistica Provincia di Rimini, Rome, Italy, 2000.
36. Unioncamere Emilia Romagna, Il sistema agroalimentare dell'Emilia-Romagna, Rapporto 2002, 2002.
37. Pulselli, F.M., Ciampalini, F., Tiezzi, E. & Zappia, C., 2006, op. cit.

U – long-term environmental damage (–)
This item is the monetary cost attributed to the increasing quantities of fossil fuels used and to the damage their use causes through emission of greenhouse gases. Cobb and Daly suggested assigning a monetary value to loss of welfare of future generations who will find themselves with few reserves of these fuels as well as increasing costs due to climate change. It is a sort of carbon tax that is subtracted from current consumption in order to compensate future generations for damage incurred. The taxes accumulate year by year in a capital account. In order to calculate this item we obtained data on consumption of fossil fuels since the beginning of the 1970s.[38] Data from before 1971 were not available and had to be estimated using regional consumption and demographic data. Once the fuel database was built, we converted the various fossil fuels into barrels of oil equivalent and applied a tax of €1.96/barrel (€ at 2003 value). Note that €1.96 equals $US 0.50 (1972 value) used by Cobb and Daly.

Table 11.17: Lasting environmental damage in the Province of Rimini.

	Annual consumption in barrel equivalents	Sum of consumption over 10 previous years in barrel equivalents	Long-term environmental damage (€, 2003 value) –*U*
1971	1,487,260	26,224,724	54,315,488
1981	2,871,016	51,289,509	106,154,629
1991	3,298,642	79,811,404	162,895,690
1996	3,765,444	97,071,816	197,641,028
2001	4,178,617	116,242,819	236,026,015
2003	4,532,576	124,705,581	253,306,788

The cost for future generations of the damage caused by burning fossil fuels was €13/person in 1971 and €33/person by 2003 (2003 value). It is not fair to distribute long-term environmental damage equally over the whole population; it is more appropriate to redistribute the welfare lost by taxing individuals in relation to their use of fossil fuels. Money accumulated from this hypothetical tax could be used to finance measures to improve environmental quality.

V – net capital growth (+)
This item is based on the amount and trend of net capital and gross fixed investments of industry in Italy and on that of employees in different sectors calculated at national and provincial levels.[39] Net capital growth in the decade

38. DGERM, Gruppo Hera S.p.A., Gruppo Società Gas Rimini S.p.A & GRTN 2003, 2003, op. cit.
39. ISTAT (Istituto Nazionale di Statistica), 8° Censimento dell'industria e dei servizi, Rome, Italy, http://www.istat.it/censimenti/industria/, 2001.

1971–1980 was estimated from the trend of gross fixed investments for each sector.[40] After reconstructing the historical series of net capital growth we calculated annual variations for all years in the study period. The values were then distributed annually for all employees at national level and multiplied by employees in the Province of Rimini.

Table 11.18: Value and trend of net capital in the Province of Rimini.

	Net capital (€, current value)	Net capital (€, 2003 value) – *V*
1971	46,173,301	634,947,535
1981	95,245,663	311,739,054
1991	221,634,096	322,012,178
1996	320,647,900	372,817,314
2001	410,212,756	430,518,287
2003	438,801,069	438,801,069

W – index of sustainable economic welfare

ISEW is obtained summing all the previous items, to provide a measure of welfare that includes social and environmental as well as economic factors. The index provides an instrument for administrations seeking to improve sustainability.

Y–Z – gross domestic product

As in the case of Modena, since we are dealing with a sub-national system, we use the acronym GRP (gross regional product) instead of GDP. ISEW and GRP[41] are now compared year by year for the Province of Rimini.

Table 11.19: ISEW and GRP of the Province of Rimini in euro (2003 value).

	ISEW	GRP
1971	3,310,983,636	2,146,126,726
1981	3,730,322,232	3,101,253,595
1991	4,182,270,291	4,372,708,451
1996	4,872,827,735	4,963,927,251
2001	5,431,635,583	6,207,182,519
2003	5,848,705,006	6,662,817,810

40. ISTAT, Investimenti fissi lordi per branca proprietaria, stock di capitale e ammortamenti, www.istat.it, 1970–2005.

41. Istituto Guglielmo Tagliacarne, Sistema Starter, Database, Roma, 1999.

Table 11.20: Monetary value of all items composing ISEW of the Province of Rimini from 1971 to 2003.

A	1971	1981	1991	1996	2001	2003
B	1,571,296,357	1,939,757,202	2,731,640,319	2,844,445,063	3,621,878,562	3,458,777,235
C	0.656	0.628	0.523	0.427	0.390	0.293
D	948,850,457	1,191,497,053	1,793,591,805	1,993,304,179	2,605,668,030	2,675,208,628
E (+)	1,375,598,442	1,527,101,563	1,081,141,162	1,263,964,484	1,180,532,545	1,255,845,356
F (+)	333,811,610	795,383,746	1,259,293,230	1,668,589,790	1,696,459,338	1,895,343,572
G (+)	5,997,605	5,900,913	7,510,689	6,994,118	8,697,463	8,040,736
H (+)	322,207,172	349,117,092	361,342,802	382,561,008	433,813,896	499,456,790
I (–)	125,929,684	185,450,248	267,552,930	338,105,685	367,604,947	344,640,899
J (–)	34,238,707	18,616,917	19,519,578	39,780,870	52,037,791	53,579,559
L (–)	55,787,274	89,264,172	136,450,568	177,726,219	189,617,020	184,255,508
N (–)	**3,247,551**	**3,379,091**	3,734,920	4,928,037	8,200,999	10,086,699
O (–)	10,688,487	12,329,511	14,067,696	12,938,377	14,297,806	25,171,170
P (–)	16,576,729	18,674,888	19,704,743	22,163,132	24,707,082	27,302,173

Continued

Table 11.20: Continued

Q (–)	7,833,981	13,387,244	19,198,058	19,830,259	21,750,664	22,364,139
R* (+)	0	0	249,119	0	0	0
S (–)	1,607,465	2,740,660	–642,529	1,583,623	9,615,820	3,222,581
T (–)	203,819	419,830	389,040	705,929	195,831	61,628
U (–)	54,315,488	106,154,629	162,895,690	197,641,028	236,026,015	253,306,788
V (+)	634,947,535	311,739,054	322,012,178	372,817,314	430,518,287	438,801,069
W	3,310,983,636	3,730,322,232	4,182,270,291	4,872,827,735	5,431,635,583	5,848,705,006
X	14,333	14,902	16,165	18,377	19,920	20,905
Y	2,146,126,726	3,101,253,595	4,372,708,451	4,963,927,251	6,207,182,519	6,662,817,810
Z	9,290	12,389	16,901	18,721	22,764	23,815
Population	231,010	250,328	258,718	265,158	272,676	279,774

A: Year; B: Private consumption; C: Gini index; D: Weighted private consumption; E (+): Services of domestic labour; F (+): Services of consumer durables; G (+): Services of road system; H (+): Public expenditure on education and health; I (–): Expenditure on consumer durables; J (–): Private expenditure on education and health; L (–): Costs of commuting; N (–): Costs of road accidents; O (–): Costs of water pollution; P (–): Costs of air pollution; Q (–): Costs of noise pollution; R* (+): Increase in area of reserves; S (–): Loss of agricultural land; T (–): Depletion of non-renewable resources; U (–): Long-term environmental damage; V (+): Net capital growth; W: ISEW; X: ISEW per capita; Y: GRP; Z: GRP per capita.

*Over the period of analysis there has been an increase in the area of reserves.

Comparison of ISEW and GRP of the Province of Rimini (1971–2003)

Comparison of GRP and ISEW of the Province of Rimini corroborates criticism of the macroeconomic indicator (GDP) and its inability to distinguish between operations that promote and depress welfare. Conceived in the early 1930s and mentioned daily in the press, GDP is the subject of bitter political debate on how to accelerate its growth and may even influence the outcome of elections. This all-important indicator is showing its limits. As we have seen, growing pollution is forcing people to buy water purifiers and increasing spending for health, which bolsters GDP, but it can hardly be said that pollution increases welfare. Similarly, a fall in energy consumption caused by more efficient use of energy promoted by the public administration in the interests of sustainability would cause spending and GDP to fall. On the other hand ISEW would increase, reflecting greater welfare as a result of lower emissions.

Like GDP, ISEW is an economic indicator, but unlike GDP it does not disregard negative factors that cause loss of welfare. Increasing inequality of income, air pollution and consumption of non-renewable resources are subtracted in calculating ISEW, while unpaid work in the home and creation of nature reserves are added, correcting the monetary model of GDP.

It is impossible to determine the extent to which ISEW reflects sustainability without making value judgements, however it can be a useful instrument for representing the time trend of welfare of a community. The study of the Province of Rimini provides a clear picture of socio-economic trends in the last 30 years, contributing to research on sustainability indicators applied on a local scale. In this period, the Province of Rimini has seen a decrease in inactive members of the population, a sign of the gradual decrease in the number of housewives, indeed the value of unpaid domestic labour has decreased since 1981. There has been an increase in the number of students. Growth of the working population and economic dynamics of different kinds have led to a more equal distribution of income.

The item *consumer durables* showed an increasing trend until the early 1990s, driven by a constant increase in car ownership and a strong real estate market. From 1991 to the end of the century, the latter was affected by a sharp downturn in the demand for second houses in the Rimini area, due to structural changes aimed at restoring the Province as a centre of international tourism. Construction of new hotels and a lively real-estate market with prices that reached €4,000/m^2 in 2006 is increasing the item *services of durables* in the province.

Public spending for roads, reserves, education and partly for health contribute, together with the above, to the welfare of a population (positive items of ISEW) and have increased in time, especially after the constitution of Rimini as an independent province.

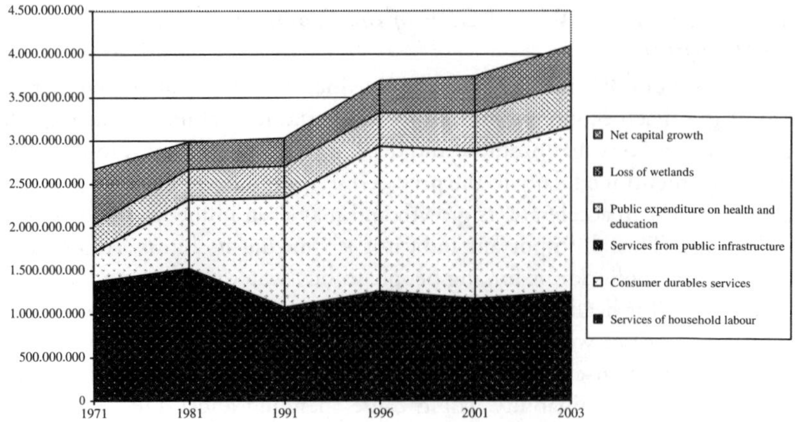

Figure 11.1: Trend of positive items of ISEW (€/2003 value.)

Capital growth, the last positive variable of ISEW, is growing again after slackening of the investments during the 1970s and the 1980s.

Figure 11.1 shows the sum and distribution of positive items of ISEW contributing to welfare of the provincial system. The trend increases in the study period, and shows the negligible influence of services of the road system and increase in nature reserves (barely visible in the graph). Spending for consumer durables, namely money spent by families to buy durable goods, follows the increase in number of cars. The large number of cars on the road, now a major problem of towns and cities, associated with air pollution, traffic and noise, has not spared Rimini. The increasing cost of noise, air pollution, road accidents and commuting is a direct consequence of this phenomenon typical of Western countries. The aim of any public administration should be to gradually reduce the number of cars in cities and increase parks, pedestrian precincts and bicycle tracks in order to improve the quality of life.

The constant increase in long-term environmental damage is also a result of profligate use of non-renewable resources, especially fossil fuels. The increase in defensive expenditures (e.g. for health) could be related to the effects of pollution.

Figure 11.2 shows the sum and distribution of negative items of ISEW that decrease welfare in the Province of Rimini. These items increase in the study period, except for a downturn in 2003. Depletion of non-renewable resources was negligible and is hardly visible in the graph.

The trend of ISEW of the Province of Rimini increases more slowly than GRP. The turning point occurred in the mid1980s, whereas in Italy it occurred

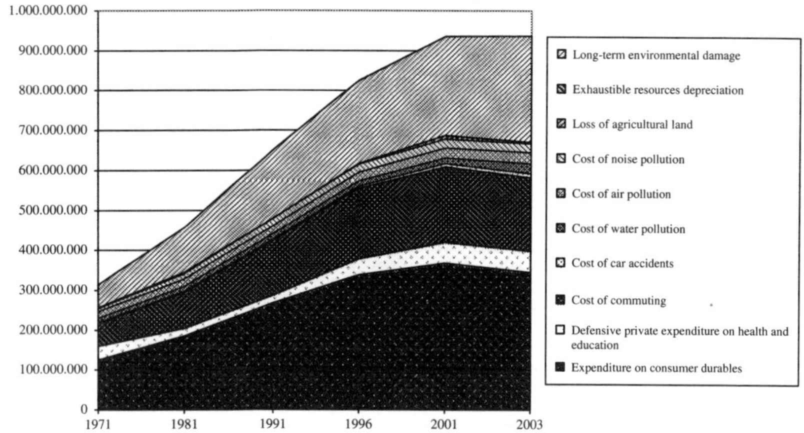

Figure 11.2: Trend of negative items of ISEW (€/2003 value.)

in the 1960s.[42] The area between the two indicators to the right of the cross-over indicates the amount that GRP overestimates welfare. It is well known that GDP does not correctly reflect the welfare of a nation and that a country or province can grow rich while social facilities and natural resources deteriorate. Now, however, there are instruments that make it possible to at least partly quantify and visualise this divergence (Fig 11.3).

The aim of this study was to invite the public and private sectors to use natural resources in a more rational way that considers the environmental and social consequence of economic growth. The fact that an instrument is now available makes it possible to monitor the true efficacy of environmental policy at local level. For example, ISEW would reflect the effects a law that limited the energy consumption of buildings to 46 kWh/m^{2}year (class A building certification). In this case it would be possible to test the sensitivity of ISEW to policies of promotion of renewable energies, showing that replacement of diesel fuel by biodiesel in agriculture (technically and economically possible) could lead to an increase of up to 3% in ISEW. This is food for thought, since in many countries elections have been won by promising 1% increases in GDP.

There is a dichotomy between what an economy or society produces or earns and the level of welfare perceived by the population. It is now possible to measure the production potential of our economic system (by GDP) and also obtain more information on the consequences of our choices in an economic,

42. Guenno, G. & Tiezzi, S., 1998, op. cit.

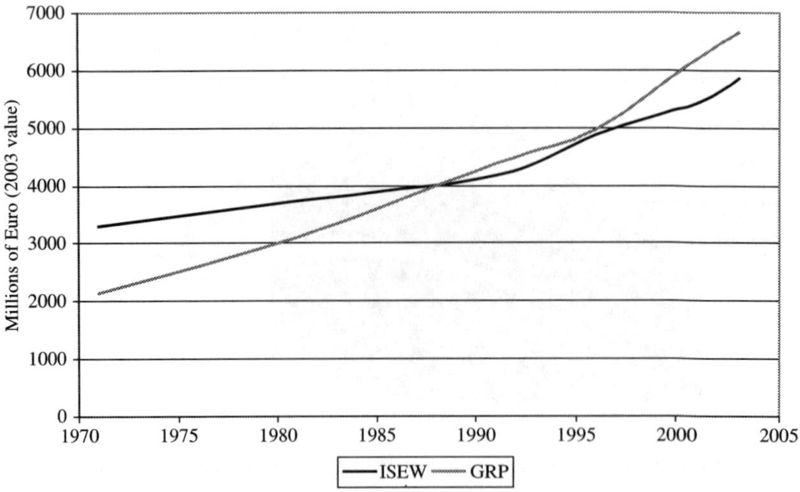

Figure 11.3: Comparison of GDP and ISEW of the Province of Rimini in the period 1971–2003.

social and environmental framework. Sustainability indicators such as ISEW can help but depend on the availability of increasingly detailed regional information. Promotion and development of advanced research using integrated indicators call for databases of high-quality statistical information of many types, especially environmental accounting data.

Chapter 12

Beyond the threshold

Economic and physical quantities

There are probably no systemic relationships more interesting that those between humans, and between humans and nature.[1] How these relationships are represented for the purposes of study must reflect their complexity and cannot be modelled in a single dimension, whatever that dimension may be. Many quantities involved in the dynamics of human activities and of the biosphere must therefore be measured, related, developed and entered in models. Clearly, economic parameters cannot do all this. As they are not the only evidence of human behaviour, measures of economic wealth must be completed with physical indicators describing the human-nature system.

In economic terms, wealth can be defined as 'a stock of assets, measured in money at a point in time, that is, cash in the bank, plus the market value of bonds, corporate shares, land, real estate, and consumer durables as of a given date'.[2] According to Edward Nell, an increase in wealth contributes to growing affluence for many, but today this happens at the expenses of environmental quality and social fairness and welfare. He maintains that the benefits related to increasing wealth rise, but at a diminishing rate, while the costs of market pressures also rise, but at an increasing rate. A point Q exists at which these must balance, but before Q is reached, there is a point Q' at a lower level of wealth, at which the additional (rising) costs of the system are no longer offset by the additional (falling) gains from it. In other words, at Q total costs are equal to total benefits and at Q' marginal costs equal marginal benefits[3] (Fig. 12.1).

1. Abel, T., System diagrams for visualizing macroeconomics. *Ecological Modelling*, **178**, pp. 189–194, 2004.
2. Daly, H. & Farley, J., *Ecological Economics – Principles and Applications*, Island Press: Washington, DC, 2004.
3. Nell, E.J., *Making Sense of a Changing Economy: Technology, Markets and Morals*. Routledge: London, New York, 1996.

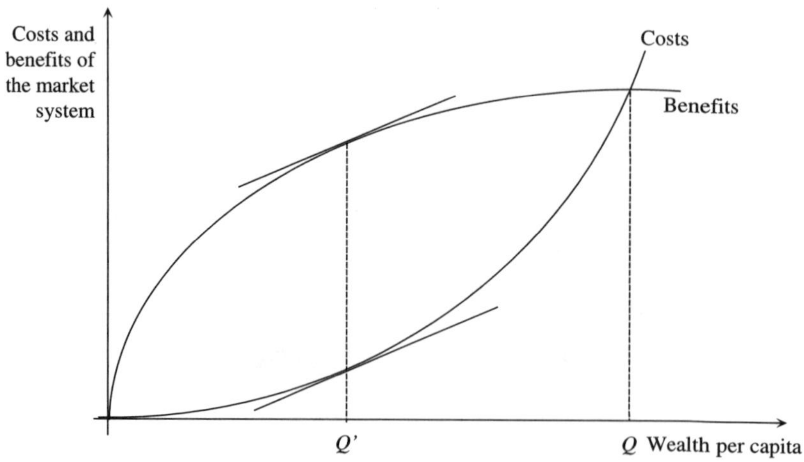

Figure 12.1: Costs and benefits related to growth (from E. Nell, op. cit.).

Nell's statements are similar to the so-called *threshold hypothesis* of Manfred Max-Neef:

> Economic growth brings about an improvement in the quality of life but only up to a point beyond which, if there is more economic growth, the quality of life may begin to deteriorate.[4]

The aim of ISEW is to measure the divergence between economic and uneconomic growth and to demonstrate that traditional economic instruments do not take into account social and especially environmental phenomena and problems. Combination of various instruments provides more precise physical measures of the problems caused by economic growth. In this chapter, we discuss a number of proposals to complete results obtained by macroeconomic analysis. For example, if the data of ISEW and the ecological footprint, or ISEW and emergy analysis are combined, new frontiers of analysis of the complex systems constituted by humans and nature are revealed.

ISEW, ecological footprint and threshold hypothesis

The following reflections come from an article published in *Ecological Economics* in 2007.[5] The idea was to analyse the temporal trends of indicators that focus on very different aspects, to see whether a relationship between them

4. Max-Neef, M., Economic growth and quality of life: a threshold hypothesis. *Ecological Economics*, **15**, pp. 115–118, 1995.
5. Niccolucci, V., Pulselli, F.M. & Tiezzi, E., Strengthening the threshold hypothesis: economic and biophysical limits to growth. *Ecological Economics*, **60**, pp. 667–672, 2007.

could be defined. The indicators were gross domestic product (GDP), a purely economic indicator, the index of sustainable economic welfare (ISEW), an ecological economic indicator, and ecological footprint (EF) and biocapacity (BIO), which are indicators of environmental sustainability.

The crucial parameter for calculating GDP, ISEW and EF is consumption of resources.

ISEW considers levels of consumption but includes environmental and social correction factors, the increasing weight of which modifies ISEW with respect to GDP. As we have seen, both aggregates show an increasing trend at first, but beyond a certain year, that varies from case to case, ISEW diverges, remaining constant or decreasing. This means that beyond a certain level of economic growth, the benefits derived from consumption are outweighed by the environmental and social pressures connected with growth. In other words, greater wealth of a nation (measured by GDP) is not always accompanied by greater welfare of the population. ISEW therefore describes the *economic threshold of growth* or the point beyond which growth no longer leads to an overall increase in welfare, because aspects such as environmental deterioration begin to be felt.

The ecological footprint translates a population's consumption of goods and services into area of ecologically productive land. It is associated with biocapacity, which expresses the wealth in natural capital of the region inhabited by the population. Comparison of EF and BIO provides an indication of environmental stress, because it compares the population's needs with the capacity of the environment of their region to provide the necessary goods and services. A high EF puts pressure on the environment, stressing biogeochemical cycles and eroding the availability of resources. It is particularly significant in industrialised countries, where demand often exceeds supply, and thus EF exceeds BIO. An increasing trend of EF is typical of these countries. The slope of the trend may vary, unlike that of BIO, which is relatively constant or in slight decline. The dynamics of this comparison generally go from a situation of surplus (BIO > EF) characterised by an abundance of resources, to one of deficit (EF > BIO) and scarcity of resources.

Combining EF and BIO, a *biophysical threshold of growth* emerges, represented by the turning point from ecological surplus to ecological deficit. From the point of view of sustainability, the biophysical threshold is more critical than the economic one. The critical threshold of an ecosystem is the point beyond which non-linear, irreversible or catastrophic changes may occur; these clearly have major environmental and economic consequences.[6] The fact that many industrialised countries are in ecological deficit today could explain the divergence between ISEW and GDP.

6. Farber, S.C., Costanza, R. & Wilson, M.A., Economic and ecological concepts for valuing ecosystem services. *Ecological Economics*, **41**, pp. 375–392, 2002.

To sustain this hypothesis, we look at the trends of EF, BIO, GDP and ISEW (or GPI, genuine progress indicator[7] if ISEW was not available) of six countries. We are concerned with the trends, not with single values of these indices, because the data sources were heterogeneous: EF and BIO data were from the same source and obtained by the same procedure, whereas the figures for ISEW and GDP were produced by different authors or institutions, based on procedures and assumptions that may not be the same.

The six nations were grouped into three cases on the basis of their results. Figure 12.2 shows the trend of the four indices: EF and BIO in black, GDP and ISEW in grey.[8]

The first case regards Sweden and Australia. Both maintain an ecological surplus by virtue of their vast natural capital (biocapacity) and low population density, despite a high EF. The time series shows that the surplus is decreasing, especially that of Australia. With regard to GDP and ISEW, the first signs of divergence become evident in the early 1980s. Since that time, GDP has increased while ISEW (GPI in the case of Australia) has remained substantially constant. This reflects the narrowing gap between BIO and EF. Conservation of natural heritage should be a primary aim of these governments. Ecological surplus is a position of strength worth maintaining. The transition from ecological surplus to deficit and its social and economic consequences should be delayed as long as possible.

The second example is the case of Austria and USA. This is an unusual and interesting case. The trends of EF and BIO show that both countries have exceeded their limits, crossing the line from ecological surplus to deficit. This occurred in 1965–1970 for USA and in 1980–1985 for Austria. Note that an American has twice the EF of an Austrian. The interesting point is that a

7. GPI is very similar to ISEW and has the same dynamics since it considers largely the same items.
8. The authors thank the Global Footprint Network (National Footprint and Biocapacity Accounts, Oakland-San Francisco 2006, http://www.globalfootprintnetwork.org), for access to information. The sources of data were: Jackson. T. & Stymne, S., *Sustainable Economic Welfare in Sweden: A Pilot Index 1950–1992*, Stockholm Environment Institute, The New Economics Foundation, 1996; Hamilton, C., The genuine progress indicator: methodological developments and results from Australia, in *Ecological Economics*, **30(1)**, pp. 13–28, 1999; Anielski, M. & Rowe, M., *The Genuine Progress Indicator – 1998 Update*, Redefining Progress: San Francisco, 1999; Stockhammer, E., Hochreiter, H., Hobermayr, B. & Steiner, K., The index of sustainable economic welfare (ISEW) as an alternative to GDP in measuring economic welfare. The result of the Austrian (revised) ISEW calculation, 1955–1992. *Ecological Economics*, **21(1)**, pp. 19–34, 1997; Guenno, G. & Tiezzi, S., The Index of Sustainable Economic Welfare (ISEW) for Italy, Worknote 5.98, Fondazione Enrico Mattei, Milan, Italy, 1998; Diefenbacher, H., The index of sustainable economic welfare in Germany. *The Green National Product*, eds C. Cobb and J. Cobb, UPA: New York, 1994; and http://www.foe.co.uk/campaigns/sustainable_development/progress/international.html.

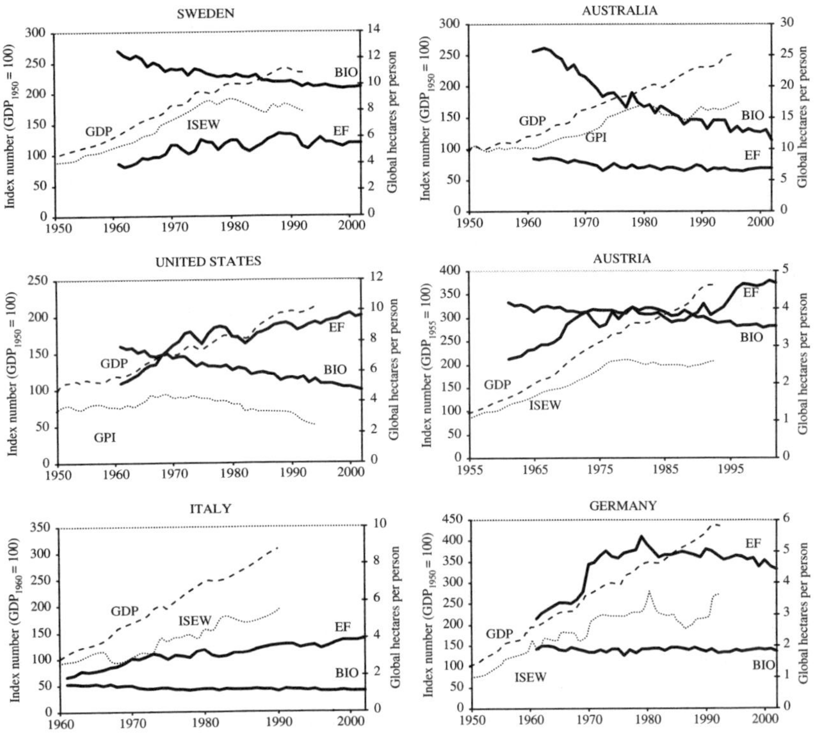

Figure 12.2: An interpretation of the threshold of sustainability. Ecological footprint and biocapacity are represented by solid lines (in gha/person – on the right), ISEW or GPI and GDP by dashed lines (index number – on the left).

major divergence between GDP and ISEW (GPI in the case of USA) began at the same time. In the case of Austria, ISEW ceased to grow; in the case of USA, GPI decreased significantly. Is it a coincidence that the transition from surplus to deficit and divergence of ISEW (GPI) from GDP occurred at the same time? A direct relation was also found between the degree of ecological deficit and the degree of divergence. Environmental aspects, especially availability of natural capital, therefore seem to be very critical elements for the health of economic systems.

The third case is that of Italy and Germany, which find themselves in a more vulnerable situation. The trends of EF and BIO showed that both countries have been in ecological deficit since before the 1960s. A difference with respect to the previous examples is evident: the economic threshold that coincides with stagnation of ISEW occurred slightly after the biophysical threshold. In Italy, the first shock occurred at the end of the 1960s, whereas in

Germany it did not occur until the end of the 1980s. As in the other cases, a correlation is evident between environmental pressure (increased gap between EF and BIO) and the discrepancy between ISEW and GDP. An increasing trend of EF was evident until the early 1980s, after which it levelled off. These two countries have lower biocapacity than the other countries considered, suggesting that the main cause of early ecological deficit was the limited availability of natural resources, a situation typical of many European countries. To make up this deficit, these countries are forced to 'import' biocapacity from other parts of the Earth, or to eat into the resource stocks of future generations. Italy and Germany presumably used their economic power to 'finance' the small but increasing gap between GDP and ISEW, contracting heavy environmental debts with other nations and with future generations.

A vulnerable point of these systems, particularly from the viewpoint of sustainability, is their dependence on the outside. Western societies are putting increasing pressure on the environment, as demonstrated by the increasing trend of their ecological footprints. This goes hand in hand with a decline in environmental sustainability, as shown by the increasing gap between EF and BIO, often due to the pressure of economic growth (measured by GDP). Increasingly often, economic wealth is growing without bringing any corresponding increase in welfare. This may be because achievement of certain levels of economic wealth is increasingly accompanied by side effects, such as environmental degradation and social pressures that lower the value of ISEW.

The above examples demonstrate that a relationship between loss of welfare and environmental problems does indeed exist. This relationship varies from case to case. Definition of the two thresholds of growth (economic and biophysical) provides important evidence of the limits of human activity in the long period. These thresholds are crucial if welfare is to be sustained in the long term; the traditional break-even points based on parameters such as feasibility, profit and market prices do not provide the necessary information. GDP is useful to quantify the economic performance of a country, but only when GDP is combined with other instruments can we know how far a country is from sustainability (environmental, social or economic). This is one of many findings that confirm that no single indicator can embody the complexity of the relationships between humans, and between humans and nature. Use of multiple indicators is therefore a good strategy to improve understanding of the mechanisms regulating these relationships.

ISEW and emergy

It is not easy to determine the sustainability of a region separated artificially from its surroundings by administrative boundaries. In order to give policy makers guidelines for good governance of their regions and natural resources, technical instruments that assess the behaviour of the region's population in the course of time need to be developed and used. Environmental accounting based on emergy considers all flows of resources supporting processes occurring in a region, providing a perspective different from traditional economic analysis. The set of results obtained are not proposed as alternatives to traditional indices but as a means for obtaining information useful for planning and management of activities and behaviour. The complementary nature of the information obtained by emergy analysis lies in its different qualitative characteristics. For example, emergy analysis is not based on market parameters but on objective physical quantities. By not using market prices but physical parameters, the problem of disregarding things not traded in markets (e.g. environmental goods and services) is solved. Environmental goods and services are only accounted indirectly in economic analysis. Emergy analysis, with its indicators, provides a series of interpretations of regional dynamics arising from relationships between human activities and natural resources.

Completion of economic values with physical parameters is rather accustomed among theoreticians. The results of emergy analysis are often compared with economic and socio-economic parameters. An immediate example is the ratio of emergy to money, or *emergy money ratio* (EMR), obtained by dividing the total flow of emergy feeding a region by the gross product of the region; the units are seJ/€. This ratio is usually calculated for national economies, dividing the emergy flow of the nation by its GDP for the year in question. The result is a measure of the number of solar emergy joules (seJ) supporting each unit of economic product (in €). In other words, it represents the amount of resources that is necessary to maintain production in a certain period of time; therefore, it should be minimised. Thus, EMR attributes an average physical value (emergy) to wealth circulating in an economy.

GDP is a good indicator of productive capacity because it counts the quantity of goods and services produced in a region in a certain period of time. As we have seen, GDP, an indicator of economic wealth, can be flanked by other economic or ecological economic indicators, in order to obtain insights into other aspects of society, such as welfare. We saw that ISEW provides information qualitatively and quantitatively different from economic performance, counting social and environmental aspects that traditional economic accounting ignores. It is therefore possible to compare a new quantity, a measure of welfare, with the amount of resources necessary to feed a regional system, which is also an economic and social system. In other words, GDP and ISEW can be compared to the flow of emergy feeding a regional system in order to have insights into the manner in which resources are used by society and the outcome of that use.

The case of the Province of Modena

An emergy analysis of the Province of Modena was carried out using data of the year 2003. All inputs supplying the system operating within the administrative boundaries were defined from a variety of sources and converted into seJ/year using the appropriate transformities. Flows of resources were then classified as local renewable (*R*), local non-renewable (*N*) or imported from outside the system (*F*) and the aggregates of each determined. Table 12.1 shows the results with the values of emergy flows for each category of resource and the total emergy flow. Analysis of the flows showed the size of the resource requirements and the types of resources, irrespective of market value (Fig 12.3). The following emergy indicators were then calculated and mapped to show the geography of resource use: environmental loading ratio, empower density, emergy per person, emergy investment ratio and emergy yield ratio. The indicators quantify environmental stress, the balance between the types of resources used and dependence on other systems. The province was found to be highly dependent on importation of resources from outside, an indicator of fragility.

Table 12.1: Emergy flows and indicators for the Province of Modena in the year 2003.

Emergy flows	Unit	Expression	Emergy
Local renewable emergy	seJ/year	R	6.22×10^{20}
Local non-renewable emergy	seJ/year	N	5.15×10^{21}
Local emergy	seJ/year	$L = N + R$	5.77×10^{21}
Imported emergy (energy sources)	seJ/year	$F1$	1.02×10^{22}
Imported emergy (goods and services)	seJ/year	$F2$	5.04×10^{22}
Total imported emergy	seJ/year	$F = F1 + F2$	6.06×10^{22}
Total emergy used within the system	seJ/year	$U = L + F$	6.64×10^{22}
Emergy indices	**Unit**	**Expression**	**Value**
Area	m^2		2.69×10^9
Population	inh.		6.52×10^5
Population density	inh./km^2		242.50
Empower density	seJ/($m^2 \times$ yr)	U/Area	2.47×10^{13}
Emergy per person	seJ/(inh. $\times$ yr)	U/Population	1.02×10^{17}
Emergy investment ratio		$F/(N + R)$	10.51
Emergy yield ratio		U/F	1.10
Environmental loading ratio		$(U - R)/R$	105.85

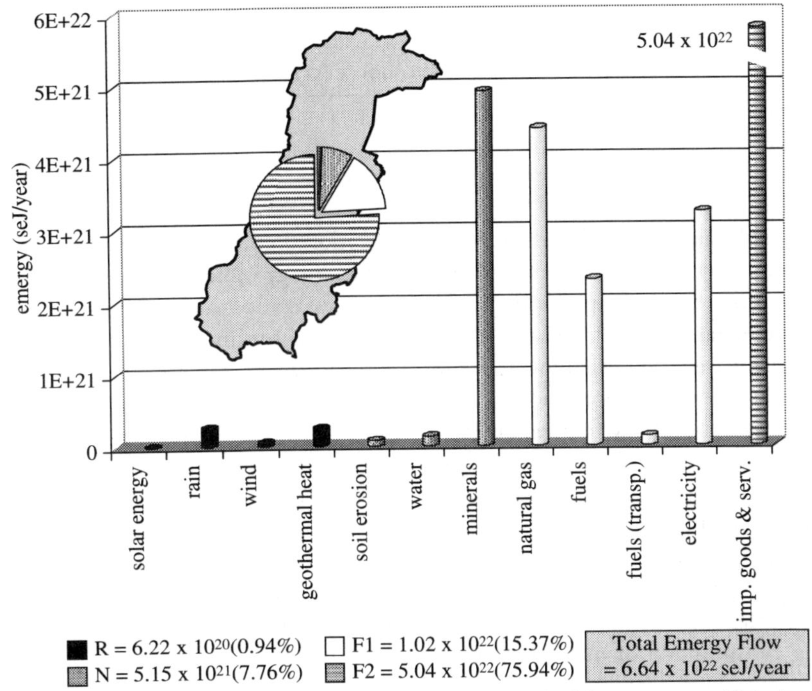

Figure 12.3: Flows of resources supplying the system of the Province of Modena and computation of total emergy.

The environmental loading ratio showed an unacceptable imbalance between use of non-renewable (local and imported) resources and (essentially environmental) renewable resources.

A similar analysis of the same province had already been done using data for the year 1997.[9] We updated and corrected the results using new conversion coefficients from recent literature in order to enable comparison with the analysis for the year 2003. In the period 1997–2003, the flow of emergy of the system increased from 4.67×10^{22} to 6.64×10^{22} seJ/year. This was due to an increase in 'imported' materials and energy (*F*) which more than outweighed the small reduction in locally extracted material (*N*) and the benefits of greater use of local renewable resources (*R*). The environmental loading ratio increased from 79.70 in 1997 to 105.85 in 2003 (105 times more non-renewable resources were used than renewable).

9. See Tiezzi, E. & Marchettini, N., *Che cos'è lo sviluppo sostenibile?* Donzelli: Rome, 1999. The data for the emergy analysis of the Province of Modena and the updated data for 1997 can also be found in a volume published in 2006 for the Amministrazione Provinciale di Modena by Enzo Tiezzi's research group at Siena University.

Table 12.2: Emergy flow, GRP and ISEW.

Year	Emergy (seJ/yr)	GRP (million €/yr)	ISEW (million €/yr)
1997	4.67×10^{22}	16,293	10,150
2003	6.64×10^{22}	17,458	12,650

We then asked whether the progressive deterioration in environmental conditions demonstrated by the trend of flows and emergy indicators was matched by positive economic performance. To do this, we compared emergy and economic parameters: total emergy flow, gross regional product (GRP, or similar index referred to for the Province of Modena) and ISEW. Table 12.2 shows the data for the two years considered. The results of emergy analysis are compared with GRP and ISEW for the year 1996 because data for 1997 was not available, resulting only in a slight overestimate of emergy/GRP and emergy/ISEW.

The increased use of resources goes with slight increases in GRP and welfare as indicated by ISEW. This means that the flow of emergy is growing faster than the gross product, reflecting increasing consumption in pursuit of (now elusive) profit. The emergy/GRP ratio increased from 2.87×10^{12} seJ/€ in 1997 to 3.80×10^{12} seJ/€ in 2003. Current economic conditions and increasing consumption of materials and energy are the main causes for the rise in this ratio in the Province of Modena.

Finally, the emergy/ISEW ratio was higher than emergy/GRP because only a fraction of the emergy necessary to obtain a certain level of wealth is translated into welfare. Welfare is costing more and more in terms of flows of materials and energy. This ratio, too, grew in the period considered (from 4.60×10^{12} seJ/€ in 1997 to 5.25×10^{12} seJ/€ in 2003), since increasing quantities of resources were consumed to meet desires that increasingly diverge from real needs.

Conclusion

Report, 28 April 2027

Ultimate Global Bank, a financial colossus, founded as a commercial bank with the aim of facilitating international transfer of capital, closed its last office five years ago. The initial project of Ultimate Global was to form an international chain of credit companies, with the consent of governments of many countries. Ultimate Global crumbled due to the work of woodworms. Its political and financial foundations were slowly eaten away, much like the effect of wave action on the buildings of Venice. The woodworms were mini-revolutions of awareness that broke out almost everywhere, forming a self-organising system that nourished the culture and welfare of the population. A new start was made with simple tools and no nonsense: microcredit where it was still needed (in poor countries) and a dense network of agreements and cooperation between families, shopkeepers and local bodies that banded together to meet the primary needs of people. Collateral and all other costs, visible and invisible, associated with the circulation of money, were eliminated. The ease of dealing with the new multiform and diversified body restored vitality to all systems, vitality that had been lost by concentration of power in the hands of a few inaccessible men. Ultimate Global had been instrumental in placing a hundred heads of government and countless ministers. Today, these men can no longer be found. A multitude of small events caused the colossus to collapse.

The decoupling of monetary policy, interest rates and investments is now almost complete. Monetary policy, which had been reduced to the creation and management of false wealth, no longer exists. As long as a century ago, Frederick Soddy defined hoarded money as virtual wealth[1] and James Tobin called money an illusion compared to tangible capital.[2] Investments are now weighed on a physical basis (energy, materials, entropy, etc.) and utility is

1. Soddy, F., *Wealth, Virtual Wealth, and Debt*, George Allen & Unwin: London, 1926.
2. Tobin, J., Money and economic growth. *Econometrica*, **33(4)**, pp. 671–684, 1965.

solely environmental, being the capacity of a system to survive in time within natural constraints. Thus Africa exports energy obtained directly or indirectly from the sun, the Congo rainforests are slowly recovering and millions of tourists visit the closed coal mines of China. Profits still exist and countless people become wealthy by the new system; however, a bill has been presented in parliament to prevent maximisation of profit, to avoid the problems it created in the past.

Many investments are made in systems operating at an economic loss. However, integrated analysis of environmental balance, which is what is now used, shows that they are worthwhile because they improve conditions and welfare and are food for prosperous survival. This is why these investments are largely public and are evaluated and proposed by persons with political, cultural and scientific expertise.

A high percentage of people can work. Agriculture has resumed production of energy and food, industry is everywhere local and typical but highly diversified and solid, administrations and states need graduates from the best universities for ambitious projects. All this has been made possible by economic resources gathered through sapient and rigorous policy: at the global level, defensive expenditures were reduced by 90%, filling the coffers of states, administrations and private firms and enabling investment in alternative projects that led to employment and long-term economic and environmental advantages. Certain advanced countries have succeeded in totally eliminating defensive expenditures from their books.

A few days ago, in a videoconference on the Internet, eminent scholars of many disciplines expressed their satisfaction with this month's events. The topic was global change (positive global change, not the global change of last century, which was usually misfortune). They discussed the virtuous behaviour of modern society, in contrast with that of their fathers and grandfathers, acknowledging, however, that their forebears did not have access to instruments that could enable them to understand. Instruments! With regard to instruments, one of the scholars raised the question, 'What will become of GDP?'

Stop press – 17 July 2027

The last dictatorial regime has collapsed. Completely autarchic and isolated, it had remained independent of Ultimate Global Bank. The event that triggered the collapse was the publication of a fragment from the 1990s, sent anonymously to a local newspaper:

> *Democracy can only exist if the natural and cultural diversity of a region is respected and conserved, and with it the sacredness of places.*
> *Democracy can only exist if there is no single dominant system of thought.*
> *Democracy can only exist if no ideology (political, religious, scientific, philosophical) oppresses the common thinking of people, preventing different ways of*

thinking and living, provided those different ways are tolerant of other diversities, and do not consider themselves superior or use their identity for power or profit.
Democracy can only exist if a country is not dominated by any power (military, religious, financial).
Democracy can only exist if the ethical and aesthetic values of places are respected and conserved.
Democracy is always the fruit of coevolution of the natural environment and human culture, and therefore varies from place to place.
Democracy is always fruit of the fertile mosaic of conservation and evolution.
Democracy is democracy if it allows science and art to express themselves without the constraints of utility, ideology, dogma, economic interest or aim. (Archimedes used to say that he was not concerned with useful things, only with the fine and beautiful).

Names index

Subject index

Disposal of Hazardous Waste in Underground Mines

Edited by: ***V. POPOV****, Wessex Institute of Technology, UK and* ***R. PUSCH****, Geodevelopment AB, Sweden*

This book contains the results of a three-year research programme by a joint team of experts from four different EU countries.

The main focus of this research was on investigating the possibility of using abandoned underground mines for the disposal of hazardous chemical waste with negligible pollution of the environment.

The research work focused on: the possibility of using abandoned underground mines for disposal of hazardous chemical waste with negligible pollution of the environment; the properties and behaviour of waste-isolating clay materials and practical ways of preparing and applying them; development of software tools to assess the stability, performance and risks associated with different repository concepts, considering the long-term safety of the biosphere; the isolating capacity of reference repositories; the different approaches for handling hazardous chemical waste. The project has demonstrated that hazardous waste can be safely disposed of in underground mines provided that adequate assessment, planning and design procedures are employed.

Information is also included on the selection of site location, design and construction of repositories, predicting degrees of contamination of groundwater in the surroundings, estimation of isolating capacity of reference repositories, cost estimation of this approach in comparison with some other approaches, and many other relevant issues.

Invaluable to researchers and engineers working in the field of hazardous (chemical) waste disposal, this title will also significantly aid experts dealing with nuclear waste.

Series: The Sustainable World, Vol 11
ISBN: 1-85312-750-7 2006 288pp £95.00/US$170.00/€142.50